HOSTAGE OF THE
word

To Roger Ebbatson,
wit, scholar, absurdist, ironist,
loyalist, Englander, unEnglander,
dour opening bat, fellow hostage,
inspiration, and friend.

HOSTAGE OF THE *word*

Readings into Writings, 1993–2013

John Schad

sussex
ACADEMIC
PRESS

Brighton • Portland • Toronto

2 4 6 8 10 9 7 5 3 1

First published in 2013 by
SUSSEX ACADEMIC PRESS
PO Box 139
Eastbourne BN24 9BP

Distributed in North America by
SUSSEX ACADEMIC PRESS
ISBS Publisher Services
920 NE 58th Ave #300, Portland, OR 97213, USA

British Library Cataloguing in Publication Data
A CIP catalogue record for this book is available from the British Library.

Library of Congress Cataloging-in-Publication Data
Schad, John, 1960–
Hostage of the word : readings into writings, 1993–2013 / John Schad.
p. cm.
Includes bibliographical references and index.
ISBN 978-1-84519-494-9 (h/b : alk. paper) —
ISBN 978-1-84519-495-6 (p/b : alk. paper)
I. Title.
PR6119.C375H67 2013
824'.92—dc22

2012029396

Typeset and designed by Sussex Academic Press, Brighton & Eastbourne.

This book is printed on acid-free paper.

Contents

Notes on the Text

The book that follows is an attempt to bring together representative pieces of my work from the last twenty years. Most of these pieces have been previously published, but there are several new texts, including five auto-biographical or, as it were, occasional poems. I should perhaps explain that each of these poems was written in response to a very specific event and were first drafted at the time but have now been dramatically revised for publication.

As you will see, the book has been organised chronologically and thus reflects, *inter alia*, one very obvious turn or 'development' in my work; namely: its movement from a broadly conventional literary-critical mode based on traditional argumentation through to an experimental kind of writing which, whilst still (I hope) very much an act of reading, is based on devices and strategies drawn from literature – plot, character, metaphor etc. It is perhaps helpful, as a kind of short-hand, to describe this more recent mode or method as critical-creative writing.

It may also help if I explain that this turn in my writing took me completely by surprise, coming about simply through the fact that, following my father's death in 1997, I was presented by my mother with a long transcript of his final words. This text was so strange and difficult that it demanded, I felt, interpretation or deciphering, and since there were no other 'professional' interpreters within the family I set about the task, drawing, as I did so, on all the usual tricks of scholarly reading in which I had been trained. As I proceeded, however, it soon became clear that the sheer strangeness of the text and the fact that it had been 'produced' by my own father demanded that I deploy a quasi-creative mode of writing or speaking, drawing on such novelistic devices as digression, irony, and hesitation. This, in the end, became a book called *Someone Called Derrida* (2007) and the first chapter is included here.

Since writing *Someone* I have, to date, persisted with this novelistic or participatory mode of criticism – participatory in the sense that it attempts to participate *in* the text it reads; for this reason, I include here, as an instance of this persistence, a new piece called 'Our Lives, Mrs Dalloway.' I have also deployed a quasi-creative mode when composing both the fore-word and afterword, and include another new piece called 'A Partial History of Bewilderment and Bedevilment etc.', which seeks to suggest that participatory criticism is far from new; this manner of reading has, I attempt to show, a long and intriguing history within mainstream academic literary criticism and theory. As ever, we are in debt to one past or another.

Talking of debts, I am of course very grateful to the various presses and journals who have given kind permission to reproduce the work that first appeared elsewhere; namely: *Critical Survey* who first published 'Waiting in Unhope: Negation in the Early Poetry of Hardy' (1993); *Modern Fiction Studies* who first published 'The End of the End of History: Graham Swift's *Waterland*' (1993); *Victorian Poetry* who first published 'The Divine Comedy of Language: Tennyson's *In Memoriam*' (1993); *Religion and Literature* who first published 'Hostage of the Word: Poststructuralism's Gospel Intertext' (1993); Inter-Varsity Press who first published 'Why Wait for an Angel: Thomas Pynchon's *The Crying of Lot 49*' in Barrett, Pooley and Ryken (eds), *The Discerning Reader: Christianity and Literature* (1995); the Modern Humanities Research Association who first published 'Reading the Long Way Round: Thackeray's *Vanity Fair*' in the *Yearbook of English Studies* (1996); Penguin Books who first published 'Half Way House' as the Introduction to my edition of Thomas Hardy's *A Laodicean* in 1997; and Continuum International Publishing Group who first published 'Leavis Spells Pianos: Coming Back to Life' in Payne and Schad, *life.after.theory* (2004). I must also thank Enfield Local Studies Library and Archives for permission to quote from early 20th century issues of *The Recorder*, and the Federation of Swiss Societies for permission to use the photograph of my grandfather and to quote from *The Swiss Observer*.

Finally, please note that reference details for all quotations are given in the endnotes which, for all pieces, appear at the back of the book.

List of Illustrations

In the beginning was the Word and
the Word was God.
(ST JOHN)

Anything may happen
to a person called John.
(OSCAR WILDE)

Not Here – By Way of a Foreword

(2013)

when a certain wise man was asked what is the method of learning he replied, ... 'a humble mind, a quiet life, silent investigation, poverty, and a foreign land.' (Hugh of St Victor)

It is customary for an author to introduce his or her own work but our author in this case is, sadly, unavailable, elsewhere, his office abandoned, his duties left undone, and the corridor shaken and uncertain as to his whereabouts. Rumours, however, abound. Some say he is in hiding, having fled like a guilty thing, others that he has taken to the hills whispering, through the rain, that his university is no longer a house of prayer. Finally, one very 'knowing' old cove is of the opinion that Schad has 'gone for to be a contortionist'; given Schad's proclivity for quotation we believe the old cove meant to say 'quotationist.'

Speaking of quotations, or epigrams, we have found two, each scribbled on scraps of paper and left within the hollow of a solitary shoe that, for some reason, stands proud upon the desk in Schad's forsaken office. Whatever his destination, he has gone or limped, we surmise, half-shoeless – like, say some, a crazed half-Moses. Whatever, we do believe that both epigrams, or sayings tell us something.

The first saying, a dark one, is this, that: 'Man has become the hostage of the Word.' These words, for all their darkness, do reflect Schad's youthful fascination, as evidenced by the earlier essays herein, with the famous prologue to St John's Gospel: 'In the beginning was the Word and the Word was God' etc. etc. Moreover, this dark saying begins to hint at why Schad has left us when we bear in mind his more recent and alarming tendency, as seen in the latter essays herein, to confuse himself and his own fate with the very texts that he studies. This tendency, by the way, we date back to the day he first read the words 'Thou thyself art the subject of my discourse,' words he found deep within Robert Burton's *Anatomy of Melancholy* (1621). It is, we fear, possible that he has read the saying 'Man is hostage of the Word' and immediately departed, imagining himself seized or abducted by language itself, or even by the very source or ground of all language – *the* Word, in other words.

There is, though, as I mentioned, a second epigram or clue to be found within the proud-standing shoe and it is this, that: 'When we are present the truth is not there.'

I

Waiting in Unhope
Negation in Thomas Hardy's Early Poetry
(1993)

What is laid upon us is to accomplish the negative; the positive is already given. (Franz Kafka)

That Hardy's early poetry, *Wessex Poems* (1898) and *Poems of the Past and the Present* (1901), anticipates Kafka's modernist injunction through a fascination for negations and absences, for the unsaid, unknown, and even unborn, becomes apparent through simply a glance at the poems' titles. I have in mind such titles as 'Postponement,' 'Unknowing,' 'The Lacking Sense,' 'God Forgotten,' 'To an Unborn Pauper Child,' 'The To-Be Forgotten,' and 'The Self-Unseeing.' Moreover, upon reading the poems, our sense of negation is soon intensified by such peculiar negatives as 'unsight,' 'unclosed,' 'unhope,' and 'unbe.' It is not, then, simply that the poems are about a series of failures and losses in the lives of Hardy's narrators; rather, the fact that happiness is no more, that a loved one is absent, or that God is silent, invariably occasions a more general consideration of discontinuity, absence, or silence. In short, to quote Hardy himself, 'nothing is much the matter' of these poems.

What, perhaps, first alarms us about this negative focus is that it is trained on the consciousness or identity of the individual. As T. D. Armstrong remarks, 'the self is always for Hardy . . . the marker of an absence in life.' The poems, that is, open up gaps and discontinuities within the ways the self thinks, knows, and is conscious; it locates, as it were, '*my* unsight.' For instance, in 'The Self-Unseeing,' the moment in which happiness is undone, the point of negation, is also the moment in which 'we' do not see:

Childlike, I danced in a dream;
Blessings emblazoned that day;
Everything glowed with a gleam;
Yet we were looking away!

Of course, what the poem's title suggests is that, somehow, in not seeing the gleam the speaker is thereby not seeing himself; as if the gap in attention – 'I danced in a dream' – opens up a gap within the very I, or subject. Clearly, if I am self-unseeing then my blindness separates me from myself, I cease to be undivided and self-identical. Hence, in part, the crisis or negation that occasionally threatens Hardy's subject; witness: 'I have no claim to be,' 'My own Being bear[s] no bloom,' and 'And gone all trace of me.'

This threat to the self in Hardy may be interpreted in both traditional and contemporary philosophical terms. Within traditional philosophy we might point to Hardy's interest in David Hume whose conviction that 'the mind is [nothing but] a kind of theatre [or space] where perceptions . . . pass, re-pass, [and] glide away' leads to extreme scepticism about the unity of the self. Similarly, the contemporary philosopher Jacques Derrida, for whom language always escapes the intention of whoever uses it, might prompt us to argue, as J. Hillis Miller does, that 'for Hardy, . . . between self and itself . . . falls the word.' The I that speaks is never, for Derrida, exactly the same as the I that is spoken about.

To explore, then, the negation or decentring of Hardy's subject we do well to talk of the overwhelming force of disparate sense-impressions and the alienating effect of words that are never quite my own. Moreover, we must also heed the implication common to both interpretations that the self is not the source or centre of its own negation but rather that Hardy's absences and gaps belong as much to the world 'out there' of sights and signs as to the self 'in here' of mind and thought. In the words of 'Departure,' a 'sense of severance everywhere prevails.' For this reason Hardy's subject does not *become* undone but, to borrow a favourite formulation of Derrida's, is *always already* undone. Hence, in part, our frequent sense that the speaker is so ghostly a presence as to be, as Armstrong puts it, 'already dead' or 'benumbed at birth' and only 'alive enough to . . . die.' The very texture of the 'reality' into which Hardy's self is born is marked, it seems, by a kind of death, or absence – an everywhere severance, as it were.

For Hardy, an agnostic of course, this absence is most obviously explained as the space traditionally occupied by God. Thus, God is not only absent from Hardy's world – 'none replies' and 'no grace I find' – but also thereby becomes the name for absence in general and unknowing in particular. This becomes obvious if for 'God' we read 'Immanent Will,' the name that Hardy gave to his absent God, or that universal mind which, paradoxically, is not conscious; as Miller writes, 'it is mind without mind . . . remain[ing] in deep sleep, evolving always that it wots not of.' This universal forgetfulness is often made quite explicit; not only, for instance, as 'Nescience' and the 'Unknowing God' but also as the 'Lord Most High . . . [who has] no remembrance of . . . the Earth of Men' and admits to his 'too oft unconscious hand.' In short, Hardy's poetry comes very close to a striking anticipation of Jacques Lacan's late-twentieth century claim that 'the true formula of atheism is *not God is dead . . . [but] God is unconscious.*'

Clearly, if God-as-Immanent Will is, for Hardy, the name for a universal Unknowing it follows that the gaps within the consciousness of Hardy's subject are repetitions, or inflexions, of this God-space. As Deborah Collins remarks, of Hardy's characters in general, 'each feels incomplete since, to borrow Feuerbach's phraseology, "God is his alter ego, his other lost half."' This becomes most apparent at the end of 'A Commonplace Day':

> – Yet, maybe, in some soul,
> In some spot undiscerned on sea or land, some impulse rose,
>> Or some intent upstole
> Of that enkindling ardency from whose maturer glows
>> The world's amendment flows;
>
>> But which, benumbed at birth
> By momentary chance or wile, has missed its hope to be
>> Embodied on the earth;
> And undervoicings of this loss to man's futurity
>> May wake regret in me.

Here the non-event that is God or, more specifically, the incarnation ('the world's amendment . . . Embodied on . . . earth') reverberates in the speaker's sense of personal lack: 'undervoicings of this loss,' we read, 'may wake regret in me.' And, of course if, as Collins argues, all the regrets and losses that beset Hardy's subjects are, in some sense, undervoicings of this loss of a God who was always already a loss ('benumbed at birth') then it would seem that Hardy's God necessarily lives on in these very gaps and absences. To put it another way, just as Friedrich Nietzsche, having first declared that 'God is dead,' then writes 'I fear we are not getting rid of God because we still believe in grammar,' so we might say that Hardy is not getting rid of God because he still believes in absence and negations.

That this might be so, that God, contrary to the dominant assumptions of Western philosophy, might be located not so much in our assertions about him but in the gaps between those assertions – i.e. not in what we do know but in what we do not – is, in fact, very much part of the New Testament Hardy knew so well. Here, of Christ we read, for instance, that 'the world knew him not' and, indeed, that in becoming flesh he 'made himself nothing'; hence St Paul's further remark that 'God [has] chosen things which are not to bring to nought things that are.'

In Hardy, this biblical equation between absence and God, respectively, is most clearly reflected in the way that both ideas, or categories, operate in the poetry as provisional names for the unconscious – that terrain of the human mind which Freud was just beginning to open up. After all, not only is the speaker's sense of lack or regret an '*under*voicing' and, similarly, the moment in which 'we were looking away' that in which 'I danced in a *dream*,' but God is 'The *Sleep*-Worker' and wields, of course, an 'unconscious hand.' In short, negation refers both directly and indirectly, via the absent(-minded) God, to the unconscious. In the 'end,' then, it may well be that, in a typically modernist turn of demystification, not God but the unconscious is to be met in the poems' gaps and absences. Nevertheless, what the poems remind us is that this is a fine distinction. And that is a point which Lacan, a key interpreter of Freud's, also appears eager to teach: 'Many people,' he writes, 'compliment me for having managed to establish . . . that God does not exist. Obviously they hear . . . but . . . what they understand is a little hasty.'

The meaning of negation, or 'what is not' in Hardy does not, however, end in hesitation between the conceptual categories of 'God' and 'the unconscious.' Instead, the everywhere severance of Hardy's world also and at the same time refers to the historically produced, or material, marginality of both the woman and the labourer in the industrialised late-nineteenth century. This becomes most evident in 'The Sleep-Worker,' where the unconscious God is not only female ('when wilt thou wake, O Mother') but has 'laboured long / By vacant rote.' Here, then, the unconsciousness and vacancy of the Immanent Will is, albeit for a moment, directly referable to the unrealised powers of the late-Victorian woman and, in particular, the alienated labour of the industrial worker. The poem clearly resonates with not only the figure of Tess at the threshing machine, her arms 'work[ing] . . . independently of her consciousness,' but also Marx's seminal assertion that, under capitalist modes of production, 'the activity of the worker is not his own spontaneous activity [but] . . . belongs to another and is the loss of himself.' Indeed, the poem's conflation of worker and woman, underlined by the reminder that both endure the pains of 'labour,' recalls Engels' observation that 'within the family man is the bourgeois; woman plays the part of proletariat.'

That the besetting negations of Hardy's vision, however abstract, in some sense relate to the suppressed voices of the late-nineteenth century, those 'strange orchestras of victim-shriek,' is a possibility underlined in other poems. In 'The To-Be Forgotten,' for instance, the complaint of the dead that most of them shall soon be 'quite forgot / . . . as men that have existed not,' there being only a 'few whose memory none lets die,' may be read as the lament of all those whom bourgeois history excluded – 'those whose story no one knows.' In his essay, 'The Dorsetshire Labourer,' Hardy drily refers to 'those unimportant scores of millions of outsiders in civilised society,' and in the poem 'Mute Opinion' the point is no less explicit. For here the speaker talks of 'a dominion / Whose spokesmen speak . . . Through pulpit, press, and song,' thereby leaving 'a large-eyed few, and dumb / Who thought not as those thought there'; nevertheless, the poem ends with a revelation of 'history . . . Not as the loud had spoken / But as the mute had thought.' Thus forgotten and muted, the story of Hardy's silent persons answers exactly to what Fredric Jameson, drawing

a Freudian analogy, has described as the not-said, or repressed of bourgeois history – an omission that constitutes, he argues, a kind of '*political
unconscious.*' In these particular poems, then, Hardy quite clearly rewrites the Nescience and 'unconscious hand' of the Immanent Will in
terms of the strategic silences and repressions of the dominant class.

If so, the speaker's plea to 'The Sleeper-Worker' reads as a Shelleyan
call for an awakening of historical consciousness. However, unlike, say,
Shelley's 'The Mask of Anarchy,' there are, for Hardy's speaker, two
possible outcomes to the awakening – not just revolution but also reform:

> Should that morn come
> Wilt thou destroy, in one wild shock of shame,
> Thy whole high heaving firmamental frame,
> Or patiently adjust, amend, and heal?

The question with which the poem ends is not so much whether or not
the world shall be released from unconsciousness but rather what a fully
conscious world might be like. After all, Hardy, like Hegel, expressed the
belief that the absolute Mind, or Idea *will*, at some point in the future,
become conscious of itself. Thus, as in 'In Tenebris I,' although 'unhope'
may be our present condition, we are at least '*wait[ing]* in unhope.'

Hardy's most positive account of that for which we are waiting is,
perhaps, 'The Darkling Thrush'; for here, as if on the very threshold of
not only the twentieth century but the world of consciousness, what the
thrush '*knew*! And [yet] I was *un*aware' is a 'blessed Hope.' In contrast,
though, in 'The Sleep-Worker' there is the possibility that the world come-
into-consciousness will be 'one wild shock of sanity.' Hardy confronts, it
seems, the possibility that coming-into-consciousness is not necessarily
the quasi-religious hope of 'The Darkling Thrush' but may just be a literally revolutionary cataclysm that the world, as constructed by the
Sleep-Worker's capitalist masters, will not survive. Hardy's Immanent
Will, when re-thought as this Worker, comes surprisingly close to the
Marxian re-writing of Hegelian history as the inevitable movement
toward consciousness of not some absolute Idea but the proletariat.
According to Marx the proletariat, of course, will one day arrive at a revolutionary, or 'Communist consciousness.'

However, there is within Hardy a third account of the world come-to-
consciousness which is neither exactly a revolution nor a 'blessed Hope.'
For, of course, insofar as such a world is born at the moment in which the
universal mind becomes conscious of *itself*, that moment has all along, I
suggest, been the subject of our study. That is to say, Hardy's negations
are thoroughly marked by *self*-consciousness. In the first place, they often
so thoroughly reverse the reader's usual, positive perception of the world
as to mark the poems with a self-conscious perversity. Secondly, and more
importantly, the effect of this everywhere severance is to inscribe all our

familiar concepts with the potential to be divided, or separated from themselves – to be, as it were, self-conscious.

This is finely demonstrated in the very first line of 'Between Us Now,' namely: 'Between us now and here,' where the position or subjectivity represented by 'us' is very obviously divided from itself; quite simply, something has come 'between us.' Just as in 'Neutral Tones,' where this something is language ('some words,' we read, 'played between us') a kind of division, or difference, has so separated us from ourselves as to make possible our being conscious of ourselves. Moreover, since something has come 'Between us *now and here*' the very concept of presentness, both temporal ('now') and spatial ('here'), is also ruptured and thus made so to differ from itself as to be, as it were, self-conscious.

Much of this closely parallels, of course, that current of contemporary, or postmodern, literary theory known as deconstruction. The deconstructive way of reading stresses, among other things, that all words and meanings – in particular, by the way, the notion of presentness – are never either pure or simple but always already differ from themselves. If so, we might say of Hardy's negations that they confront us with not only 'the ache of modernism' that is absence but also the ache of *post*-modernism that is difference.

No, I was Not Born

(November 1st 1991)

*An ectopic pregnancy is a complication of pregnancy in which the foetus
implants outside the uterine cavity and, if not treated properly, will lead
to maternal death. Treatment usually takes the form of surgical
intervention to remove the foetus*

As if,
as if,
your face
in the dark,
an operatic mute,
one passing by,
or, or,
a thousand of Croatia,
I
froze
some where
greater love
and
all my life
has
no
man seen
being
laid down.

Live,
live,
you will now live
without
this
face.

May 2012

II

The End of the End of History

Graham Swift's *Waterland*

(1993)

> The historian is a prophet facing backward.
> (Walter Benjamin)

The most obvious lesson of *Waterland* is that the grand narrative of history ends more than once, or rather is always already ended. It first ends with the French Revolution which, as Tom Crick informs his pupils, in rejecting the past and tradition thereby rejected history itself. Tom, then, is already relating the end of history when, in a chapter entitled 'About the End of History,' he suddenly departs from the grand and objective narrative of the Revolution to narrate the small and subjective narratives of his own life. In short, the 1789 end of history does itself come to an end. Indeed, no sooner has Tom's own post-historical narrative begun than it in turn is interrupted by the pupil Price who declares that '"the only important thing about history . . . is that it's . . . probably about to end."' As Tom himself remarks, Price has contrived to '"disrupt disruption,"' to end the end of the end of history.

The significance of all this, needless to say, is that it brings into question the very idea of 'the end of history.' And it is, of course, a self-confessedly ironic formulation; Baudrillard, for instance, even when using the phrase, 'distances himself,' writes Douglas Kellner, 'from the very concept of "the end of," claiming it is embedded in a linear view of history.' In much the same way, *Waterland* does not allow us the consolation of an end to the grand narrative of history since, it is implied, there never was such a narrative. The reader of *Waterland* finds herself, like Tom when being told stories by his mother, 'in the middle of nowhere' rather than at the end of somewhere. '"There are no compasses for journeying in time,"' remarks Tom; or, as Michel Foucault puts it, 'the true historical sense confirms our existence among countless lost events, without a landmark or a point of reference.'

According to *Waterland*, what makes the-end-of-history landmark (for that is what it is) so particularly problematic is that insofar as it entails any kind of nostalgia it is implicated in what Tom identifies as the founding mechanism of some of the grandest narratives of history:

> history . . . creates this insidious longing to go backwards. It begets this
> bastard . . . child, Nostalgia. . . . How we pine for Paradise. For Mother's
> milk . . . [for] the Golden Age. . . . [Even] revolution contains within it
> . . . the idea of a return.

Should, then, it entail the slightest nostalgia, the postmodern end of
history has only returned, suggests Swift, to the very source, or beginning
of history. As Gianni Vattimo observes, 'the dissolution of *metarécits* is
itself a kind of *metarécit*.' Alan Sinfield touches upon this problem when
remarking of American deconstruction that 'it is often in danger of slipping into a nostalgia for the very metaphysics it claims to displace.' What
Waterland reminds us is that nostalgia is itself a metaphysic, indeed a
grounding metaphysic, of traditional, teleological history.

The point is made by not only Tom but also the embodiment of this
'bastard . . . child, Nostalgia': namely, the bastard child Dick whose
actions are informed, according to Tom, by both a desire for his dead
mother and a pre-evolutionary fascination with water. Through Dick, or
rather the Dick inscribed in Tom's post-historical digression, the novel
suggests that the 'Nostalgia' written into the very notion of the end of
history will perpetuate not just logocentrism – Dick is born, it is said, to
be the 'saviour of the world' – but also phallogocentrism. Dick by name,
he is also Dick by nature, endowed with a large and much envied penis.
Indeed, when it comes to attempting sex with Mary he proves, as the
chapter title puts it, 'Too Big' for what Tom and the others refer to as her
'hole.' It is as if the post-historical 'Nostalgia' personified by Dick constitutes a phallogocentrism which is, by analogy, 'Too Big' for the hole or
void that is the novel's postmodern world. Not only is the Fenland 'a landscape which, of all landscapes, most approximates to Nothing' but the
'Reality is that nothing happens.' If, then, the postmodern world-as-
absence is too small for the 'Nostalgia' inscribed in the end of history, the
latter is once again problematised, this time from a feminist-cum-decon-
structive perspective.

The event which, in the first and most obvious place, articulates the
post-historical conviction that nothing happens is Mary's abortion: just
before the abortion Tom talks of how they are '"waiting for . . . Nothing
to happen. For something to unhappen."' It is, moreover, a scene in which
'what the future is made of' is thrown into a bucket. What, though, really
might persuade us to interpret the abortion as a version of the post-historical is not only that its subject is a woman – as Christine Crosby remarks,
'Women are the unhistorical other of [traditional] history' – but also that
it represents what Nietzsche, as interpreted by Foucault, terms *wirkliche*
or non-traditional history: namely, a history that 'shortens its vision to
things nearest to it – [in particular] *the body*.' This '[post]historical sense,'
remarks Foucault, 'has more in common with medicine than philosophy.'

The abortion scene perhaps confirms its association with the postmodern end of history simply through being so appalling as to be unthinkable. Or rather, it is *almost* unthinkable; for, crucially, it does not quite resist all predication: Tom does manage both to dream and narrate the abortion. On an allegorical reading, then, the scene suggests we can just about *think* the post-historical void. According to Baudrillard, of course, this is not so; for him, the 'desert,' or nothing of pure signs beyond the end of history, is *un*thinkable and therefore apolitical, particularly when he calls that desert 'America.' In significant contrast, the abortion scene in *Waterland*, the scene in which Nothing really happens, is bound up with the paradigmatic political act of revolution:

> But Mary [is] . . . sitting still as stone . . . and quite inside herself. And inside Mary who's sitting so inside herself, another little being is sitting there too.
> And then from out of these doubly locked-up regions Mary says:
> 'I know what I'm going to do.' . . . So one day, after teaching the French Revolution, I come home to find that my wife's committed a *revolutionary* . . . act.

The contrast with Baudrillard is clear. Indeed, to put the case in Marxist terms, it seems that the posthistorical void represented by the abortion *cannot* escape 'Sartre's vision of history as a nightmare' that bore – and for such as Jameson still bears – a revolutionary imperative. 'The nightmare of history,' Jameson maintains, 'is the fact and intolerable spectacle of . . . labour itself.' In the abortion scene we could say, in fact, that Sartre's nightmare metaphor is literalised and Jameson's assertion undergoes a feministic inflection. For, while Tom is having an appalling dream, Mary suffers what is, after all, an intolerable *parody* of labour, the labour that is giving birth. Indeed, at the very moment of abortion she repeatedly cries out '"Mary *Mother* . . . Mary Mother of God."'

Of course, as a feminist inflection of the Jamesonian nightmare, labour-as-childbearing enjoys a very obvious pertinence to that Marxist-feminist dialogue which has sought to marry the situations of both worker and woman. *Waterland*'s equivocation upon the double sense of 'labour' serves, that is, as an obvious gloss on Friedrich Engels' claim that 'within the family man is the bourgeois, and the wife represents the proletariat.' Indeed, the same equivocation serves also as a reminder to contemporary feminism (tempted as it is to dissociate itself from a Marxism under pressure both from historical events in eastern Europe and from deconstructive developments in Western thought) of the indissolubility of the sufferings of production and *re*production. In short, in a faint echo of the Genesis account of the Fall where the curses of male and female labour – work and childbearing, respectively – are cognate, the novel effectively suggests a response to the familiar objection that the sphere of production, as privileged in Marxist thought, is a necessarily male preserve. For if the abortion-scene account of the post-historical void cannot quite escape the historical nightmare, or subtext, of labour, even less does that later version, the novel's final scene. It reads in this way simply because Dick has discovered that, as the retarded offspring of an incestuous relationship, he should not have children and that Henry is not his real father. Thus dislocated from any tangible familial past or future, Dick retreats to what Tom interprets as the present, or the now – and so to what both Aristotle and Derrida have understood as the time which of all times most approximates to nothing: 'If . . . the now,' writes Derrida, 'is given simultaneously as that which is no longer and . . . not yet . . . [then] it is what is not and is not what it is.' Dick has returned, even though it is a Sunday, to his place of work, the silt dredger:

> He's here. He knows his place. He knows his station . . . The noise of the churning machinery drowns the fleeting aerial clamour of global strife . . . the smell of silt is the smell of . . . amnesia. He's here, he's now. Not there or then. No past, no future.

Although adrift from 'global' or, as it were, historical time, in an almost Nietzschean forgetfulness of history, Dick's situation describes a post-historical vacuum that is still, very obviously, set in relation to the Jamesonian nightmare of history: namely labour. Quite simply, Dick is enduring what Tom elsewhere calls the dredger's '"dredgery *drudgery*"'; and, as he tellingly remarks here, Dick '"knows his place. He knows his station."'

Through first the abortion scene and then this final scene, the novel develops an account of the post-historical that, even as its barrenness increases, is also inching toward the representation – however metaphorical, or displaced – of the suffering of labour. Thus, the novel to some extent confirms *and* to some extent defies Spivak's postmodern assertion that '"History" is . . . a metaphor without an adequate literal referent.'

Waterland argues, then, that there is some kind of political subject beyond the end of history, that there is, as it were, a politics of nothing. Moreover, and here lies the argument's dénouement, this politics is profoundly bound up with a *theology* of nothing. The abortion, for example, is both 'a revolutionary [*and*] . . . miraculous act.' Again, at the very moment of abortion, Mary prays over and over '"Holy Mary Mother of God"'; and since the foetus, for all that Dick or indeed we know, might as well have originated through, as Tom remarks, an '"immaculate conception,"' it is almost as if we are witnessing the very abortion of God. In short, the post-historical void, as depicted by the abortion, has as its non-literal referents the suffering of not only labour but also God. In this way the novel puts into question Vattimo's assertion that 'the end of history . . . [is a kind] of "desacralisation"' and, instead, foregrounds the 'mystic' within Ihab Hassan's claim that 'postmodern literature moves, in nihilistic play, or mystic transcendence towards the vanishing point.' To cite Hassan again, the abortion scene 'display[s] the resources of the void.'

Much the same may be said, *a fortiori*, of the final scene when Dick dives from the dredger to his death and thus empties *the now* (his amnesiac 'sanctuary') of human presence. He would seem to complete thereby the novel's deconstruction of time and, therefore, to bring history to an end. But, of course, in so doing Dick not only escapes the 'dredgery drudgery' of labour but dies in the place, as it were, of the guiltier Tom. Thus, in diving into the water Dick both achieves a kind of emancipation and finally becomes the sacrificial 'Saviour of the World' that his grandfather always predicted he would be.

Clearly, we are very close to Walter Benjamin's Judaeo-Marxist belief that 'every second of time . . . [is] the straight gate through which the Messiah might enter.' Dick's death may well compel us to add '. . . or exit.' But therein lies the event's pertinence to postmodern theories of history, for the presence/absence of the 'revolutionary [or] Messianic' referent or signifier (since that is all Dick is) points toward a convergence beyond the end of history of the once grand narratives of Marxism and Judaeo-Christianity. Just as the two are united by their presence-through-absence from the very end of *Waterland* so what unites them in a postmodern context is the problem of representation, of maintaining the grand referent under the pressure of absolute epistemological scepticism. For example, in much the same way as Steiner acknowledges that 'in natural and unbound discourse God has no demonstrable lodging' so Jameson observes of the Marxist hermeneutic that 'its "master-code," or transcendental signified is . . . given as an absent cause, as that which can never know full representation.' Jameson's Althusserian, or postmodern, account of Marxism is taken even further by Dick Hebdige in an article responding to Baudrillard: 'It is no longer possible,' he claims, 'for us to see through the appearance of, for instance, a "free market" to the structuring "real relations" beneath (e.g. class conflict and expropriation by capital of surplus value).'

That Swift is conscious of this problem of representing the political, or revolutionary is clear: '" Where,"' asks Tom, '"do we place the revolutionary will? . . . Where is the revolution truly embodied? . . Its social location is elusive."' However, for Swift, the problem of representing the revolutionary is not thought independently of the problem of representing God. Witness, for instance, the last paragraph where, with Dick's disappearance into the water, the novel presents us with the conspicuous absence of both saviour and labour: 'the dredger, unmanned, still determinedly dredges.' And if the '*un*manned' dredger constitutes production without labour then, on an allegorical reading, we are also in a world without Man:

We row back against the current, tie up to the *Rosa* and climb aboard. No wet and shivering Dick (our last, thin hope) who has tricked us all and, swimming in a circle, clambered back on deck. Stan Booth shuts off at last the bucket-ladder engine. The sudden, dripping quiet strikes like a knell. 'Someone best explain.' We trip over empty bottles. Peer from the rails. Ribbons of mist. Obscurity. On the bank in the thickening dusk, in the will-o'-the wisp dusk, abandoned but vigilant, a motor-cycle.

'Unmanned' and with 'our last, thin hope' gone we are now in a world that comes close to that of the postmodernist, marked as it is by the 'dehumanization of the Planet' and the 'End of Man.' And the resemblance is furthered as first the dredger's engine is turned off, thus suggesting a post-industrial world, and then as the first-personal pronoun vanishes and, with it, all obvious trace of the subject. Indeed, all that seems to be left is, just as Baudrillard would predict, the object, or thing: namely, the motor-cycle. But this is not quite the 'empty triumph of the object,' for whilst Baudrillard declares that beyond the end of history 'the irony of the object lies in wait for us' here the object awaits us with hope, or at least the irony of hope, in that it is a '*vigilant . . . motor-cycle*.' It alone seems to believe that Dick, 'the saviour,' will return. In short, the object or reified sign is not quite empty; rather it is motivated by the stubborn hope of resurrection; it is, after all, a Sunday. One is put in mind of Baudrillard's 'twenty-first century metaphysic founded not on God or man but in the material world,' a kind of postmodern *deus ex machina*.

However, whilst what might distinguish the end of *Waterland* from Baudrillard's materialist metaphysic is that the material object, the vigilant motorcycle, still depends, however faintly, on God and Man for its value, both semiotic and economic. At the semiotic level, it depends on the Resurrection conventionally signified by Sunday; while at the economic level it depends on the labour by which Dick earned the money to buy it. In fine, though conspicuously absent at a literal level from this post-historical ending, the once grand narratives of Christianity and Marxism maintain a precarious existence.

One recalls Jameson's anticipation of 'not the disappearance of the great master-narratives, but their passage underground.' Jameson does not make explicit whether Judaeo-Christianity is one such narrative but the briefest glance at the postmodern debate suggests it is. As Phillipa Berry has argued, within the work of theorists such as Levinas, Irigaray, Kristeva, Baudrillard, and Derrida, the 'trace of the holy survives . . . postmodernism in persistent echoes of that cultural legacy to which it declared itself the murderous heir.' According to Berry, 'the ghostly pressure of this supposedly invalidated concept [the holy] seems to have become especially acute with the gradual collapse of intellectual confidence in Marxism'; however, in *Waterland*, at the end of history the Christian narrative is not so much an alternative plot to the Marxist plot as coincidental with it. For not only does the postmodern void, as represented by the abortion, have as its non-literal referent the sufferings of labour and God alike but, when represented by the supermarket where Mary steals the baby, this same void becomes the ironic site of both the incarnation and revolution: Mary believes that 'God came down to Safeways' and Tom talks, on their return, of the '"mobs [of] . . . revolutionary Paris . . . [and] a Lewisham lynching."' The two narratives coincide, it seems, at the point at which, displaced or ironised, they are as much absent as present. In *Waterland*, then, the failing of Marxist discourse may not be dissociated from the failing of Christian discourse. As Tom himself recites, '"Vox populi, *vox Dei*"'; or, as a pupil translates, '"The voice of the people is the voice of God."' And perhaps that is never more the case than at the postmodern moment in which both voices fall silent: for just as 'God doesn't talk any more' so, we learn, 'there are no more real revolutions.'

Of such a coincidence neither contemporary theology nor contemporary Marxism makes much explicit acknowledgment. Nevertheless, insofar as critics like Jameson and Eagleton have combined the postmodern conviction that one cannot in any sense know the world with a continuing and paradoxical commitment to it so, I suggest, they have adopted modes of rhetoric and reasoning that, like those of Derrida, are comparable with negative theology. That both Jameson and Eagleton draw in part on Adorno's proto-deconstructionist *Negative Dialectics* clearly makes such comparisons feasible; indeed, their postmodern Marxism is arguably *closer* to negative theology than is deconstruction in that its doubts and paradoxes are, in the end, explicitly affirmative.

All the same, only Eagleton among contemporary theorists gives much serious attention to the theological resonances of the doubts and indeterminacies within Marxism. In his discussion of what he, at one point, actually terms Benjamin's 'negative political theology' Eagleton has recognized both a very general analogy between 'negative theology [and] . . . much of the negativity of Marxism' and a more specific correspondence: 'just as the pious Jews,' he writes, 'were forbidden on pain of idolatry to fashion graven images of the God of the future, so political radicals are prohibited under pain of fetishism from blueprinting their ultimate desire.' Eagleton's account of the ironies of dialectic is drawn still closer to theological paradox in an essay on Kierkegaard. Seeking a way to think the self/other opposition dialectically, as both resolved and yet kept open, he turns to the Kierkegaardian account of faith, concluding that 'the knowledge of faith is a sort of unity-in-conflict, as the subject binds itself unconditionally to an objective reality [that is, God] it recognises as problematic.'

Such syncretism may well come close to *Waterland*'s intuition of the coincidence of Marxist and Christian discourses; what separates the two is that, in marked contrast to Eagleton's recourse to Kierkegaard, the *Waterland* coincidence is finally located not in the self, or subject but on the more properly postmodern site of the thing, or object – namely, Dick's Velocette. Note that this bike is not only a 'chromium-plated confessor' but, as a 'motor *cycle*,' is also a reminder of revolution. Admittedly, on both counts the bike means what, literally, it is not; thus it is only a site of politico-theological coincidence as a thing that is not itself, or a kind of nothing. However, in this way, the bike contrives to point up the general fact that, for *Waterland*, the void, along with all its resources, is – as the word '*Nothing*' itself suggests – most specifically thought under the sign/absence of the thing.

For instance, it is as a version of the historical nothing that is woman that the thing most thoroughly unites the Christian and the Marxist. Already feminized as the reputed object of Dick's sexual desire, the 'motor cycle' cannot but act, for the reader, as a trace or displacement of 'menstrual cycle,' a cycle that in Mary's case had 'stopped cycling.' That woman is the 'unhistorical other' and, therefore, the nothing of traditional history is echoed in Tom's apprehension that the baby-snatching Mary '"is where history dissolves."' And what makes the female void so resourceful is that, in the synechdocal guise of the 'menstrual cycle,' woman provides the novel, at its very ending, with a bodily subtext and thus a hint of both the Christian and Marxist Utopian moment. Note that, for Marx, 'the suppression of private property is the complete emancipation of all human *senses*'; while, for Christianity, the Kingdom is, self-evidently, the extension of the *body* of Christ (that is, the Church). Here we are perhaps close to what Adorno meant when he wrote that 'at its most materialistic, materialism comes to agree with theology. Its great desire would be the resurrection of the flesh.' Indeed, in both theology and historical materialism the flesh that marks the Utopian moment is female: the body of Christ being also his bride, while Marx writes of 'the new society with which the old collapsing bourgeois society itself is *pregnant*.'

Neverthless, the female body, identified as it is with the un- or post-historical, is as much an erasure of the utopian moment as it is a signature. In *Waterland* this is indexed most obviously in the opposition between women and much that, in conventional narratives, produces such a moment: namely, both a determinate, lineal account of history and a male subject of that history. For not only does Mary's baby-snatching threaten to make 'chronology go . . . backwards' but, since no one is ever quite sure as to who is the father of the aborted embryo, Mary's womb becomes a kind of *aporia*. It becomes, that is, the point at which both patrilineal and, therefore, lineal or causal accounts of history break down – a breakdown that is paralleled by the later reduction of the Henry/Dick relationship to that of a 'nonfather' to a 'son-who's-not-a-son.' As regards the male subject of such history, women are similarly disruptive; just as Mary's abortion, in parodying the experience of child-bearing, acts as both a punning metaphor and displacement of the intolerable spectacle of male labour so 'the landgirls . . . [serve] as replacement labour' for the men who had previously worked the farm. And that both cases act as a distant refraction of the observation that 'the more modern history becomes developed, the more is the labour of men superseded by that of women' is underlined by the novel's equating of femininity with the machine. Not only is Dick reputed 'to . . . get down with [his bike] on the grass and . . . ' but the dredger is called 'Rosa.' As Andreas Huyssen has observed, ever since the nineteenth century's denigration, and even demonization, of the machine 'writers [have begun] . . . to imagine the *Machinenmensch* as women.'

According to *Waterland*, woman leaves history with neither its conventional linearity nor subject in tact – she leaves it, in other words, as a kind of void; but, consistent with the Benjaminian logic of a negative political theology, this same post-patriarchal space uncovers a surprising point of intersection between once-grand narratives. For, in centring as it obviously does on Mary and in particular on her 'hole,' the void that is woman is inevitably inscribed with that imaginative leap by which Mary's pregnancy constitutes a parodic version of the 'Virgin Birth.' The uncertainty surrounding the father thus produces a negative episode that is crucial not only to the Christian narrative but Marxist rhetoric. After all, when Marx writes of a 'bourgeois society [that] is *itself* pregnant' with 'the new society,' or Eagleton of the '*womb* of history,' or, again, Adorno that 'the attempt to change the world *miscarried*,' the implication, if history be driven by the internal logic of dialectical materialism, is that there is no transcendental or teleological progenitor. In Althusserian terms, there is an 'absent cause,' an insight paraphrased by Raman Selden as 'no originating seed.' In short, the Virgin Birth, in the light of its negative, *Waterland* interpretation – as not the incarnation of God but the absence of cause – is identified as a crucial, though tacit, moment in Marxist rhetoric. And that is perhaps never more clearly the case than in Marx's assertion that

> under the capitalist mode of production . . . capital becomes a very mystic being since all labour's social productive forces appear to be due to capital, rather than to labour as such, and seem to issue from the womb of capital itself.

One is reminded of Jameson's observation that Marxism can and does 're-write certain religious concepts . . ., [including] the pre-theological system of primitive magic, as anticipatory foreshadowings of historical materialism.' What, then, happens with respect to the Virgin Birth is that Marxism effectively produces a deconstructive rewriting of Christian 'magic' in order to think a central contradiction within historical materialism: namely, that history is determined yet without a determinant. We are back to the presence of a negated, if not quite negative, theology within Marxist discourse – religion, if you like, as a rhetoric of scepticism.

Pertinent here is Benjamin's parable of 'the puppet called "historical materialism" [that] is to win all the time . . . if it enlists the services of theology, which today, is wizened and has to keep out of sight.' Just as, for Benjamin, theology is the wizened and hidden half-presence that gives a name to the spaces and hollows within the puppet of materialism so, I am suggesting, religious discourse operates within Marxism as a means of articulating its areas of indeterminacy and doubt.

Recall, for instance, Eagleton's recourse to Kierkegaard's 'subject of faith' to think the paradoxes of a revolutionary self, or Adorno's declaration that 'the revolution has suffered the same fate as the Second Coming,' or again how Marx uses the illogic of the Trinity to comprehend the dialectical relationship between value and surplus value: 'Value differentiates itself,' he writes, 'as original value from itself as surplus-value, just as God the Father differentiates himself from himself as God the Son.' With contemporary Marxism, under the especial pressure of postmodernism's critique of grand narratives, dwelling increasingly on its discontinuities, it comes as no surprise that theorists such as Eagleton are beginning to acknowledge Marxism's dependence upon the negations and paradoxes of theological discourse.

As for understanding what might now come of this acknowledgement, *Waterland* repays further attention, particularly since, as I say, it accommodates Baudrillard's death of the subject by thinking the post-historical void under the sign/absence of the thing, with even woman being identified with the machine. The conclusion to my study develops, then, out of specific attention to *Waterland*'s post-historical no*thing*. What, above all, prompts the novel to think the thing as nothing is that it understands the thing as commodity. For, as commodity, the object enters the ceaseless circulation of exchange and thus, writes Marx, 'instead of possessing a direct self-identity . . . is only a relation with something else'; present and absent simultaneously, its meaning is always elsewhere. As then a kind of no-thing, the commodity may easily represent the entire post-historical void; hence, of course, talk of consumer capitalism. However, according to *Waterland*, the commodity's version of the void is just as resourceful as that of, say, the abortion scene or Dick's death; the novel conceives, that is, of the commodity in the form of the stolen baby – Mary believing that 'God came down to Safeways, and left her a gift, a free product.' Thus conceived, the no-thing that is the commodity is inscribed with not only theological discourse ('"I got it from God"') but also political discourse: to take the baby was a 'revolutionary act.' Indeed, as the 'babe in the bulrushes,' it is at once both salvific and revolutionary since Moses' liberation of his people from Egyptian slavery is interpretable in theological and political terms alike. That the commodity should be so inscribed is not, though, an idiosyncrasy of *Waterland* but rather a commonly observed characteristic. Its quasi-sacred aspect is well noted by Marx who writes of the commodity 'as abounding in theological niceties,' as 'something transcendent,' and as possessing a 'mystical character.' As for its radicalism, Eagleton writes that 'the commodity is [both] transgressive [and] promiscuous in its levelling passion to exchange with another of its kind.' But, of course, to be more specific, the mystico-radical dynamic of the commodity is referable to the absolute relativism and hallucinatory (il)logic of an exchange economy. As Eagleton implies, it is a logic according to which any object may, potentially, be exchanged for any other object in what is a wild parody of both universal equality and, as Eagleton remarks, 'the creative naming of God.'

Indeed, just as *Waterland* typifies the commodity in the baby-as-product, so it personifies the logic of exchange value in the aptly named Price. With his 'white greasepainted' face and resemblance to Tom's grandfather, the '*ghostly* Price' effectively mirrors not only the '*ghostly . . . charges*' on the sign of the disused ferry but also what Marx calls 'the phantasmagoric form of a relation between things' that is exchange value. Moreover, as one who announces 'the end of history,' Price personifies the specifically post-historical logic of exchange value; and, consistent with *Waterland*'s understanding of that logic, he represents ghostly and, as it were, deconstructed, traces of both revolutionary and sacred narratives. Price, we read, 'wants to change the world. Yet Price knows that all the old authentic revolutions are over.' He thus embodies both the logic of late capitalism and the problematic position of the revolutionary within that logic.

So much for Price, or exchange value and revolutionary narrative. As for sacred narrative we turn to the novel's end. For, come the reduction of the Henry/Dick relationship to that between a 'non-father' and a 'son-who's-not-a-son,' not only does Dick endure a fate akin to that endured by the other 'Saviour of the World' but the ghostly Price, recalled to our minds by the 'ghostly . . . charges,' almost becomes (by triangular, Trinitarian association) *holy* ghostly. The association is directly analogous to that which in a novel with a 'Tom' and a 'Dick' cannot but produce, in the reader's mind, a 'Harry.' Like this virtual 'Harry,' the third person of the Trinity is, at most, a conspicuous absence; but then, of course, such elusiveness is only characteristic of the Spirit. Indeed, that the ghostly Price should in himself tie together the workings of an exchange economy and the contradictions of the Trinity is, arguably, just an extension of Marxian rhetoric. Note that in order to articulate the mediatory character of exchange value Marx refers to 'Christ the mediator between God and man – [the] simple means of circulation between one and the other'; and, as we know, Marx also writes that 'value differentiates itself as original value from itself as surplus-value, just as God the Father differentiates himself from himself as God the Son.' Once again, theology may be seen to serve Marxism as a discourse of impossibility; the two intersect, as it were, at the point of contradiction.

Such intersection is nicely reflected in the way that the very contradictions of Price's revolutionary project gesture toward the sacred. His initial and paradigmatic act of revolution is also, that is, a counter-revolution, since in interrupting Tom's already interrupted lesson on the revolution he 'disrupt[s] disruption.' As then, an act of contradiction, the ghostly Price's interruption is referable to what one contemporary theologian calls the 'disruptions of the Spirit or *holy* ghost.'

This reference, I submit, has considerable theoretical significance in that it suggests a connection between the contradictions of revolution and a negative theology of not just rhetoric but practice. To operate according to 'the Spirit [that] bloweth where it listeth' is, self-evidently, to engage in a positive practice of *un*certainty, or *un*knowing. Thus, just as a species of negative theological rhetoric may be seen to help make Marxism a hesitant and paradoxical body of thought, so might the Spirit represent, metaphorically if not literally, one way for Marxism to continue as a *praxis* despite or even because of its new-found self-doubt, one way not to just think the paradoxes and indeterminacies of historical materialism but to live them as a revolutionary practice.

To theorize a little further, I would argue that such a Spirit-disturbed revolutionary practice of doubt is most nearly realized by liberation theology. Defining salvation in political and socioeconomic terms, liberation theology may be interpreted as a practice of not just revolution but also systematic doubt. For the Christ of liberation theology is never identical with his historical or theological self but rather is always elsewhere in the Christ of the poor or oppressed: '"Inasmuch as you have [served] the least of my brethren ye have done it unto me."' In short, since 'He' is always already 'them' there can be no centre to liberation Christology; indeed, since '"ye [shall] have the poor always with you"' neither can Christ ever be fully, or finally known. Under the sign of Christ, unknowing thus turns into a revolutionary practice.

III

The Divine Comedy of Language

Alfred Tennyson's *In Memoriam*

(1993)

> I sometimes hold it half a sin
> To put in words the grief I feel;
> For words, like Nature, half reveal
> And half conceal the Soul within.
> (*In Memoriam*)

In Memoriam concerns Tennyson's grief not only for the dead Hallam but also for the failure of language to articulate that grief. Although a convention of elegy, the poet's consciousness of the limits of his words becomes in *In Memoriam* a thoroughly theoretical concern for the nature of language in general. We are told, for example, not just that it is only 'lesser griefs that may be said' but, quite categorically, that 'truth in closest words shall fail.' As Isobel Armstrong remarks, 'there is a fundamental anxiety in *In Memoriam* about the dissolution of language altogether.' The poem, we might even say, is as much an elegy for language as for Hallam, particularly since, as Elizabeth Hirsch points out, Hallam is frequently eulogized 'as, above all, the most eloquent of speakers, the power of whose voice marks him as a veritable reincarnation of the logos.' That language might be the real subject of the elegy is effectively suggested by Alan Sinfield, who writes that 'the loss of the imaginary wholeness which . . . [Tennyson] associates with the loss of a loved person coincides with the inability of language quite to restore . . . [that] wholeness.' One obvious mark of this coincidence is that the poet speaks of language just as he might a friend: as 'dear words,' 'familiar names,' and 'closest words.'

'The sad words' of *In Memoriam* are marked, then, by a sadness not just for Hallam but also for themselves; a sadness that seems almost internal, or intrinsic to language. Not only is the poet's 'measured language . . . [a] sad mechanic exercise' but when, like 'an infant crying in the night,' he is left 'with no language but a cry,' it is quite as if words have been returned to an elegiac or tragic premise. 'In the beginning was not the word but the cry,' comments Gerhard Joseph.

Such a premise comes close to Jacques Lacan's thesis that 'the symbol manifests itself first of all as the murder of the thing,' since the infant only cries or, later, speaks when the thing desired is not immediately present. But, of course, a sense of absence has been with us ever since Saussure's divorcing of sign from referent; and, as Derrida points out, it is a fundamentally elegiac sense: 'this structuralist thematic of broken immediacy is,' he writes, 'saddened, *negative,* nostalgic, and guilty.' Moving closer, chronologically, to Tennyson, the notion of an elegy on the inside of language recurs with Wordsworth's reference in *The Prelude* to 'the sad incompetence of human speech.' The elegy becomes more properly a kind of tragedy within Shelley's characteristically Romantic understanding that 'when composition [i.e. language] begins, inspiration is already on the decline'; an understanding which may well owe something to the theological conceit by which not only does the Word Himself undergo a kind of tragedy but language, along with the rest of creation, is called to 'partake . . . of Christ's sufferings.' Hence, in *The Faerie Queene*, Una's 'bleeding words' or again, in Hopkins' 'The Wreck of the Deutschland,' 'the word of it Sacrificed.' Indeed, just as Christianity might understand the dissolution of language as a function of tragedy so Structuralism might view tragedy as a function of the dissolution of language. 'Recent research,' writes Roland Barthes, 'has demonstrated the constitutively ambiguous nature of Greek tragedy, its texts being woven from words with double meanings that each character understands unilaterally (this perpetual misunderstanding is exactly the "tragic").'

Of course, with such conspicuously Romantic, theological, and tragic pre-histories, *In Memoriam*'s elegy for language does not so much anticipate as challenge 'the structuralist thematic,' avowedly anti-essentialist as it is. Moreover, if the dissolution of language is inscribed with the contours of elegy, and therefore with affective significance, meaning arises out of the very loss of meaning. And so long as there is a grieving within the linguistic void that void is not complete. In the 1833 version of 'Early Spring' Tennyson writes, 'Let tears of wonder fill / Thy void of speech'; as Sinfield paraphrases, 'the void which speech opens up can be filled . . . by tears.' This Tennysonian claim foregrounds, in fact, an obvious problem within poststructuralism's articulation of the void, or emptiness of the sign; as both Joseph and Sinfield point out, Derrida *et al.* find it all but impossible to rid their thought of the elegiac ghost. The work of the Yale critics, writes Sinfield, 'is often in danger of slipping into a nostalgia for the metaphysics it claims to displace'; indeed, even in Derrida's assertion that deconstruction 'must be conceived without nostalgia' there is, argues Sinfield, 'a hint of stoicism.' To adapt a remark of George Steiner's, there is no word less deconstructible than the name of sadness; as Derrida's assertion suggests, sadness is the very last meaning to go as deconstruction finally abandons the consolations of meaning. Sadness's embarrassment of deconstruction is significant; its philosophical force should not be underestimated.

The Victorian poets, and Tennyson in particular, knew this well; elegy,

their characteristic mood and mode, is not just testimony to the passing
of belief in transcendence but also a last-gasp perpetuation of that same
transcendence. Hence, for instance, Emily Bronte's 'divinest anguish,'
Matthew Arnold's preoccupation with 'the nobleness of grief,' and
Tennyson's reference to 'some divine despair.' Arnold, in fact, laments that
'the nobleness of grief is gone,' and so contrives to grieve even for the
departure of grief, thus illustrating elegy's capacity to survive its own
deconstruction. Arnold's line serves, then, as a gloss to 'the far-off interest
of tears.'

The 'interest,' or significance, of *In Memoriam*'s tears for language is
not, though, limited to elegy's philosophical force or irony. For these are
tears over a void which is not just the 'doom assigned' to language in all
times and all places but also an effect of specific historical circumstances
– in particular, the mid-nineteenth century's mechanization of printing.
This is, from the outset, implicit in that the poet's 'measured language
. . . [is a] sad mechanic exercise.' Armstrong is very helpful here through
her observation that with the emergence of 'what Carlyle called "movable
type"' there was both a 'technologising of the sign and a new account of
alienated language.' In this context the meaning of 'type' when used of
Hallam-as-logos comes under distinct pressure, particularly since we are
told that it was a 'remorseless iron hour / [that] Made . . . earth of thee.'
Interestingly, the iron hour of the machine also contributes to the alienation of language in *Maud* where the protagonist sees a strange apparition
that might almost be a page of print: for 'plagued' he is

> with a flitting to and fro,
> A disease, a hard mechanic ghost,
> That never came from on high
> Nor ever rose from below
> But only moves with the moving eye.

Of course, to be now suggesting that the sadness of language, as
conceived by *In Memoriam,* is in some sense referable to the extrinsic and
alterable conditions of Victorian culture means that the poem's tears carry
an implicit appeal for change. If so, language constitutes not so much a
pure tragedy as one that entails at least the possibility, however 'far off,'
of the comedy of change.

After all, Tennyson did write that *In Memoriam* 'was meant to be a
kind of *Divina Commedia*'; to adapt Clough's axiom, language's tragic
plot has a comic counterplot. Indeed, for *In Memoriam* 'plot' is no casual
term, rather it has a very special pertinence to that legerdemain by which
the tragedy of language becomes, in part, a comedy. For, though

> truth in closest words shall fail,
> . . . truth embodied in a tale
> Shall enter in.

Where arguments fail the words that tell a story shall succeed. It is as if there is something intrinsically successful or comic about stories, so much so in fact that Armstrong suggests '*In Memoriam* longs to be a narrative.' What is so special about the 'tale' by which truth is 'embodied' is, it seems, that words become flesh; hence the ensuing declaration: 'And so the Word had breath.' That, for *In Memoriam*, the comedy of language relates to its materiality, or what Foucault calls the 'phonetic premise,' is, in effect, Hirsch's point when she observes that 'in both the climactic section 95 and the epithalamion . . . [the poem recovers or] returns [to] a scene of speech [that] revivifies an otherwise lost voice.' It is not, then, just the comic Word Himself that takes flesh and has 'breath.' For Tennyson draws on the incarnational premise – 'Man's word is God in man' ('The Coming of Arthur') – not to perpetuate an idealist account of language, as can happen in, say, Max Müller's writings (e.g. 'The word is thought incarnate'), but rather to help conceive of 'matter-moulded forms of speech.' Indeed, in so doing, *In Memoriam* serves to recall us to the specifically theological force of what tends to be, for contemporary literary theory, a largely secular formulation: namely, the materiality of the sign. We tend to marginalize the fact that, as Clark and Holquist point out, Mikhail Bakhtin's seminal 'conviction that the sign has a body corresponds to . . . [his] ontotheological view that the spirit has a Christ.' One critic who has, in passing, acknowledged this correspondence is Terry Eagleton who, in his early, Catholic phase, writes that 'Christ, uniquely, is both a body and a language.' Like Bakhtin or the early Eagleton, *In Memoriam*'s very Christo-logocentrism helps to produce, in a conspicuous swerve away from logocentrism per se, a decidedly materialist linguistic.

The parallel with Bakhtin's material sign extends, in fact, to the sense of carnival and even laughter which accompanies that sign: 'the most ancient forms for representing language,' writes Bakhtin, 'were organized by laughter.' For just as the poet declares 'ring out my mournful rhymes, / But ring the fuller minstrel in,' so the internal sadness of words is to some extent counterpointed by a certain levity or minstrelsy. Note, for instance, that 'Sorrow . . . sports with words,' that only 'lesser griefs . . . may be said,' that 'Love . . . played with gracious lies,' and that 'grief with symbols play[s].' There is, then, the suggestion of an irreducible levity within language; as Armstrong remarks: 'the poem . . . sport[s] with words.' Armstrong, in fact, adds that such 'play is a necessity'; and so it is, to the extent that words are seen as merely the phonetic or material surface of the mind: 'My words,' we read, 'are only words, and moved / Upon the topmost froth of thought.' Much the same phonetic surface is implicit in the assertion that 'The lightest wave of thought shall lisp.' As the 'froth' or 'lisp' of thought, the phonetic materiality of the sign appears to trouble, or disconcert, all attempts at absolute gravity, even Sorrow's. Moreover, this phonetic levity even extends, in the characteristic form of the pun, to the silence of the written word, as happens when the poet describes the signatures of his sister and her newly-wed husband as 'Mute symbols of a joyful morn.' Though the signatures may be 'mute,' the word 'morn,' in the context of elegy, is most obviously not; inscribed then with the ensuing oxymoron, 'joyful mourn,' the line entails – in its 'froth' or 'lisp' – a double contradiction or irony. As the poet remarks, 'there oft seemed to live / A contradiction on the tongue.' Thus, the poem's phonetic dimension, or what Sinfield calls its 'intense effects of sound and rhythm,' are not, as he goes on to claim, simply 'Tennyson's strategy for limiting the arbitrariness of the sign.' Knowing as it does that contradiction lives on the tongue as much as on the page of movable type, *In Memoriam* departs – *pace* Hirsch – the thoroughgoing phonocentrism of Tennyson's fellow Apostle, John Donaldson. To this extent the poem anticipates Derrida's deconstruction of speech.

However, *In Memoriam*'s account of the spoken word makes it the site not so much of pure contradiction or *différance* but of struggle; as with Bakhtin, the poem's sense of the materiality of the sign, though in part a phonetic minstrelsy of 'froth' and 'lisp,' is also and at the same time radical and politically subversive. I acknowledge that this perception of speech as 'matter-moulded' derives from mid-nineteenth century accounts of language whose materialism has to do with either the empiricism of Locke or the naturalism of Chambers; nevertheless, the same perception acquires or develops a specifically radical meaning. In this respect it parallels the subversive significance of the new philology and its startling reversal of language study's traditional preoccupation with the written word. As G. W. Cox commented, 'the vulgar dialects that had formed a kind of undercurrent rise beneath the crystal surface of the literary language and sweep away, like the waters in spring, the cumbrous formation of a bygone age.'

Notwithstanding this obvious parallel the political force of *In Memoriam*'s 'matter-moulded forms of speech' is most conspicuously formulated out of the poem's very Christo-logocentrism; for 'the Word [that] had breath' also

> Wrought
> With human hands the creed of creeds
> In loveliness of perfect deeds
>
> . . . .
>
> Which he may read that binds the sheaf
> Or builds the house, or digs the grave.

Thus formulated, the paradigmatic Word ascribes to language not just a phonetic materiality but also the materiality of manual labour or production; not only does 'the Word [operate] with human hands' but he that may read the Word 'binds the sheaf.'

Of course, if *In Memoriam*'s incarnational premise does indeed identify language with production -'without him [the Word] was not any thing made that was made' – then it constitutes a comic counterpoint to that 'sad mechanic exercise' of language alienated by the mid-Victorian technologising of the sign. As we know, for Shelley it was poetry that restored language to its originary condition and thus to its moment of production, as it were; poetry, after all, is 'a making.' As part of the Romantic tradition, Tennyson does share this hope; as Sinfield remarks, it seems to have been Tennyson's customary assumption 'that in poetry the defect of words is remedied.' Nevertheless, it is perhaps a measure of *In Memoriam*'s distance from high Romanticism that the restoration of language to the moment of making means not so much a celebration of poetry as a dim apprehension that all language is a form of production or craft. Thus it is that the poet talks of poetic capacity as the 'practice . . . expert / In fitting aptest words to things' and, in relation to Hallam's fame that never was, of 'force that would have forged a name.' There is, then, some significant concurrence with Raymond Williams' Marxist understanding that 'signification . . . is a practical material activity . . . indeed, literally a means of production.'

Such concurrence, even its possibility, comes as something of a surprise, particularly alongside the now familiar claim that Victorian poetry in general, in its preoccupation with language and the transcendent, perpetuates a bourgeois elision of language's material situatedness. However, there is some evidence that Victorian poets knew better. For instance, in Browning's *Sordello* we read not only that there is not 'so pure a *work* of thought / As language' but also that 'the poet [is] . . . welding words into the crude / Mass from the new speech round him.' Like Tennyson's 'practice . . . in fitting . . . words to things,' Browning's 'welding [of] words' effectively counterpoints the 'sad mechanic exercise' not because they conceive of a sign any less technological but because they lay bare a moment of production and, therefore, of labour. The contrast with Lord Macaulay's assertion that 'language [is] the machine of the poet,' or W. J. Fox's similarly utilitarian reference to 'the machinery of a poem,' is not so much technological as political; the poets' own metaphors constitute a telling shift toward the labourer who *works* the machine.

In Memoriam's intuition of 'the Word . . . with human hands' is, then, both a half-witting reversal of the contemporary alienation of language and also a radical reimagining of the politics of industry. In short, the poem's tragedy of language is answered by not just a comedy but a kind of revolution, albeit as much feared as hoped for.

Hence the way that the elegy, for both Hallam and the logos he represents, is at times opposed by the contemporary threat of Chartist revolution. Note, for instance, the rhetorical cry,

> Is this an hour
> For private sorrow's barren song,

When more and more the people throng
The chairs and thrones of civil power?

That the people taking to the streets represents a comedic antithesis to the poet's own bourgeois tragedy is perhaps echoed by the lines, 'He is not here; *but* far away / The noise of life begins again . . . On the bald street.' For comedy in general to be thought under the sign of collectivity is, of course, a commonplace; as Northrop Frye remarks, 'comedy tends to deal with characters in a social group.' But what is specific to Tennyson's elegy is that this collectivity extends to the comedy of language; for, in an echo of Adam Smith's axiom that it is labour which fills up the monetary sign, the linguistic sign in *In Memoriam* proves to be, in part, replenished by a kind of proletarian collectivity. Hallam represents, that is, not just an abstract idealization of language (i.e. the *Logos*) but also a specific and dominant discourse, or register of language: he bears 'the grand old name of gentleman' and 'shape[s] the whisper of the throne.' Thus, when the reminiscing Tennyson returns to Hallam's rooms in Cambridge to find '*another name* was on the door' it is quite as if some kind of social revolution has thereby been effected; particularly since 'all within was noise / Of songs, and clapping hands, and boys / That crashed the glass and beat the floor.' Just as in the England of 1848 'the people [literally] throng / The chairs . . . of civil power,' so here they metaphorically throng the realm of names, or language, now vacated by Hallam.

The force of labour again throngs and indeed replenishes this realm (though this time it is the poem's own language) when we read that 'life is not as idle ore,

But iron dug from central gloom,
  And heated hot with burning fears,
  And dipt in baths of hissing tears
And battered with the shocks of doom
To shape and use.

Here the industrial analogue, foregrounded by both its modernity and length, serves to eclipse the conventional wisdom that suffering maketh man; in Lacanian terms, the stanza's philosophic signified slides under the industrial signifier. Even as the stanza is emptied of its literal significance so it is replenished, as it were, by industrial rhetoric. And much the same drama recurs whenever the working or living conditions of the 'people' – pressing upon the poem by way of association, allusion, or rhetoric – contrive to displace the explicit subject of the poetry. Consider, for instance: 'like coarsest clothes against the cold'; 'sealed within the iron hills'; 'every kiss of toothed wheels'; 'out of darkness came the hands'; and 'all . . . is toil cooperant.'

Although, in general, Victorian poetry was 'offered . . . the space . . .

left when the main business of the world had been done elsewhere,' very often that business threatens to reclaim the aesthetic space. To be more specific, the rhetoric of labour threatens to replenish the very gap formed by the exclusion of the fact of labour. Indeed, on the evidence of the decree in Robert Browning's 'Rabbi Ben Ezra' that 'Not on the vulgar mass / Called "work," must sentence pass' or Carlyle's claim that 'the under-classes [are] . . . wild inarticulate souls unable to speak,' it seems only inevitable that all Victorian discourse is to some extent marked by the absence of labour. Thus it is that in *In Memoriam* the emptiness of the sign is understood as not only a timeless semiotic tragedy but also an ideological formulation. It becomes, that is, a partly historical tragedy of domination in which the word is alienated from the referent just as consciousness, under capitalist modes of production, is alienated from social and economic realities.

A semiotic extension of Marxist analysis comes, of course, as no surprise; Raymond Williams, for example, associates 'the radical distinction between "language" and "reality" [with that] . . . between "consciousness" and "the material world,"' while Eagleton has argued that Saussure's notion of an arbitrary, non-referential sign is essentially bourgeois. What does surprise, however, is the intuitive rehearsal of such analysis in *In Memoriam* where, on occasions, the distinction between sign and referent is quite clearly hierarchical, or socio-economic. For example, we read, on the one hand of 'noble letters,' 'noble type,' and 'the wealth / Of words' and, on the other, that 'griefs that may be said . . . Are but as *servants*.' We may précis this semiotic intuition with a phrase from *Maud*: 'she had given,' we read, 'her *word to a thing so low*.' In short, that which cannot be spoken is not so much beyond language as beneath language. Tennyson's well-documented preoccupation with 'the Nameless' cannot, then, be dismissed as a merely metaphysical project, for it is also and at the same time an apprehension of the silenced and subordinate. What George Eliot calls in *Middlemarch* 'that roar which lies on the other side of silence' might just, for Tennyson, be the roar of the silenced. We read, that is, not only of 'nameless trouble' but also, in *Maud*, that 'I am nameless and poor.' For the Victorians, I suggest, the Unnameable cannot be thought of independently of that unspeakable threat, the militant poor; witness Carlyle's description of Chartism as 'a new name for a thing which has had many names, [and] which will yet have many.'

Of course, if the working classes do merge, in the Victorian mind, with that which stands outside language, then that extra-linguistic realm becomes inscribed, by force of the analogy, with a near-revolutionary energy or threat. In short, the Victorian mind is bound to entertain, however unconsciously, nothing less than a revolt of the referent. In *In Memoriam*, for example, though 'the lesser griefs that may be said . . . Are but as servants [it is] in a house / *Where lies the master newly dead*'; 'that [which] may be said' enjoys, it seems, an emancipation from the mastery and mediation of saying, or language – now those servants 'speak their feeling as it is.' Thus, though the poet often despairs that the word silences or fails the thing, he also declares that 'I cannot think the thing farewell.' Similarly, in Browning's *The Ring and the Book* as the discussion moves from the ring to the book we read, of the former, ''Tis . . . / A thing's *sign*: now for the thing *signified*.' Nearer still to *In Memoriam*'s referent in revolt is Browning's 'A Death in the Desert' where we read of 'objects brought too close, / Lying confusedly insubordinate, / For the unassisted eye to master.' According to Martha Vicinus, the insubordinate thing is symptomatic of the Victorians' increasingly commodified and automatised world, 'a world where,' as in the novels of Dickens, 'so many objects were out of control.' The parallel with Jean Baudrillard's description of our own late-capitalist culture as 'the triumph of objects over subjects' is obvious; 'the obscene proliferation of. . . [the] object world . . . surpasses all attempts,' he argues, 'to understand, conceptualize, and control it.'

As the parallel with Baudrillard suggests, the insurrection of the thing does not necessarily entail a simple or conservative restoration of the sign-referent relationship. For, although a dramatic affront to both Saussurean and indeed Victorian anti-representationalism, the insurrection is not quite identical with the Romantic, or symbolic, reunion of language and reality that critics have often attributed to Tennyson. The revolt of the referent must be thought of in somewhat different terms, for it is motivated not only by the threat of working-class insurrection but also by the force of desire. To put it briefly, in *In Memoriam* desire or sentiment has the capacity, just for a moment, to make thinkable a space or horizon outside language.

For example, no sooner has the poet compared 'that [which] may be said' to 'servants [whose] master [is] newly dead' than he declares 'My lighter moods are like to these [servants] / That out of words a comfort win'; in short, if the master is language, the text generates the possibility of a comfort that is won 'out[side] of words.' Not limited, though, to gesturing toward an extra-discursive space, the affections or desire also fill up that space with a sense of the thing; in two consecutive lines, that is, the poet declares that, though 'My words are only words,' 'love reflects the thing beloved.' Thus, in the instant before we read the word 'beloved,' desire appears to inaugurate nothing less than a new mimetic all of its own. Admittedly this mimetic is only fleeting, but later – at what is often thought the poem's climax – desire is part of a force that appears to roll back the realm of the sign. For just as 'word by word, and line by line,/ The dead man touched me' so the poet encounters a combination of 'love's dumb cry' and 'doubts that [together] drive the coward back / . . . through wordy snares to track / Suggestion to her inmost cell.' In so driving back both reader and language, love dramatically exceeds the expectations of

Tennysonian and Lacanian alike, both of whom locate desire very much within discourse. Dwight Culler, for instance, remarks of language in Tennyson that 'love . . . is its animating soul' and Herbert Tucker writes that 'the only consummation [is] the mating of word with punning word'; while, for Lacanians, language and desire are identical in that 'man's desire,' writes Lacan, 'is a metonymy,' an 'effect of the signifier.'

Needless to say, the question then is this: by what logic does *In Memoriam* understand 'love's dumb cry' to elude language's 'wordy snares'? Admittedly, the logic is, in part, that of the metaphysics of self-presence: when Hallam's 'living soul was flashed on mine' the poet's soul comes '[up]on that which *is*'; however, the moment's logic is also that of subversion – it is, in fact, more force than logic, more political than metaphysical. For love's dumbness is not so much the silence-beyond-language of mysticism as the silenced cry of Victorian (homo)sexuality – it recalls, that is, 'the wish too strong for words to name.' Moreover, love's silenced cry 'tracks,' or locates 'Suggestion . . . [in] her inmost cell' – imprisoned, it seems, in language's 'wordy snares.' Doubly identified, then, with the repressed, love's cry is situated *beneath* language; a position that, we should now note, is marked as feminine -'Suggestion' is tracked to '*her* inmost cell.'

That the extra-discursive space should shade into the feminine agrees, of course, with Julia Kristeva's assertion that '"woman" [is] that which cannot be represented, that which is not spoken.' This now familiar equation of the feminine and silence is made by the poem itself when, following the final wedding celebrations, the poet remarks that 'Dumb is that tower which spake so loud'; insofar as the tower is a kind of phallus it is as if the voice which has ceased is specifically male, particularly since the poet then concludes with an address to a traditionally feminine principle: 'And rise, O moon, from yonder down.'

If, though, the 'dumb tower' may be said to make silence in the image of the feminine, then silence must also be inscribed with the memory of *Babel*, another 'tower which [once] spake so loud.' Indeed, there is something distinctly multivocal or Babelic about the silence upon silence of 'love's dumb cry': 'And strangely on the silence broke / The silent-speaking words.' Such Babelic silence (or rather silenc*es*) is very far from the undifferentiated, self-identical silence of traditional accounts of the extra-discursive. Even at this the poem's mystical and comic climax, *In Memoriam*'s silence is too diacritical to appeal to a metaphysic of presence.

Indeed, made as it is in the image of both woman and Babel, such silence comes very close to Hélène Cixous' *écriture féminine* which 'lets the other language speak – the language of 1,000 tongues.' No doubt closest to personifying such a writing is 'Suggestion . . . [within] her inmost cell' and 'wordy snare.' What, though, distinguishes both 'Suggestion' and *In Memoriam*'s other silences is that, unlike Cixous' *écriture*, which 'work[s] on the difference,' they contrive to locate, if only for a moment, some kind of extra-discursive horizon. In short, as part of a more general and comic revolt of the referent, these feminine and Babelic silences effectively objectify Cixous' project; a project which does itself, in claiming all possible subject positions, push subjectivity to the very verge of objective realisation. Thus while Cixous' *écriture* makes the feminine subject 'capable of [being] others . . . of him, of you,' *In Memoriam*'s silences make the feminine capable also of 'it,' or facticity.

This capacity is inscribed, once again, within the poem's incarnational premise by which language is conceived of as both feminine ('loveliness') and factual, or material ('deeds'): 'the Word,' we read, 'wrought / . . . the creed of creeds / In loveliness of perfect deeds.' However, the notion of a discourse that is at once feminine and material is most precisely inscribed in the Prayer Book definition of the Church as both 'the spouse and body of Christ' – in other words, as the Word made feminine flesh. It is, then, by way of this theology of the Church that *In Memoriam* proves most nearly to realise and historicise Cixous' *écriture* – particularly since she insists that 'woman must write her *body*.'

In his early book *Body as Language*, Eagleton effectively paraphrases this theology by talking of 'that articulate body of signs we call the Church' and, of course, in *In Memoriam* that structure's most prominent sign is the person or figure of the bride, Tennyson's younger sister, Celia. Moreover, though never conspicuous, the Church is present not only as the site of the buried Hallam, that 'single church . . . folded in the mist,' but also dispersed across a whole sequence of signs or signifiers: namely, 'priestess,' 'chalice,' 'altar,' 'catacombs. . .crypts,' and 'endless feast.' Thus dispersed, the Church enacts or endures what it means to be the Word's body and spouse; what it means, that is, to be, like Derrida's *différance,* a metaphor for the differing and deferring that is language: the Word's body and spouse is, by definition, never quite the Word itself. In short, 'the dark church like a ghost' both signifies and endures the flickering presence/absence of the Derridean sign. However, far from giving us purely and simply the comedic *ir*resolution of deconstruction (what Derrida calls 'the joyous affirmation of the play of . . . signs . . . without truth') the Church motif is bound to the comedic *resolution* of marriage. Moreover, the bride is all but identical with a conspicuously redemptive language; for not only are 'the most living words of life / Breathed in her ear' but 'Her sweet "I will" has made . . . [bride and groom] one.' The irreducible resolution inscribed within the trope of the bride prevents the Church from allowing a wholly Derridean account of the sign. This resolution consists, though, of not so much a metaphysical appeal as a specifically female 'will to power'; for what makes bride and groom *one* is, to our surprise, not God or priest but rather 'her sweet "I will."' In this sense the bride gives a wilful and assertive twist to her theological correlative, the Church; indeed, in willing the marriage, she begins to represent not so much the bodiliness of the Word as the body *political*-ness of the Word. In short, the bride-as-Church suggests a comedic and empowered rewriting of that earlier and tragic vision of the Word made political: namely, 'The fool that wears a crown of thorns,' a 'civic crown' worn 'in . . . the public squares.'

Of course, if the Church-as-bride constitutes an account of language that resists deconstruction by virtue of its almost feministic 'will to power' then it may usefully be read, I suggest, as a politicized (as well as histori-cized) *écriture féminine*. And indeed, in the last stanza, the Church's resistance increases, albeit along with deconstruction's threat; for here, in finally essaying a public religious discourse ('One God, one law, one element') and thereby affecting the language of liturgy ('One body . . . one Spirit . . . one Hope') or hymnody ('One Church, one Faith, one Lord'), the poem aspires to that status mapped out for literature by Carlyle: 'Literature,' he had declared, 'is fast becoming . . . our Church.'

The means here are, though, as important as the Carlylean end; for, in so obviously imitating liturgy and hymnody, the poem finally makes the Church the implicit site or location of its language. Whilst, earlier in the poem, the Church was, 'like a ghost,' dispersed along a chain of signifiers from 'priestess' to 'bride,' here at the end she makes as if to stand outside discourse as its very site or place. Like the poem's other comedic terms – labour, desire, and the feminine – the Church rehearses that comedic coun-terplot which momentarily locates or rather endures some extra (or sub) discursive horizon. In fact, in this final stanza it is even as the 'divine event' of eschatology is deferred and 'far off' that the 'divine event' of the histor-ical Church becomes most present. In short, the nearest 'divine event' is that which situates discourse in place and time. Tennyson's divine comedy, it seems, is identified more surely with the material situation of the stanza than with its deferred and 'far-off' metaphysics.

To theorize this moment, the materiality of the sign is closer to being the site of the sacred than the more obviously theological (that is, *nega-tively* theological) differing and deferring of the sign. Thus, just as for Bakhtin the sign's body 'corresponds to the belief that the spirit has a Christ' so here the sign's body is the body of Christ, the body of Christ that is the Church. In short, what for Bakhtin is an analogy here approaches a tautology.

IV

Hostage of the Word

Poststructuralism's Gospel Intertext

(1993)

> In the beginning was the Word, and the Word was with God,
> and the Word was God.
> (St John)

That God and speech share the same impossible beginning and, therefore, are always already identical, or coextensive, is the apparent heresy of the prologue to the Gospel of St John. As Michael Edwards has reminded us, not only is the Greek text without any distinguishing capital for '*logos*,' but the Logos proceeds to speak *logoi*; in short, the same word is used to describe both Christ and utterance or speech. For some, if God is neither prior to nor outside of speech then religious conviction is undone. Terry Wright, for instance, writes that the 'belief that language does point to a "real" referent, however indirectly, seems to me to be crucial to Christian faith.' For others, it appears easy enough to believe that God might be identical with the very signs and meanings in which we move and have our being. Robert Scharleman writes, 'God *is* what language *means*, and language is what God means.'

However much one might share Wright's understanding, the Johannine prologue itself is surely much closer to Scharleman; for here we are confronted with the end of a God who defines himself and thus stands outside discourse: we are not told that 'God was God' on the model of 'I am that I am,' as in Old Testament Exodus. Instead, what we are given is 'the *Word* was God,' an account of speech as not a closed system but an infinitely open and literally God-like field of meaning. This sense of a speech-that-is-absolute coming into being even as an absolute-outside-speech passes away is effectively articulated by Charles Winquist: 'The death of God,' he writes, 'is the birth of the Word.' Winquist, of course, here speaks not only *from* a postmodern position but also *about* that position or situation. Johannine incarnation (on the one hand) and the postmodern or poststructuralist situation (on the other) might be described, it seems, in one and the same way; as Jacques Lacan demonstrates when declaring that 'Man has become the hostage of the Word because God is dead.'

This coincidence comes as no surprise in the sense that poststructuralist discourses often rehearse or rewrite the Johannine prologue. 'In the beginning is hermeneutics,' suggests Derrida; 'it was certainly the Word (*verbe*) that was in the beginning,' writes Lacan; while according to Kristeva, 'In the beginning was love.' Indeed, in *Glas*, Derrida sustains a continuing dialogue with St John's Gospel, at one point offering us a page-long précis of the whole narrative, albeit 'violently selected [and] fragmented.' Picking up on this dialogue between poststructuralism and gospel, my essay explores the ways in which each discourse may be read as an allegory or rewriting of the other. My premise is that they are intertexts, that we cannot think one without thinking the other. On behalf, as it were, of the poststructuralists, Lacan declares: 'For us the word has. . . come into the world and contrary to the saying . . . in the Gospel, it is not true that we have not received it. We have recognised it.'

My premise is that both discourses, both theology *and* theory, are necessarily at risk, in danger of being displaced or even appropriated by the other. Until recently it has been rather assumed that it was theological discourse which was the most in danger. Roland Barthes, for instance, writes that 'literature . . . by refusing to assign . . . an ultimate meaning to the text . . . liberates . . . an anti-theological activity. . . . To refuse to fix meaning is, in the end, to refuse God.' Likewise, Lacan argues that his rewriting of 'the Other . . . as the place of speech was a way of exorcising our good old God'; while Derrida observes that 'the intelligible face of the sign,' that face or side which is always already deferred, 'remains turned toward the face of God.' Clearly, if the possibility of intelligible or determinate meaning is indeed an ever-receding horizon then so too is the face of God. For Derrida, language admits no possibility of a final or fixed meaning that we may call 'God'; there is no such concept in which we can ground or make sense of the ideas and meanings, whether religious or not, amidst which we live.

Such a thesis is without doubt alarming for the believer, questioning as it does any talk of a God of identity. However, as Kevin Hart and others have been arguing, though such a God may well be the God of philosophy and theology, he is not the God of faith. Hart's point is that Derrida's project is not so much a critique of God but of logocentrism, that habit we have of centring the way we think or speak on any one point of reference which may, admittedly, be 'God' but could equally be, say, 'truth,' 'reason,' or 'Man.' Hart goes so far as to summarise Derrida's position thus: 'one may hold that there *is* a God but that there is no *concept* of God . . . that can ground one's discourse about God or the world.' Hart is perhaps overstating the case simply by stating it (the copula 'is' would, for Derrida, be under erasure) but we do well to heed him. For, surely God could never be limited to the centre of our discourse, never be limited merely to guaranteeing or holding together whatever Christianity declares him to be. This may well make creeds and, perhaps, belief very difficult; but unless my faith may always be ambushed by the language in which it is expressed I am not fully open to the God whose name is speech. To quote Edwards again, 'John's Gospel . . . declares that . . . God is the Word, not [mere] Reason, or the vague Ground of our being.' Just as Heidegger distinguishes between Logos and logic so the Christian would differentiate, as René Girard does, between the Hellenic Logos (more nearly the logos of logocentrism) and the Johannine Logos. As Derrida himself remarks, '[although] John writes in Greek, the Gospel . . . is by a Greek Jew.'

What then Hart, Edwards, and Girard are arguing is that our sense of God need not necessarily be logocentric, or even theological, by which Derrida usually means monological, or totalising. In other words, the 'good old God' who both guarantees our meanings and whose meanings can be guaranteed may never have really existed outside philosophy. Properly (mis)understood, as Jean-Luc Marion has argued, the Judaeo-Christian God always has been what Emmanuel Levinas seeks: namely, 'a God not contaminated by being.' In the words of Heidegger, another key figure for deconstruction, 'faith does not need the thought of Being.' So much in fact is acknowledged by Derrida when he writes that the 'original, heterogeneous [i.e. non-Hellenic] elements of Judaism and Christianity . . . perdure throughout the centuries, threatening and unsettling the assured "identities" of Western philosophy.' Derrida's point is not difficult to illustrate. For instance, the Judaeo-Christian God is never purely or simply present, whether as Yahweh in the Old Testament or, in the New, as the one choosing the 'things which are not, to bring to nought things that are.' Instead, he is always in some sense other or absent, other than we say and absent from our understanding. Quite clearly, this way lies negative theology, a mode of discourse often compared to deconstruction and indeed discernible, as postmodern theologians have stressed, within even Christianity's most positive theology. One might cite, for example, Simone Weil: 'I am quite sure,' she writes, 'there is no God in the sense that I am sure there is nothing which resembles what I can conceive when I say that word.'

Of course, insofar as Weil – or, for that matter, the negative theologian – affirms that God is some kind of super-essentiality beyond the reach of the sign, they must part from Derrida, for whom God, like every other sign, is dispersed across or along the chain of signification. What, he asks Levinas, 'if God [were but] . . . an *effect of the trace*?' Though perhaps unfamiliar, this attenuated and evanescent God of semiotics is surely closer to John's Gospel than the ineffable God of negative theology. This is a fine but important distinction, hinging on the prologue's implication that Christ, as the Word, does not so much put himself beyond language but rather that he endures all its frailties. Indeed, his very life, characterised as it is by discontinuities, displacements, and misinterpretation, parallels closely the fate, or itinerary, of the Derridean sign. 'Ye shall seek me,' Christ declares, 'and shall not find me.'

On this reading, and here I draw in part on hints and suggestions from postmodern theology, many aspects of the gospel narrative acquire new significance. The Incarnation, for instance, becomes an account of how the Word's very presence (in human flesh) is always already compounded by his absence (from the Father). Likewise, Christ's subversion of the Mosaic Law from within becomes a Derridean contest between the total-izing Book and the enigmatic text, or *écriture*; it is not for nothing that when the woman is caught in adultery his tacit protest takes the form of writing in the dust. Again, Christ-crucified is also Christ-written in that he endures not only a cross but the trilingual rubric, or legend, 'King of the Jews,' thereby suffering what Derrida terms the 'outer darkness,' or 'Violence of the Letter.' 'What I have written, I have written,' says Pilate of this text, a text that accomplishes both the irony and Babelic divided-ness of *écriture*. If we continue this allegorical reading, the Resurrection becomes the Word's refusal of all limits including that of presence; as the angels say at the empty tomb, 'he is not here' but, as it were, always already elsewhere. If so, then the Johannine Paraclete becomes, as Stephen Moore suggests, yet 'a further Substitution,' or deferral of the Word; to quote a more conventional Bible commentator, the Spirit is 'the presence of Jesus when Jesus is absent.'

That the trajectory of the Word might parallel that of the Derridean or poststructural sign is an intuition not peculiar to post-modern theology but shared by the poststructuralists themselves among whom the Johannine narrative operates as a kind of subtext; as when Derrida describes how writing 'risk[s] death in the body of a signifier that is given over to the world and the visibility of space.' The debt to the Judaeo-Christian tradition is, indeed, an acknowledged debt: 'Have we ever left the Church?' asks Derrida; while Lacan declares that 'God has not made his exit.' For evidence of this it is common to point to the Jewish Derrida who playfully signs himself as 'Reb Derrissa' or 'Reb Rida,' and who in a series of essays since 1980 'has been exploring,' writes Graham Ward, 'th[e] . . . unerasable nature of the theological.' Indeed, Geoffrey Hartman has not only described *Glas* as a 'graveyard, [or] perhaps Golgotha, of dissociated names and notions' but also, playing on the name of Derrida's publishers, declared it to be 'of the House of Galilee.'

Beyond Derrida we should note that Bakhtin's influential rewriting of the logos as *dialogos*, and thus all discourse as a carnival of dialogic meaning, is decisively related to the figure of the mocked Christ whose 'crown of thorns . . . is an anti-crown.' That the work of Bakhtin, a life-long adherent of Russian Orthodoxy, has important theological resonances is just beginning to be recognized. Much the same could be said of poststructuralism's various critiques of the Cartesian subject. Rewritten as not the cause but merely the effect of discourse, the post-structural 'I' becomes disseminated across an endless series of substitutions. As Barthes puts it, 'I am dispersed,' suggesting that for the first time since Descartes Western thinking is not automatically founded on the humanistic premise of the subject. That this development makes space for an otherness or alterity that might just be God is clear to Lacan, who writes that 'Descartes inaugurates the initial bases of a science in which God has nothing to do.' Indeed, the early Bakhtin argues that 'where I do not absolutely coincide with myself, a place for God is opened up.' As Edwards has observed, we are approaching an epistemological version of Saint Paul's 'yet not I, but Christ,' particularly since 'Christ,' we read, 'made himself nothing' – in other words, made himself the very space vacated by the subject. All this is explicitly recognised by Luce Irigaray, who argues that to undo a masculine logic which appropriates all accounts of the subject requires that the woman make a mystical virtue of the impossibility of subjecthood; and this manoeuvre, Irigaray suggests, finds a paradigm in the kenotic Christ.

Whether, then, it be as a Galilean subtext in Derrida, a holy fool in Bakhtin, or a model for subjectlessness in Irigaray, the Word quite clearly endures, if not thrives on, the displacements, subversions, and dissolutions of poststructuralism. We should here echo Hart's observation that 'Christian theology – in some of its elements at least – is a process of deconstruction.' As John Dominic Crossan argues, 'It is where our language-world . . . breaks apart that God can be found,' not *beyond* our meanings but, as it were, *between* them. This 'new version of a "God of the gaps,"' as Wright puts it, is clearly an intriguing possibility for faith, particularly since for Derrida and Lacan language is nothing other than a tissue of differences. But would faith suggest that contemporary discussions of the emptiness of the sign are always unwitting meditations on, say, the kenotic Word? I think not.

In the first place, all the major theorists, with the possible exception of Bakhtin, would themselves refute such a possibility. Derrida, for instance, finally rejects the comparison with negative theology, instead describing his work as a 'negative atheology.' Likewise, Kristeva concludes *Au commencement était l'amour* with an assertion of the fundamental atheism of psychoanalysis. A still more important reason, however, for withdrawing from a theological appropriation of poststructuralism is that it is not necessarily in the nature or rather history of the servant Word to issue in a master discourse. Indeed, reminding us that 'the world knew him not' and 'his own received him not,' Girard goes so far as to argue that 'the Johannine Logos . . . is forever expelled, an absent Logos that never has had any direct, determining influence over human culture.' We must reject, it seems, the possibility that deconstruction, inscribed as it is on the very body of Western culture, may accede priority to the Johannine Word.

If Christianity recognizes any coincidence between itself and deconstruction, it must, then, be at the risk of losing itself, of being decentred and displaced by the play of the sign. But, of course, insofar as the Word himself is always expelled or pushed aside, so Christian discourse, far from being abolished by its own displacement, might just thereby discover its subject more fully. Such an irony lies behind David Jasper's suggestion that 'living with the sad critical logic we have been taught [may be] . . . the most unexpected road back to that which we thought we had lost.' Indeed, unless we are prepared to lose the Word, as he himself was prepared to be lost, perhaps we shall not gain him. It is may be for this that he says to Mary 'do not hold on to me.' As Meister Eckhart puts it, 'I pray God he make me free of God.'

Following then the example of the Word, Christian discourse may well end up risking itself. We cannot speak, as Eric Ives does, of 'deconstruction . . . [as] a bad master but a . . . necessary servant.' Instead, as a hostage of the Word, the Christian's very fate is deconstruction; or rather, and here my argument turns, *part* of her fate. For while the Johannine Word does not stop short of deconstruction he does, as it were, exceed it. I refer to the stubborn fact that, for all Christ's ambiguities, he also regularly makes statements that presuppose both their own truth and clarity. For example: 'this is the condemnation . . . men loved darkness rather than light'; or, 'Verily, I say unto you, I am the door'; or, again, 'these things I command you, that ye love one another.' Moreover, Christ emphatically separates himself from the negations and indirections of Jarwehism by the sheer directness of his addressing God as 'Abba' or 'my father.' To this extent, the Gospels put into question what Norman Brown calls 'a Dionysian Christianity,' in which meaning is absolutely unfixed. Or rather, such a Christianity must put itself into question since, like any other thorough-going scepticism, if it really is open to the *absolute* uncertainty of things it cannot exclude the possibility of certainty.

Both the gospels and the very logic of scepticism compel me to suspect that if I make the Word in the likeness of postmodern relativism this relativism might itself be relative. Perhaps it is no more than an inflection, as Fredric Jameson suggests, of the cultural logic of late-capitalism. There has certainly been a tendency for postmodernists to heroise what Lacan might prompt us to call a subject presumed *not* to know. We talk, that is, of the agonies of uncertainty and yet also remark, as Crossan does, that 'we do not mourn that we see through a glass darkly, [but] rejoice in the dark loveliness of the glass.' Of course, if I do not see through the glass it acts as a mirror, and that appeals to my vanity. Moreover, the biblical verdict is that we rejoice in the dark, even dark loveliness, because our deeds are evil; or, at least, that the reason I prefer uncertainty to conviction is that it is less likely to commit me to changing either myself or the world. Eagleton has been making this point from a Marxist position for some time; 'deconstruction,' he claims, 'is, among other things, an effect of . . . indifference [and] privilege.' In the context of postmodernity it may well be that the 'foolishness of God,' a foolishness that presumably changes as often as the wisdom of man, is the disturbing trace of clarity and fixedness that runs throughout the trajectory of the Word. Perhaps we should now reverse Franz Kafka's aphorism: 'What is laid upon us,' he wrote, 'is to accomplish the negative; the positive is already given.' For postmodernity, it seems, it is the negative that is given.

To put it another way, the hermeneutics of suspicion has taught us to suspect the positive, to expose it as that nostalgia for presence which Derrida criticizes so relentlessly. John's Gospel, however, compels us to think otherwise, in that the Word's fixedness, or determinacy, inheres not so much in declarations of monologic authority – even 'I am the way, the truth, and the life' appears to be misunderstood – but rather in the dialogic positions and oppositions in which he is situated. In declaring 'I am the truth' he is not identifying himself *with* the truth, as something prior or given, but *as* the truth. He thus rewrites the truth so that it becomes not something we may know but whose side we may take: 'everyone,' he says, 'on the side of truth listens to me.' What is most certain about the Word is not what he means but how he is received, that he may be either accepted or rejected. 'I am come,' he says, '[not] to give peace . . . but rather division'; and in John we more than once read that 'there was a division among the people because of him.'

The point, then, at which the Word finally hardens into certainty refers not to the logocentrism of the absolute truth claim but to the relative or provisional conditions of both his reception and also, more generally, his situation. Note, for instance, that the Word is bound not only by extrinsic power, 'I will not talk much with you; for the prince of this world cometh,' but also by history: 'My time is not yet come.' Thus constrained by his material situation, the Word endures a fixity or determinacy that the Gospel expresses in terms of the limits of the body. 'The Word,' we read, 'became flesh.'

That the Word's determinacy should be so expressed realigns it with the itinerary of the poststructural sign, or rather with recent Marxist-cum-materialist readings of that sign. For, following Bakhtin and Foucault, such readings see the undecidability of the text arrested by the fact that the 'sign,' to quote Bakhtin '[always] has some kind of material [or situational] embodiment.' Indeed, what is often overlooked is that, for Bakhtin himself, the materiality of language is inextricably bound up with the Russian Orthodox stress on the Word becoming flesh. As his biographers put it, 'this conviction that the sign has a body corresponds to Bakhtin's ontotheological view that the spirit has a Christ.' One might argue, in fact, that the same doctrine haunts Eagleton's linguistic and cultural materialism, since in his early Catholic period he argued that 'Christ, uniquely, is both a body and a language. In him, language and bodiliness finally converge.'

The poststructural sign, it seems, is a hostage of the Johannine Word at the point of not only its undecidability but also its materiality. Indeed, the Word's very trajectory is something of a mirror image of the material sign. For just as the school of Foucault has stressed that the sign, redefined as a site of struggle, is ultimately motivated by a Nietzschean will to power, so the Word that became flesh, choosing as it does the way of the Cross, is finally motivated by a will to weakness. The gloomiest Foucauldian moment within contemporary theory is, then, analogous to Golgotha. But where the Christian plot departs from the Foucauldian is with the Resurrection, which suggests that meaning, like the Word himself, does survive absolute weakness and is, therefore, something more than just an effect or victim of power.

But that is to move too hastily to the Resurrection; and, strange as it might seem, that is to some extent the mistake of deconstruction. What I mean is that, for Derrida, meaning can no more be fixed or decided by power than by presence, and so will always in the end escape the death of determination. Just as Derrida is anxious lest his 'double science' of reversal and displacement might 'overlook the phase . . . which brings low what was high,' so I am concerned that deconstruction tends to pass too quickly the Golgothan moment in its rewriting of the Christian plot. To put it another way, deconstruction only half acknowledges the Golgotha which is, in fact, inscribed within it. And it is with this inscription, and its several discrete meanings, that the rest of this essay is concerned.

My interest, in the first place, is with those moments in which the broken immediacy of the sign is thought in terms so elegiac – what Derrida calls the 'saddened, negative, [and] nostalgic . . . side of the thinking of play' – as to invoke the rhetoric of the death of God. Carl Raschke, for example, writes that deconstruction is 'in the final analysis the death of God put into writing'; while Derrida himself asserts that only 'the death of God will ensure our salvation.' What distinguishes the Derridean death of God from its counterpart in the gospels is that the former is always thought provisionally, or under erasure: it never quite happens. 'It would not,' writes Derrida, 'mean a single step outside of metaphysics if nothing more than a new motif of. . . "God's death" . . . were the result of. . . [the deconstructive] move.' It is never fully appropriate within deconstruction to talk of God's death since the play of the sign, and therefore the possibility of meaning, can never be completely arrested. For Derrida there is no 'ground of nonsignification.'

By contrast, the gospels do confront us with the death of God and, indeed, the ground of nonsignification. For not only does the divine Word die but, in a moment of absolute kenosis – 'My God, my God, why hast thou forsaken me?' – he is emptied of his very meaning. He could not, as it were, mean less. The concept of God dying entails, that is, the absolute absence of sense, a point that finds its paradigmatic expression in the letter to the Philippians where the cross is described as that unthinkable moment in which the Word 'made himself nothing.' In short, he becomes precisely that ground of nonsignification which is, for Derrida, quite impossible. In this one important respect the trajectory of the Word is far bleaker and more austere than ever is the itinerary of the Derridean sign. Although there is a 'saddened and negative . . . side to the thinking of play,' a side that corresponds to Golgotha, it is always doubled, for Derrida, by that 'other' and, as it were, resurrection 'side [which] . . . is the joyous affirmation of the play of the world and the innocence of becoming.' In the gospels, however, Golgotha is always three days away from Resurrection. Even though *Glas* cites Hegel's insistence that 'Good Friday must . . . be restored in the . . . truth . . . of its Godlessness,' it is not deconstruction but the gospel narrative which is fully and knowingly inscribed with the death of God.

I say 'fully and knowingly' because, if specifically interpreted as the absolute 'foolishness' of the Golgotha of First Corinthians, the 'death of God' *is* to be found in deconstruction, but only as a kind of blind spot. The Corinthian Golgotha privileges non-sense in a way that recalls the analogous prioritising of play in the practice of deconstruction, though not perhaps in Derrida's own writing. This prioritising, particularly in the work of Paul de Man, entails an effective privileging of uncertainty – if you like, the certainty of uncertainty, or what Derrida calls the 'unquestioned possibility of the question.' 'Nontruth is the truth,' he ironically declares. It is just this contradiction, which deconstruction outside Derrida rarely acknowledges, that the Golgotha of apotheosised foolishness can locate. In *Glas*, Derrida describes Jean Genet's *Miracle of the Rose* as 'a violent, parodic [and] . . . implacably derisory interpretation of Golgotha.' Golgotha, however, proves to be a troublesome text for deconstruction in the sense that the cross does *not* simply illustrate deconstruction's concerns, as Hartman and also Raschke seem to think, but rather inflects or even exceeds them.

Indeed, not limited to locating within deconstruction a second-order certainty, Golgotha may also be read as a metaphor for that first-order certainty which Derrida argues is merely desired or dreamt but which the gospels view as a terrible reality. The cross, that is, may be read within deconstruction as not just the certainty of uncertainty but also as that *certainty of certainty* to which Derrida gives the name of death. 'Is not,' he asks, 'the centre, the absence of play and difference, another name for death? The death which reassures and appeases, but also . . . creates anguish and puts at stake?' A correspondence between Golgotha and this death identified as determinacy is easy to trace, both in Derrida's talk of anguish, or putting at stake, and in the crucifixion narrative itself. For at Golgotha the Word's mission or meaning is circumscribed by not only the Pharisaic will to power but also his own acute sense of an ending: 'It is finished,' he cries. Moreover, since he also cries 'My God, my God, why hast thou forsaken me?', the Word, we must presume, is absolutely alone and thus appallingly self-identical, totally unable to defer, or pass the buck of what he now means, namely, sin. He is totally unable, in Christ's own terms, to have the 'cup pass from me.' In short, the crucified is precisely that 'one naked man' whom Derrida, in a fascinating passage on Levinas, entertains as a terrible hypothesis. The passage is a discussion of how, for Levinas, only the infinite (as infinitely other) keeps the world from the violence of totality and its logic of the Same. 'The structures of living. . . experience described by Levinas,' writes Derrida, 'are the very structures of a world in which war would rage . . . if the infinitely other were not infinity, if there were, by chance, one naked man, finite and alone.' For the Christian, of course, this naked and absolutely lone man, infinitely finite (if you will), is not just an hypothesis.

My point, then, is that the hell which Christ endures may be interpreted, within a Derridean frame, as the dead centre of meaning, or what Derrida himself calls 'the bad solitude of solidity and self-identity.' The crucified Logos, we might say, endures the impossibility of logocentrism. In this particular sense Derrida errs when he writes that 'God's name holds death in check.' Invoking the Derridean 'logic' of the signifier, we may say that Golgotha's absolute saviour becomes Hegel's '*savoir absolu*': witness, in *Glas*, Hegel's phrase the 'Calvary of absolute Spirit.' Certain knowledge, it seems, could not be further from the security and shelter that so much poststructuralist theory presumes it to be.

We begin, perhaps, to understand what Frank Kermode, in his discussion of the studied impenetrability of Christ's parables, terms 'the shrine of the single sense.' That even the believer is always to be in part excluded from this shrine reflects, I suggest, not the perversity of God but the mercy. What Golgotha teaches the theorist about single sense is that it is not necessarily an Eden from which she is exiled but rather that it might just be a place of commitment or belief to which, as a Lacanian hostage of the Word, she is called. 'If any man will come after me, let him . . . take up his cross.'

In fine, we might conclude that although the Johannine Word shares the same fate as the poststructural sign it also, and at the same time, suffers what the sign can never endure. He suffers, that is, the Golgotha of certainty, both the certainty of uncertainty that is the beam in the eye of deconstruction, and the certainty of certainty. Thus the importance of this Golgothan account of determinacy is that, in a quite radical irony, it suggests deconstruction to be too sanguine. For in always impossibilising the death that is certainty, deconstruction's affirmation of an endless play of meaning reads, alongside its Johannine intertext, like a resurrection without a crucifixion.

By contrast, for all his undecidability, the Johannine Word is completely vulnerable to the death of determinacy. Hence the way that as the Word made flesh, or situation, he is always already determined by position and opposition: a master to the disciples, a healer to the sick, a blasphemer to the Pharisees. Indeed, the absolute determination of Golgotha comes about as a direct result of these situational or local determinations: the two species of determinacy are intimately related. Thus the call to take up a cross is in part a call to endure the constraints of single sense; for example, the constraints of formulating creeds, taking sides, accepting authority, naming my sin.

And if these moments of single sense may be thought under the sign of Golgotha then two things follow. First, that they share not only in the sufferings of that place but also in its transforming or redemptive energy; somehow, as well as leading to transformation, faith's single senses are in themselves transforming. And second, that like Golgotha, these single senses are, finally, provisional. It may still be Friday, but Sunday is coming. Thus the certainties, positions and meanings to which the believer is called always stand on the brink of a deconstruction whose Johannine or Christian name is resurrection; as Derrida almost acknowledges when talking of 'the joyous . . . affirmation of a world of signs without fault' or 'a certain laughter and a certain step of the dance.' Deconstruction's Christian name is resurrection in the sense that the resurrected and liberated Word does not just defeat every limit but, in so doing, anticipates Pentecost and that loosening of tongues, which marks the birth of the Church.

Might, then, we share in that birth? The only proviso it seems is that the Golgothas of faith's single senses must first be our death.

LAND LOCKED

(MARCH 11TH 1993)

On the birth of two, in Swansea bay.

No,
you cannot possibly
see
she who labours
for you
while
I
and
the
sea-side mid-wives
come and go
talking of
what had been a land.
Yugoslavia,
one had called it.

No,
you cannot possibly
see me see
your secret hearts
dance
on the screen
as
I
hide North of
the bay
to whose arms
you head
on broken waters,
your face
and
your face

two small pictures
of a
sadness
I think no state
to be
born
in.

MAY 2012

V

Why Wait for an Angel?
Thomas Pynchon's *The Crying Lot of 49*
(1995)

> I define *postmodern* as incredulity toward metanarratives.
> (Jean-François Lyotard)

Postmodernism is characterized, above all, by incredulity, a perpetual questioning of not just the grand narratives, or meanings by which we make sense of our lives but also of any certainty, or truth. For the Christian, for one who follows one who declared, 'I am . . . the truth,' such radical scepticism must itself be subject to scepticism. The problem, though, for the Christian reader of contemporary literature is that so often our reading seems to echo the postmodern call to uncertainty. This is, perhaps, particularly true of *Lot 49*, since not only is the novel itself an unresolvable problem, but its central figure, Oedipa Maas, finds her very world to be a riddle without solution.

If you have not yet read *Lot 49*, let me put you in the picture, or rather the question. The novel, which is set in 1960s California, opens with Oedipa learning that she has been named as an executor of the late Pierce Inverarity. In exploring this estate she seems to discover more and more clues suggesting the existence of an anarchic organization called the Tristero, which seems to have its own secret system of communication and, indeed, a secret symbol described as 'a muted post horn' and reproduced thus:

'Communication,' declares Nefestis, 'is the key.' He refers to his improbable machine and its supposed reception of the messages of Maxwell's demon, but his dictum is pertinent to the novel itself. For here we are given a world crammed with all sorts of communications, or messages; not only letters, newspapers, books, acronyms and signs on walls but also phone-calls, television, radio and neon signs. However, just as Oedipa, the protagonist, 'wait[s in vain] . . . for the Demon to communicate' so we often wait in vain for these communications ever to be fully understood or even received. The television, for instance, may be on but not necessarily watched; the phone may ring at three in the morning but there is no real message; and, in the supermarket, 'muzak' plays – music, of course, to be heard but not listened to. In a sense, then, the whole of San Narciso (the novel's fictional Los Angeles suburb) shares the condition of the homeless who spend the night 'swung among a web of telephone wires' and 'thousands of unheard messages.' Indeed, when Oedipa looks down at the geometric street layout of San Narciso she thinks of 'the time she'd opened a transistor radio . . . and seen her first printed circuit.' The American city, it seems, is not so much a place as a vast network for the circulation of disembodied messages, hence 'Telegraph Avenue.'

This is, of course, what cultural theorists have come to call the postmodern universe, a world dominated by the constant flow of unauthored and unaddressed messages, or signs. Such a world may well be frighteningly empty; when Oedipa rings from a pay booth but gets no reply 'The phone buzzed on and on, into hollowness.' However, just as the novel also gives us the '*miracle* of communication' so postmodernist theory, for all its talk of absence, often bears witness to the stubborn persistence of some kind of sacred presence. As Philippa Berry remarks, 'The trace of the holy survives within postmodernism in persistent echoes of that cultural legacy to which it declared itself the murderous heir.' Echoing Berry, several critics and theorists have recently argued that the holy has survived the disruption of all the guarantees and assurances of traditional Western culture; in particular, the guarantee that words yield meanings, that messages have content, that letters have destinations. In short, Roland Barthes may well have got it wrong when, in 1968, he famously declared that 'to refuse to fix meaning is, in the end, to refuse God.' Though the texts and signs among which we live may not make sense, that does not necessarily mean that there is no God. The Christian God is not wedded to sense, or meaning; or, at least, meaning as something definite, or univocal.

This is something, indeed, of which *Lot 49* reminds us. For it is charged with the possibility that there might just be 'another mode of meaning'; moreover, the novel is positively fascinated with that moment in which the gospel bursts out in not one considered voice but many and spontaneous tongues – namely, Pentecost. Not only does *The Courier's Tragedy* (the Jacobean play that is being performed and researched during the course of the novel) include a grotesque and 'frightful Pentecost' of literal 'tongue[s] aflame,' but, as Edward Mendelson has pointed out, Pentecost comes *forty-nine* days after Easter. Admittedly, the Christian reader might, at first, read these intimations as just one more instance of postmodernism rewriting Pentecost in its own, multivocal image. We might, though, suggest that *Lot 49* contrives to defamiliarise the biblical event, to rediscover the shock of a God who speaks through many to many and in many voices.

Clearly, our sense of God *is* going to be defamiliarised by a novel which gives us not only a 'zany paraclete' but an 'epileptic Word,' not to mention a Jesus (the character Jesús Arrabal) who is an anarchist. To be more specific, these teasing formulations disrupt our received, and largely Enlightenment, sense of a God whose actions and speech are consistent with reason and order. The chief biblical source for such a rational account of God is, of course, the prologue to John's Gospel where Christ is identified as the *Logos*, meaning – for the later Greeks – reason, or concept; *Lot 49*, however, with its 'epileptic Word' gestures toward a quite *un*reasonable, or *dis*ordered *Logos*. And indeed, the communications of the holy do seem quite as bizarre as all the other communications. Oedipa's first 'revelation,' for instance, is an 'odd, religious instant' experienced in a Chevvy along a San Narciso freeway, and her last, we anticipate, is in an auction room; in between, she is prey to 'all manner of revelations.' That the Word is not, in *Lot 49*, its usual, privileged self is clear enough; but lest we miss the point, the novel's single most important sign, its Word as it were, first appears to Oedipa on the wall of a public convenience. For the Gospel of John we may read the 'ladies' John.'

Strange, though, as it may seem, such an exchange does not necessarily represent a loss or reduction, since, as Oedipa tells herself, there is a 'high magic to low puns.' In other words, the very fact that the American slang for 'toilet' should happen to coincide with the name of the fourth gospel does not so much bring down Scripture as raise up urinals. We might, then, say that the 'sacred' has nothing to lose and much to gain from sharing the same symbolic world as the 'secular.' This understanding is crucial to any reading of *Lot 49*, a novel in which these two realms, or discourses, constantly interrupt each other. The disc-jockey, for instance, 'cue[s] . . . the next record with movements as stylized as the handling of . . . [the] chalice might be for a holy man'; the movie *Cashiered* features 'father, son, and [a] St Bernard'; and in the laundromat 'the odour of chlorine bleach [rises] . . . heavenward, like an incense.' Moreover, in this context the very verb 'to communicate' becomes charged with a second, eucharistic sense (according to the Anglican Prayer Book, in taking the bread and wine we 'communicate'). As then the Word grows epileptic, as the sacred is exposed to all the fitful disorders of the novel's sheer intertextuality (its radical mixing of narratives and voices) so that sacred shares in the 'high magic of low puns.' According to David Seed, Oedipa 'seek[s] . . . the Word' though 'finds only words,' but if *Lot 49* teaches us anything it is that this is a distinction which overlooks the potential within 'mere' words for the high magic of the sacred.

Can, then, the Christian reader relax in the assurance that since she has a God whose name is Word, or speech, this same God only increases with the novel's multiplication of words and signs? In short, if communication is indeed a miracle or sacred magic, are all words made in the image of *the* Word, or at least the epileptic Word? I think not; *Lot 49* knows too well that, as Michel Foucault has argued, words and meanings are never purely or simply themselves but are always distorted by power. For even as Oedipa, in her pursuit of the Tristero, increasingly finds San Narciso's world of signs charged with alarming connections and coincidences so she comes to suspect the dead hand (or dead letter) of Pierce Inverarity: is she simply being set up by the novel's most powerful character? She is beset, if you like, by the Foucauldian conviction that this world of signs – however Californian, however 'free,' however postmodern – finally reveals not truth, but power or will. As Oedipa remarks of the radio circuit, there is 'a hieroglyphic sense . . . of an intent to communicate'; there is, in more senses than one, a will to communicate, namely Pierce's. In fine, Oedipa-the-interpreter comes to fear that the 'high magic' of coincidence and connection might turn out to be no more than low cunning, something 'willed' into existence.

This anxiety is rather too close for comfort for anyone who reads the novel with an eye to its theological patterns. We scarcely need reminding that what makes these patterns possible might just be an intent, or will – this time, our own. Like Oedipa, we are compelled to ask if, caught in an hermeneutic circle, our interpretations are merely projections? As Oedipa herself puts it, do we merely '*project a world*'? If so, then, like the Cardinal in *The Courier's Tragedy*, who has his big toe cut off and is 'made to hold it up like a Host [consecrated bread] and say "This is my body,"' do we 'communicate' not with God but only with ourselves? Indeed, given the place-name 'San Narciso' (Saint Narcissus) the novel inevitably prompts the suggestion that the fate of the Christian (whose biblical name is, of course, 'saint') is necessarily narcissistic. This suggestion is underlined by the description of the appropriately named *Echo* Courts; for here the narrator casually remarks upon 'the stillness of the pool,' and in doing so prompts, albeit for a moment, associations not only with the mythological pool in which Narcissus (Echo's beloved) becomes enamoured of his own reflection but also the biblical pool of Bethesda where the waters are still until the angel descends. We have to wait, of course, until the very end of the novel for even the possibility of 'a descending angel'; in the meantime, then, it is as if we, the readers of theological patterns, are, like Narcissus, seated beside a still pool gazing at our own reflection, the projection of our own world.

'Greet them that be of the household of Narcissus, which are in the Lord.'
(Romans 16:11)

Pool-gazing may be the tragic end of the story of Narcissus, but it is not the end of the story of Bethesda. According to the gospel narrative, though the stillness of the pool means no angel it does not prevent the arrival of Christ. Thus, though the novel leaves us still waiting, in effect, for the angel to descend, is it just possible that, by the high magic of analogy, we have already been visited by Christ? Is it possible that we are like Oedipa who, come the end of the novel, is still waiting for the answers to her questions and *yet* (almost without knowing it) has already met Jesus, Jesús Arrabal the anarchist? Are we who await so eagerly, and yet vainly, for an end to the novel which will complete our theological speculations, overlooking the fact that we have already met the very subject of those speculations? To be blunt: why wait for an angel when the novel has already given us a Jesus? The theological point of the Bethesda sub-text, perhaps, then, is this: that we must not be so preoccupied with the 'promise of hierophany' that we miss the Christ who has already come to us; the Christ, indeed, who we have always already encountered. Exactly what it might mean to say that Christ is never purely or simply present (in both senses of the word) will become clearer as we continue. What *is* obvious now is that we are reminded of the danger of not recognizing Christ. We are reminded of the danger of being like Oedipa, who at first misunderstands and then completely passes over Mr Thoth's claim that he 'feel[s] him close to me.' 'Your grandfather?' she asks. 'No, my God.'

The irony of still seeking what one may, in fact, have already found continuously haunts Oedipa's quest for the Tristero. For, in passing through the San Narciso underworld – the gay night-club, the 'busful of Negroes,' the Inamoratti, and so on – does she perhaps encounter the very community of which the Tristero is an elaborate metaphor? ('It was a Negro Neighbourhood. Was The Horn so dedicated?') Is it possible, then, that the Tristero exists not so much *beyond* the urban web of hints, clues and muted post horns but *among* them? If so, we are confronted with the more general and philosophical possibility that all human discourse, however hollow or contentless, entails within itself the faint outline of mutuality, or community. To put it another way, just as Oedipa, when poring over the single mention of 'Tristero' in one edition of *The Courier's Tragedy*, pursues 'the . . . face of the word,' so the whole question of the Tristero promises to lay bare the faces *among* the words. The Tristero, that is to say, names the decidedly *un*postmodern possibility that community is the inner *telos* of communication, that signs, however opaque, do not come between us but bring us together. And perhaps that is the real 'miracle of communication.'

We come closest, no doubt, to just such a miracle when, in a dream-like passage, Oedipa encounters 'a circle of children in their nightclothes' playing a jump-rope game involving not only a post horn chalked on the sidewalk but the chant 'Tristoe, Tristoe, one, two, three'; thus, quite unknowingly, they at once perpetuate the circulation of the Tristero sign and form a kind of society: they 'told her they were dreaming the gathering . . . and needed nothing but their own unpenetrated sense of community.' For all the haunting beauty of this gathering, it is formed, we presume, without parental consent and so is charged with a subversive, almost Blakean, energy. And much the same can be said of all the communities intimated by the Tristero; it comes to possess, that is, something of the danger and threat of the myriad counter-cultural movements within 1960s America. To invoke 'the high magic of low puns,' while communications in *Lot 49* entail the vague promise of *revelation* the community inscribed within those communications entails the promise or threat of *revolution*. This revolution is not necessarily that 'anarchosyndicalist' insurrection which Jesús Arrabal represents but the revolution which goes by the philosophical name of Otherness, or alterity. The Tristero is given this name by Emory Bortz when explaining how, for the Scurvamhites, only one part of creation 'ran off the will of God' while the rest ran off 'some opposite Principle': they 'felt,' concludes Bortz, that 'Trystero . . . symbolize[d] the Other quite well.' Oedipa develops this theme when, just a few pages later, she remarks of the Tristero that 'a network by which X number of Americans are truly communicating' quite independently of 'the official government delivery system' would, if it does exist, constitute 'a real alternative to the exitlessness, to the absence of surprise to life, that harrows the head of everybody American.'

Exitlessness is not, though, a peculiarly American fate but rather one shared by those of us who read *Lot 49*, particularly if we are Christians. The novel, that is, threatens not only to characterize us as a kind of (San) Narcissus looking 'out' on nothing save our own theological speculations but also, come the very end, as those doomed to repetition: 'Oedipa settled back,' we read, 'to await the crying of lot 49.' Caught in a novel which promises no way out, we share, it seems, in the exitlessness of America, an America which has so completely dreamt the world in its own image that there is nothing that is not America, and therefore no way out of America. All this, of course, is brought more sharply into focus by the Tristero since, as Oedipa concludes, 'there either was some Tristero beyond the appearance of the legacy America, or there was just America.' In short, this postal system which operates quite apart from the official state system symbolizes not just a very general Other but also, and more specifically, America's Other. After all, in contrast to Oedipa's America where 'the oldest building' dates from only just 'before World War II,' and life is dominated by property and inheritance, the Tristero has a history which goes back to sixteenth-century Europe and is a community that styles itself as 'El Desheredado, the Disinherited.' In short, 'Tristero's empire' comes to represent both a time that is other than now and an economy that is other than our own, other than property-based; it is structured not by a law of the same or continuity but of difference and discontinuity. In this sense the Tristero is like the mirror in which Oedipa 'tried to find her image' but 'couldn't.'

While Oedipa's interpretive pursuit of the Tristero mystery is always haunted by the possibility of narcissism her encounters with the miscellaneous outcasts who people the urban maze of post horns are quite different. The facially deformed welder, the scarred negro woman, and the soap-eating night watchman, to name but three, are very obviously *not* made in either her visual or her socio-economic likeness. They represent, that is, an 'alternative to the exitlessness' of Oedipa's hermeneutic circle. This is never more obvious than when she meets the old sailor with the post horn tattoo; in pausing, touching and even holding the old man she encounters for once not just another clue, or sign, but the person of the sign – or, if you like, 'the face of the word.' In doing so, indeed, she not only looks into a face that is, for once, not her own but also thereby opens up a profoundly ethical space within the conspicuously *post*-ethical continuum of California; for when she whispers, 'I can't help . . . I can't help,' even while holding and rocking the old man, we cannot avoid reading, 'I can't help *but help.*'

The rude otherness of the Tristero here locates, it seems, something whose existence the novel might otherwise teach us to doubt – instinctive generosity. And it is a generosity that we are moved to value not just in moral terms but also Christian. Oedipa's outstretched arms acquire, that is, a certain Christlikeness in the sense that, although the stamp on the sailor's letter portrays, as usual, 'a jet flying by the Capitol dome, . . . at the top of the dome stood a tiny figure in deep black, with its arms outstretched. Oedipa wasn't sure what exactly was supposed to be on the top of the Capitol, but she knew it wasn't anything like that.' To quote an earlier question of Oedipa's, 'A cross? Or the initial T?' Has Oedipa once again met a Jesus? 'Inasmuch as you have [served] one of the least of these my brethren,' declares Christ, 'ye have done it unto me.' This particular Tristero outcast seems to constitute not just 'the face of the word' but also the face, as it were, of the Word. Here the Tristero names the possibility not only that communication entails community but also that the poor give us Christ.

By the end of the novel, though, the Tristero outcast does not simply give or embody Christ but, to be more precise, represents a *memory* of him, a memory of Christ. For when Passerine 'spread[s] his arms' we do not simply speculate, with Oedipa, whether this gesture is that of 'the priesthood' or 'a descending angel'; our response is more complex, since we are also reminded of the sailor's stamp and that 'tiny figure . . . with arms outstretched.' Once again, theological speculation – this time, of priesthoods and angels – is to some extent foreclosed by the possibility that we, like Oedipa, have already come across Jesus, that he is encountered not so much through interpreting as remembering.

To remember is no easy task among the almost exclusively post-war architecture of San Narciso; nevertheless, the Tristero mystery simply *compels* Oedipa to remember, to develop an historical consciousness. Not only does she trace and research its 400-year history but in the middle of her night 'spent . . . finding' everywhere 'the . . . Tristero post horn,' we read the arcane declaration that '*She was meant to remember*' – 'I am meant to remember,' she echoes. Who or what she is to remember is not clear, but two pages further on into 'the night's profusion of post horns' we read that 'Oedipa . . . had remembered Jesus' – not, we should note, 'Jesús.' Remembering Jesus is, of course, written into the novel in the form of its preoccupation with that 'perpetual memorial,' the Eucharist; like the name 'Oedipa *Maas*' (originally 'Mass'), the novel's fascination with 'the intent to communicate' possesses, as we know, a double significance. After all, as well as the disc-jockey handling records like a 'holy man' handling a 'censer,' and Wharfinger's cardinal holding up his amputated toe 'like a Host,' there is that haunting remark at the end of chapter four: 'As if the dead really do persist, even in a bottle of wine.'

If, though, the novel as a whole 'remember[s] Jesus' in an eucharistic sense, the Tristero also remembers him in the punning sense of re-membering, or re-fleshing; for, strange as it may seem, the Tristero may be interpreted, *among other things*, as the *body* of Christ – that is to say, the church as imaged by St Paul. It is no accident that what we anticipate to be the Tristero's final revelation of itself is comically reduced to the body: '"Your fly is open," whispered Oedipa. She was not sure what she'd do when the bidder revealed himself.' The reader's own investigation of the Tristero puzzle is also interrupted by a body, the metaphorical body of Christ. We tend to share, that is, Oedipa's difficulty in distinguishing the Tristero's 'initial T' from 'a cross,' if only because, as Mendelson has pointed out, the word 'Calavera' in the founding Tristero's name, Hernando Joaquin de Tristero y Calavera, is the Spanish form of 'Calvary.' Moreover, at times the church and the Tristero seem inextricably intertwined; witness the curious involvements of both the Vatican and the Scurvamhites in the text of *The Couriers's Tragedy*. At other times, it is more that church and Tristero seem equally ubiquitous: as we know, at the laundromat with a post horn tacked to the bulletin board 'the . . . chlorine . . . rose . . . like an incense'; again, in Bortz's library Oedipa reads about the Tristero brigands at a 'tabernacle'; and yet again, Jesús' anarchist party operates not only under the sign of the post horn stamped on to their newspaper but also, 'like the church we hate' (to quote Jesús), in the name of rebirth – the paper is called '*Regeneración.*' In short, just as Oedipa fears that the Tristero has been inscribed, or rather 'encrypted' into Inverarity's will so, we might say, church – by association with 'crypt' – is written into the Tristero.

The notion that an alternative system of communication might constitute a kind of church is with us from very early in the novel: the disc-jockey *cum* celebrant is, we read, 'really tuned in to . . . the music . . . as were all *the faithful* it went out to.' We have, then, some idea of what Mendelson means when he remarks that 'the Tristero [also] carries with it a sense of sacred connection and relation.' Needless to say, though, the church described by the Tristero is not one with which we are particularly familiar; it is, rather, one we are 'meant to *remember*,' one that requires an historical consciousness. To be precise, it is the early, pre-Constantine church that most obviously constituted an 'underground' system of communication, employing, like the Tristero, both acronym and cryptic ideogram. For W.A.S.T.E., that is, we might read, ICHTHUS, and for the sign of the post-horn we might substitute the sign of the fish.

Admittedly, to do so is to indulge in Christian interpretation of the kind that the novel characterises as a form of narcissism, as gazing in the pool at Bethesda. However, what distinguishes the church as the focus of a Christian interpretation of *Lot 49* is that it can survive the discrediting of that interpretation. For just as the Tristero is not so much a puzzle that Oedipa fails to resolve but a community that she has already encountered, so the church, for the Christian reader, is quite obviously not so much a sub-text to be deciphered as the very community, or body, out of which she reads. In other words, *Lot 49* finally returns the Christian reader to that body.

Indeed, perhaps the same may be said of *any* reader, whether Christian or not, who, at Passerine's (anti-)climactic gesture, is reminded of the 'tiny figure' on the airmail stamp; for if a reader is thereby caused to 're-member Jesus,' then – by 'the high magic of low puns' – do they in some sense bring into being the very body of Christ? For the reader who would not, before reading the novel, have called herself a Christian, this possibility might well come as a surprise, perhaps even a revelation. For the avowedly Christian reader it is surely a call to draw back from our pool-gazing to remember the strange and estranged body of Christ – to embrace the alcoholic sailor.

Postscript

When this essay was first published it was part of book called *The Discerning Reader: Christian Perspectives on Literature and Theory*, and so I was invited to conclude by 'demonstrating how I arrived at a Christian reading.' What follows was my attempt to respond to this invitation.

First, I am not sure how helpful it is to speak of a 'Christian reading.' Can the way that I read ever be 'Christian' in the same way that I might be? In one sense, then, the answer to how I arrived at a Christian reading (if I ever did) is by being a Christian – being a Christian not only when reading but also when not reading. Indeed, to read as a Christian is often to be called not to read; as *Lot 49* reminds us, though Christ is the Word (and thus a text, or complex of meanings, with which I must engage) the Word has a face, he is someone I must encounter.

To start again, then: how did I, as a Christian, read *Lot 49*? To be honest, my first and intuitive impulse was always to save the text, to read it as a crypto-Christian novel. At times, I suspect, this led to wilful misreading, looking for Christian patterns at the expense of apparently counter-Christian moments. Insofar as this was the case, I was neither a discerning nor a Christian reader. Nevertheless, at the same time as seeking to save the text I also sought to lose it; that is, to allow the novel to rewrite the text that is Christianity without my beliefs foreclosing that process. If one name for the Christian God is 'the Word' or speech, then in one sense there is, in language, no outside of God. I could, therefore, suspend belief in the sure hope that, whatever Thomas Pynchon's intentions, I would somehow encounter the high magic of the living and epileptic Word amid all the chances, changes and low puns of *Lot 49*. Insofar as this was what happened, then my reading may be characterized as a kind of Christian deconstruction.

> 'It is more proper to speak of a trick than a method.'
> (Walter Benjamin)

VI

Reading the Long Way Round

W. M. Thackeray's *Vanity Fair*
(1996)

It may, perhaps, have struck her that to have been honest and humble
. . . to have marched straight forward on her way would have brought
her . . . happiness. . . . But just as the children at Queen's Crawley went
round the room, where the body of their father lay, if ever Becky had
these thoughts she was accustomed to walk round them.

When *Vanity Fair* finds itself among the 'famous events' of Waterloo,
'hanging,' that is, 'on to the [very] skirts of history,' it declines, like Becky,
to march straight ahead and narrate the battle, opting instead to circumvent it altogether: 'We do not claim to rank among the military novelists.
. . . When the decks are cleared for action we go below and wait meekly.'
The novel, it seems, chooses not only the 'skirts of history' but also to skirt
the historical; to put it another way, the novel's European sortie proves to
be not so much a Grand Tour (such as Thackeray himself went on) as a
grand detour. Not, of course, that this surprises the reader for by this point
s/he is well used to the novel's digressions, circumlocutions, and narrative
refusals. *Vanity Fair* has more than just one 'Roundabout Chapter'; in
fact, the whole novel, we might say, is another of Thackeray's
Roundabout Papers. It is long, therefore, not only in a conventional linear
sense but also in the sense that it often goes the long way round. Despite,
that is, Carlyle's declaration that 'narrative is *linear*,' *Vanity Fair* disrupts
what Derrida calls the 'the time . . . of the line or the line of time.' Time
and again, 'we are [left] wandering' as this history 'go[es] backwards and
forwards' reflecting our narrator's 'amiable object' which is simply 'to
walk' with us 'through the Fair,' and then to 'come home.' As a 'novel
without a hero,' without a centre, there is (as at Queen's Crawley) a
conspicuous absence to circumvent.

This absence, and the detour it entails, is never more conspicuous than
when Becky is introduced to the King and the narration, in mock rever-
ence, 'backs away':

What were the circumstances of the interview between Rebecca Crawley
. . . and her Imperial Master, it does not become such a feeble and inex-

perienced pen as mine to relate. The dazzled eyes close before that Magnificent Idea. Loyal respect . . . tell[s] even the imagination . . . to back away . . . making profound bows out of the August Presence.

Vanity Fair, it seems, is a novel without not only a hero but also a King; the irony, though, that attends this political absence is that it goes by the name of 'Presence.' Here then, in its ironisation of 'Presence,' and indeed of the Platonic 'Idea,' a typically Thackerayan digression takes an almost Derridean turn. It is not for nothing that Thackeray writes that *Vanity Fair*'s characters 'live "without God" in the world.'

There is, however, another and very different 'August Presence' from which the novel might just also back away; namely, the so-called 'Peterloo' massacre of August 1819 which, as the very soubriquet testifies, was indelibly written into the nation's memory of Waterloo. After Peterloo, the memory of Wellington's famous victory was, in a sense, never quite the same. Note, for instance, that in Dickens's *Our Mutual Friend* 'Veneering . . . instructed his driver to charge the Public . . . like the Life-Guards at Waterloo.' As the historian David Thomson remarks, 'the "massacre of Peterloo" . . . did much to offset the Tory credit for Waterloo.' The associations with Waterloo are, indeed, many and various; not only was the massacre carried out by a troop of the 15th Hussars wearing their Waterloo medals but their victims, the parliamentary reformers gathered to hear Henry Hunt, were organized and even drilled by other Waterloo veterans. To compound the irony, one of the eleven killed was, famously, another comrade-in-arms from Waterloo, one John Lees.

Is it possible that such historical intertextuality lies behind the fact that, as Clive Emsley observes, 'so little nineteenth-century literature deals with Waterloo'? If so, is *Vanity Fair*'s ostentatious avoidance of the battle in some sense an unwitting reflection, or parody, of this more general departure from the straight line of Tory history? Certainly, for Thackeray, writing *Vanity Fair* at the very height of the Chartist movement for parliamentary reform, to have considered Waterloo quite independently of Peterloo's appalling 'August Presence' would clearly have been difficult; particularly given that, when the final and largest Chartist demonstration of April 1848 so alarmed the government, the defence of the capital was entrusted to none other than the Duke of Wellington. It is not, perhaps, for nothing that the victors at Waterloo become, in a moment of Thackerayan bathos, 'august jobbers.'

I suggest, then, that just as the children at Queen's Crawley very deliberately 'round' the dead body of their father so *Vanity Fair* takes us the long way round the many dead bodies of Waterloo partly because the novel is, at some level, mindful of the eleven dead bodies of Peterloo. The reader's experience of the novel's length is, to this extent, marked by the evasions and indirections of Tory historiography.

However, to read the grand detour that is *Vanity Fair* is also, and much more obviously, to go the way(s) of women; when, that is, the novel comes to the battle of Waterloo and we 'go no farther with the —th than to the city gate' we, instead, 'come back to Major [Dowd]'s wife, and the ladies.' Like Becky, the narration here chooses not to 'march . . . straight forward,' not to follow the straight line of military history; we are, remember, 'hanging on to the *skirts* of history.' What is more, 'our women' or, at least 'their bodies,' are prone to 'go abroad,' to go astray – that is, to wander. In short, if to read *Vanity Fair* is to experience the length not so much of the line as of the detour then is that experience in some sense marked as feminine? After all, to read a long novel with the primary purpose of getting to the end as quickly as possible is clearly aligned with Dobbin's conventionally masculine desire for Amelia: upon finally winning her we read that 'this is what he pined after. Here it is – the summit, the end – the last page.' Moreover, given that we, as readers, are not exclusively concerned with Dobbin's pursuit of Amelia (we are also mindful of a woman, Becky, who is still 'abroad'), our experience of the length of the novel evidently strays from this masculine model. And what doubtless confirms our departure from a masculine line is that from the death of George onwards we have been reading a novel without its most likely hero; like the children at Queen's Crawley we have been skirting round a male corpse – 'skirting' in the sense that if anyone is the focus of our attention it is a heroine: namely, Becky.

Of course, given that Becky is not only half-French but spends much of the novel as a woman who is quite literally 'abroad,' she causes us to depart from not only the male line of patriarchal narrative but also 'the English line' of the Victorian novel. As Robin Gilmour remarks, 'The sense of history in the great Victorian novels is almost invariably domestic, local, urban or regional.' By contrast, in *Vanity Fair* 'the English line' is both drawn and broken abroad, on the battlefield of Waterloo: '[The] final onset . . . came at last: the columns of the Imperial Guard marched up the hill of Saint Jean . . . unscared by the thunder of the artillery, which hurled death from the English line.'

That Becky is a kind of Napoleon waging war on the codes and mores of the English bourgeoisie is a critical commonplace; however, the English line from which she departs is not only social but semiotic. When she flings *Dr Johnson's Dictionary* from a moving coach Becky violently rejects a potent symbol of standardized English. Indeed, in doing so she foregrounds that more general disordering which Carlyle bemoans: 'The whole structure of Johnsonian English,' he declares, '[is] breaking up from its foundation.' Underlining Becky's complicity in this disruption is the fact that her second going abroad takes the novel and, therefore, the reader on a linguistic detour: a departure from the English line of language. When Jos, Amelia, Dobbin, and young George all leave London on the annual 'Continental tour' only to cross paths with Becky once again the reader must negotiate not just a number of French or German phrases but also what can only be described as, variously, German-French: 'des sangviches,' English-French: 'Newmero kattervang dooze' and, indeed, German-French-English: 'the little Engländerinn seems to be *en bays de gonnaissance*.' It is no accident that the 'tour' left London from 'the Tower,' a line that, via an interlinguistic detour (in French 'tour' means, *inter alia*, 'tower'), already begins to turn the tour into a very particular tower, namely the Tower of Babel. Moreover, within a couple of pages we are introduced to the Babelic character, Kirsch, the interpreter who, 'though he was familiar with all languages . . . was not acquainted with a single one.' If Becky's violent rejection of the dictionary corresponds to Carlyle's fear of the break-up of Johnsonian English then this Babelic (de)tour in which Becky latterly involves both novel and reader rehearses Carlyle's influential characterization of the nineteenth century as 'Innumerable Philosophies of Man contending in boundless hubbub' and 'confusion of tongues.'

To return, though, to the line of our argument: this same (de)tour might also be said to inform our sense of the length of *Vanity Fair* in that it requires us to *read* the long way round; to read, that is, out of the way of 'the English line' and into an interlinguistic space of not just Babelic farce ('sangviches' and so on) but also knockabout catachresis. Note how Thackeray caricatures a series of German names, from 'Count de Schlüsselback' to 'Princess Amelia of Humbourg-Schlippen-Schloppen.' To read around in this way is to undertake not a Grand Tour but rather something more like Becky's bathetic, low-life parody of this already declining convention, a low de-tour as it were.

Of course, from a deconstructive perspective it is always already the case that we read the long way round, the sheer Babelic intertextuality of all discourse being such that signification necessarily entails an almost infinite detour. No one sign, it is argued, can mean without, in some sense, first referring to every other sign. Hillis Miller makes more, then, than a simply calligraphic point when observing that 'letters in the alphabetic sense are made of lines . . . which turn back on themselves in one way or another' so that the 'intelligibility of writing depends on this twisting . . . of the line.' It is no accident that, as the American translator of Derrida's '*Des Tours de Babel*' remarks, 'taken together, *des* and *tours* have the same sound as *détour*.' Admittedly, for Derrida, signification is a detour without return and therefore not, strictly speaking, a detour at all; nevertheless, we may still say that the Derridean sign, like the letter, 'can always *not* arrive at its destination, [and] . . . must bear within itself a . . . straying of the destination.' That meanings must go astray is implicit in Becky's violent rejection of the dictionary; all dictionaries enshrine the fiction that there is a direct and inviolable line between sign and referent. Indeed, in returning to Europe, Becky violates this line for the second time by living, as Dobbin puts it, as 'a lady who is separated from her husband, [and] who [therefore] travels not under her own name.' The irony that her name was never her own, in that it was always already her husband's, should not be lost on us.

To live in the breach opened up by the rejection of the dictionary is, it seems, to go abroad. Indeed, by the end of the novel, 'our little wanderer' has become 'this little Ishmaelite,' and is compared to an 'Arab' 'career[ing] across the desert.' She goes, that is, not just abroad but nowhere; in the desert you are not so much displaced as in a non-place. Of course, if Becky's wandering mimics our experience of reading *Vanity Fair* then we too are cast as going nowhere, a possibility with which we have always read in that our novel's very title implies a failure to arrive – a failure to arrive at the Celestial City. The nowhere in which we read is not, then, the nowhere that is utopia (*u-topos*, 'no-place'); the utopian nowhere we never reach is the Celestial City precluded by our title. In its stead, the novel introduces us to the nowhere that is madness; when Lord George grows 'queer' we read that 'he was nowhere: he was gone out.' Indeed, checked as it is by a '*Strait*-Waistcoat' this nowhere very specifically maps *our* departure, as readers, from the straight line of narrative.

Developing this conceit, the novel intimates that to go the long way round might just be to avoid the memory of childhood trauma; after all, it is her own 'thoughts' that Becky 'was accustomed to walk round, and not look in[to].' Moreover, given the analogy with the movement of children around the 'body of their father,' those thoughts may be (mis)read as thoughts about Becky's own father and, therefore, her own childhood. That Becky has a past the memory of which she might wish to avoid is, of course, strongly hinted at. Only ten pages earlier we had learned that 'Rebecca thought about her . . . youth and the dark secrets of those early tainted days'; indeed, 'she had been a woman since she was eight years old' and had not once 'blushed.' For all the dark suggestion of these remarks, though, Becky is not portrayed as wholly exceptional. Rawdon, for example, joins her in 'thinking of old times' (in his case 'about Eton,' his 'frigid' mother, and 'a sister who died') whilst the narrator makes the general observation that with some persons the 'awes and terrors of youth last for ever and ever.'

That we who read might just be among such persons is a possibility with which the novel confronts us in the sense that it very conspicuously takes its first, Victorian readers back to the scene of their childhood. This it does not only by finally addressing them as 'children' and by the use of nursery-style names (from Mr Hammerdown the auctioneer, through Sir Huddlestone Fuddlestone, to Sir Something (Creepy?) Crawley) but also simply by virtue of dealing with Waterloo. As the narrator reminds his readers, 'you and I [. . .] were children when the great battle was won and lost.' Given the 'awes and terrors' of youth, each reader is left to wonder whether the battle in question might just have been for her or his childhood. The novel's very deliberate circumvention of Waterloo may mime, then, my own repression of this private battle ground. If this psychic detour is merely hinted at by Becky's 'walk [a]round' her own thoughts then it is more strongly, albeit unwittingly, signalled by casual narratorial references to 'each respected reader's private circle' and 'reader[s] of a sentimental turn.'

That disturbing childhood experiences do indeed press upon the very margins of our novel is never more evident than when the narrator hastily resumes his narrative whilst in the middle of recounting an old man's nightmare: 'If the Doctor . . . had appeared bodily to him, . . . and had said "Boy take down your pant —" Well, well Miss Sedley was exceedingly alarmed at this act of insubordination.' To cease reading a narrative driven by the need to avoid repressed memories is, of course, to be returned to those memories: we note with discomfort that our narrator desires not only 'to walk' with us 'through the Fair' but also that after 'we should all come home . . . and be perfectly miserable in private.' Here our reading, it seems, is no more nor less than a studied circumvention of a private sadness; *Vanity Fair*'s tendency to go the long way round cannot, that is, be separated from each reader's very private circle and turns. The novel is, in some sense, as long (or as short) as these same circles and turns. To read the long way round *Vanity Fair* is to read the long way round my past.

It is also, however, to read the long way round my future, or rather the one certain event within that future, namely: death. For not only do we avoid death in skirting round the Battle of Waterloo but simply by virtue of reading a novel entitled *Vanity Fair* we are implicated in a nine-hundred-page deferral of the 'Celestial City' and the death it entails. Like the children at Queen's Crawley I have to make my way around death. The death that I seek to avoid is not, though, something abstract or that happens to others; it is, rather, my own death. What Jack Rawlins describes as 'Thackeray's pervasive argument *ad mortalitatem*' is, in *Vanity Fair*, addressed specifically to the reader. The death of Mr Sedley, for instance, prompts the narrator to a meditation on that moment when 'the doctor will come up to us too for the last time. . . . Your end, brother reader [will come].' Part of the pleasure of reading a long novel is, though, to defer the end and thereby also to defer, somehow, my own end. In this respect our experience of the novel's length is rehearsed by our reading of Lord Steyne's ridiculously long death sentence:

> Two months after the French Revolution of 1830 . . . the Most Honourable Gustavus, Marquis of Steyne, Earl of Gaunt . . . Knight of the Most Noble Order of the Garter . . . First Lord of the Powder Closet . . . died after a series of fits.

If writing, following Scheherazade, is, as Foucault remarks, 'a protection against death' then so too is reading, particularly in a novel which reminds us of 'our own funeral.' For Derrida, the addressee is always already informed by his own death in the sense that 'writing that was not structurally legible – iterable – beyond the death of the addressee would not be writing.' In *Vanity Fair*, however, death does not have everything its own way since through the motif of Becky's walk around her own thoughts, mapped as it is onto the movement of the children around their father's corpse, the novel describes as circuitous both its own and our avoidance of death. In short, our experience of *Vanity Fair*'s argument *ad mortalitatem* answers nicely to Freud's contention that, in resisting the death instinct, the 'living substance . . . diverge[s] ever more widely from its original course of life and . . . make[s] ever more complicated *détours* before reaching its aim of death.'

On this Freudian reading the linearity of the novel becomes a kind of death instinct, a function of death as a kind of *telos*. This is not, however, quite how the novel itself describes the relationship between death and the line; or at least that is not how it is described in the description of Jane Osborne's apartment following the death of her brother, at which point the room's two mirrors seem to have nothing to reflect but each other:

> The great glass over the mantelpiece, faced by the other great console glass at the opposite end of the room, increased and multiplied between them the brown holland bag in which the chandelier hung; until you saw these brown holland bags fading away in endless perspectives.

These endless perspectives are, presumably, in an endless line; here death issues in linearity, though not as Freud's final and causal presence, but rather as a ceaselessly recurring absence, the absence of someone to reflect. Moreover, the linearity of these endless perspectives is an illusion, a trick performed by mirrors. But what else would we expect of a novel called *Vanity Fair*? The word 'vanity' implies not only the work of mirrors but also a certain absence, *vanus* meaning 'empty.' It should, then, be no surprise that, through these endless perspectives, Freud's teleological notion of death undergoes a kind of deconstruction. Indeed, the virtual linearity with which we are left, predicated as it is upon absence, puts into question Derrida's contention that the line is necessarily inscribed within the metaphysics of presence, that what is thought as deconstruction 'cannot be written according to the line.'

Of course, given that the absence of George is marked by Jane's 'mournful sadness,' it is almost as if here the line is (to adapt a phrase of Lacan's) *hollowed into desire*, the long shading into long*ing*. And, if we are to believe Freud, longing once again takes us the long way round; in *Beyond the Pleasure Principle* he remarks on 'the long *indirect* road to pleasure,' a formulation nicely anticipated by our narrator's talk of London society's 'annual tour in search of pleasure.' For 'indirect road' read, of course, 'tour.' However, as regards the reader, for 'tour' in turn read 'endless perspectives'; for though Dobbin's eventual winning of Amelia is described, as we know, in terms of reading a long novel ('here it is . . . the end, the last page') it is the mirrors' endless perspectives that more nearly reflect our experience of a novel which is finally long in the sense of endless longing: 'Ah! *Vanitas Vanitatum*! . . . Which of us has his desire? or, having it, is satisfied?'

In the next and final sentence, however, our experience of the novel is not of longing but also of being longed for: 'Come, children,' we read. Someone or something, it seems, desires us. To what extent it is death ('our play is played out'), or Christ ('suffer the little children to come unto me'), or even the seductive father ('Come back. Do come back. Dear Becky do come,' pleads the elderly and lascivious Sir Pitt) is impossible to say; we do not, therefore, know whether to feel comfort or terror. What we do know, though, is that we are hailed, or interpellated, that even as we know so we are known (known, indeed, as 'children') and that, therefore, we are not wholly free. Hitherto, of course, our reading has been character-ized by our apparent freedom to circumvent such terrors as death and childhood distress; here, though, we know better or at least otherwise. Here we know that our subjectivity might also entail subjection for we are now 'children,' and children must obey. Indeed, insofar as this 'Come' recalls that 'G.O.' which is scratched in the window of George Osborne's old room we are faced with the possibility that the written word has always commanded us – now to 'come,' then to 'GO'.

Nevertheless, if 'Come, children' *does* echo Christ's 'suffer the little children' then it is also haunted by another biblical 'Come' – namely, that invocation of St John's at the very end of Revelation, the invocation with which *Jane Eyre* (published just one year before) concludes: 'Even so, come Lord Jesus.' St John's 'come,' addressed as it is to Christ, is of course the mirror-image of 'suffer the little children'; here, then, is a biblical 'come' that we may, like Jane Eyre, choose to make our own, and in this sense we *may* finally desire (desire Christ) as well as be desired. We do so, however, at the cost of entering into a potentially ceaseless dialogue of desire in which (St John's) 'come' only echoes (Christ's) 'come,' in which longing only echoes longing, thus giving a whole new meaning to Thackeray's 'which of us has his desire?' We have, then, before us the peculiar prospect of entering into something like the 'endless perspectives' of the empty apartment's two mirrors; something like, in fact, an utterly hollowed-out mirror stage; we are now 'children,' of course.

At the end of *Vanity Fair* there is, as it were, another and virtual 'vanity fair'; unlike, though, the novel we have finally completed, the dialogue of desire threatens to be as endless and as empty as the mirrors' perspectives. This is, I fear, a species of hell.

WHEN DID YOU LAST
SEE YOUR FATHER?

(OCTOBER 28TH 1996)

The death of my father, a minister of religion, followed several years of
a wasting illness in which he completely withdrew into a waking
nightmare that caused him to see and say the strangest things.
News of his death reached me whilst I was reading the
end of T.S. Eliot's **The Waste Land,** *a poem that Eliot*
originally intended to call 'He Do
the Police in Different Voices.'

Father
When did you? When did you last see?
See with your blind-boy eyes?
See the poor wretch
come reading?

I
though
did see you,
you
in your unmade bed
curled,
like a comma,
turned,
like a
metaphor;
but then,
as you once said, in
order to crack
a joke,
'What's a meta for?'

Yes,
what *is* it for,

all this,
all this?

Ah,
but I see
now
that you are not here
but there, there,
Da Da.

I see,
you see,
how you da the peace
the peace
indifferent
voices.
Da Da.
Da Da.

MAY 2012

VII

Half-Way House
Thomas Hardy's *A Laodicean*
(1997)

Philosophy . . . represents . . . itself as . . . an art of architecture.
(Jacques Derrida)

Architecture/Philosophy

More than any other of Hardy's novels *A Laodicean* draws upon the author's own professional experience of architecture; it is also, claims Martin Seymour-Smith, 'Hardy's most sheerly intellectual novel' – a curious combination, as one contemporary reviewer observed, of 'melodrama and philosophy.' Indeed, anticipating Derrida, *A Laodicean* is concerned with uncovering an ancient analogy *between* architecture and philosophy; it is no accident that the architect Somerset is the grandson of 'a notable metaphysician.' The novel gives renewed significance, if you will, to the ancient notion of the 'philosopher's stone.'

For Hardy and his first readers, the connection between architecture and philosophy would have been very pertinent in the sense that the period's 'stylistic eclecticism was,' as J. B. Bullen writes, 'frequently related to philosophical relativism.' Fittingly, Paula Power (the heroine) is not only criticized for her eclectic approach to the restoration of Stancy Castle but also suspected of relativist religious views. In fact Paula, the waverer or Laodicean of the novel's title, so lacks a fixed ground or centre as to be very conspicuously at odds with the foundationalism of both architecture and philosophy. To develop the point: the character of Paula, reflecting 'the bottomless depths [of] . . . her eyes,' hints at a groundlessness of thought that undermines philosophy's habitual perception of itself as a firm and grounded structure. This groundlessness is not, though, just an absence of ground but also, in part, a release from it. Paula is capable, we learn, of 'flights of thought'; and for her, looking out on the city of Strasburg, it is not the firm and grounded houses but the storks flying above them that are 'philosophical.' Freedom from ground is something that Paula very obviously represents both in her high-flying gymnastics and in the dance she hosts in which 'human beings shak[e] . . . themselves free of all inconvenient gravitation.' Given too her capacity for the playful reworking of philosophy, she seems, like Hardy's contemporary the radical philosopher Friedrich Nietzsche, to have 'kill[ed] the Spirit of Gravity' in more senses than one.

To suggest the same of the author of *A Laodicean* is to refer both to the novel's comedy and to the curious fact that, during its composition, Hardy suffered from an illness which, for several months, 'compelled [him] to lie,' as he himself expressed it, 'with the lower part of his body higher than his head.' With Hardy himself so literally groundless there is a bizarre biographical logic to the novel's riddling references to 'an enchanted submarine palace' and 'unpedestaled Dionysus.' At one point we do read that 'a man [at the castle] searched for old foundations' but, strangely, nothing more is said; it is merely an aside and thus a silent dismissal of the architectural-cum-philosophical preoccupation with foundations.

In *A Laodicean* what Annie Escuret describes as Hardy's 'refus[al of the] . . . world . . . of the architect' intersects with what Michael Millgate describes as Hardy's 'lack [or suspicion] of . . . systematic philosophy.' The result is a novel which both identifies and questions the often invisible assumption that the house is *the* space of philosophy, the only way, if you like, to imagine thought in spatial terms. It is an assumption towards which the novel twice glances in the opening scenes: first with the phrase 'it was brought *home* to his intelligence,' and then with the description of the castle walls as 'of a thickness sufficient for the perpetuation of grand ideas.'

That Hardy has an intuitive suspicion of the architectural pretensions of philosophy is, perhaps, most obvious in a letter of 1892 where he condemns 'metaphysic' (caught, as he sees it, between 'Deism and Materialism') as 'a halfway house.' The halfway house (the house that is not quite a house) appears, though, to be already on Hardy's mind when composing *A Laodicean*. Not only is the castle as much a military as domestic space, but Woodwell's dreary cottage is 'without any natural union with [the earth]' whilst, at Sir William De Stancy's, 'sun and air riddl[e] . . . the house everywhere.' The whole novel, in fact, serves to riddle, or complicate our notion of a house; for with its curious references to lighthouses, trading houses, a 'house of cards,' and 'the house of . . . Jacob,' *A Laodicean* seems, at times, to be primarily an answer to the riddle: when is a house not a house?

This is particularly the case with respect to Charlotte De Stancy, to whose family the castle no longer belongs but who, as Paula's companion, effectively lives there; as Somerset observes 'This is [both] home to you, and not home.' So interpreted, Charlotte's relationship to the castle very precisely anticipates Freud's account of the uncanny (or *Unheimlich*) as that which is at once both homely and *un*homely. And of course if, as Freud argues, '"*Unheimlich*" is the name for everything that ought to have remained . . . hidden but has come to light' then the castle is uncanny in the sense that it houses (and thereby both hides and discloses) the quasi-lesbian relationship between Paula and Charlotte. '"They are more like lovers than girl and girl,"' remarks one local.

The castle is again marked by the unhomely revelation of a sexual relationship in a very strange scene where Somerset sits down to sketch his plan for the restoration; as he does so Paula, who is elsewhere described as 'sinister,' bends over him and, with 'the breath of her words fann[ing] his ear,' murmurs, '"Ah, I begin to see your conception."' For an uncanny moment we are tempted to misread her words as a reference to the conception *of* Somerset, to some distant but primal scene, with the architect's conception becoming not a mental or intellectual event but a sexual one. For this moment, architectural creation risks losing all the metaphysical significance with which it has been traditionally invested. Note how, in order to explain Plato, one seventeenth-century commentator writes that, 'From the beginning the Architect conceives in his spirit . . . the Idea of the edifice; he then makes the house . . . in the way in which he has decided in his mind.' The house, it seems, has long been *the* exemplar of the metaphysical understanding of the world as merely a material presentation of prior and immaterial ideas. Much, then, is put at risk by the sheer ambiguity of Paula's 'I see your conception.' The pure and prior intelligence that architecture has traditionally represented is opened up to the possibility of an outrageously impure and posterior intelligence.

Architecture is similarly opened up in the casino at Monte Carlo which, like the castle, is a house that is also not a house ('casino' is the diminutive of *casa*, meaning 'house'). Indeed, it comes close to being the '*unheimlich* house,' or unhomely home which Freud himself translates as the '*haunted* house'; for, described as a 'phantasmagoria,' the casino is, from the outset, marked by a suggestion of phantasms, or phantoms. And this suggestion only grows as we read of 'half-charmed spellbound' gamblers 'familiar with many forms of utterance,' and arranged in a 'hollow circle' of 'murky intelligences around a table.' The image thus parodically conjured up is of a séance, a central motif of the spiritualist boom in the late-nineteenth century. But if the diminutive house of gambling is haunted then so too is the big house of architecture, of which the casino is also a kind of parody. Not only are its tables covered in 'figures . . . lines [and] . . . diagram[s]' but here Somerset re-encounters none other than William Dare, his former and disgraced architectural assistant, who declares that the probability of his finally winning is grounded – architecturally, as it were – on a '"vast foundation of waste chances."' Thus parodied by a casino which is at the same time a parody of a séance, architecture seems a long way from its traditional analogy with philosophy. To put it another way, it is not Somerset's relationship to a 'notable metaphysician' that here strikes us but his relationship to a notable charlatan, the disreputable Dare, whom Somerset, it seems, can never quite escape. Architecture (traditionally the analogue of all that is grounded and rational) is here doubled by all that is groundless, irrational and specious.

What, though, is so intriguing about this is that it does not come to us as a total surprise. Paula, for instance, has already pointed up architecture's capacity to depart from conventional ways of knowing; it is, she remarks, 'an art which makes one . . . independent of written history.' Indeed, as the Victorian fashion for eclecticism made clear, architecture may also make one independent of *linear* history. Witness the Saxon abbey with Gothic arches 'built ere the art was known'; in this instance, architecture is not so much science as a kind of *pre*science. It is, admittedly, an unusual moment, but nevertheless one that reflects the novel's more general attempt to disentangle architecture from metaphysics, the philosophy of knowing. For example, whilst metaphysics is preoccupied with abstraction, certainty and, above all, presence, Paula's encounter with the stonework in the castle chapel is characterized by touch, doubt and, above all, absence. She is concerned with 'deep hollows' in the ornamentation which, to appreciate, she must touch rather than view:

> She pulled off her glove . . . her hand resting in the stone channel . . . [and] the ideas [were] derived through her hand [before] pass[ing] into her face.
> 'No. I'm not sure now,' she said.

Absence and doubt again beset the classically architectural relationship between stone and idea, castle and character, when Somerset reads a newspaper announcement of Paula's engagement:

> In his meditation he stood still, closely scanning one of the jamb-stones of a doorless entrance, as if to discover where the old hinge-hook had entered the stonework.

What occupies Somerset is, of course, the announcement and not a hinge-hook that is no longer in a doorway that no longer has a door; here, the relationship between mind and stone constitutes what is almost an edifice of negations, an edifice that is completed just a few lines later as Paula declares that the announcement itself has 'no foundation whatever.'

In *A Laodicean* the architectural relationship comes close, it seems, to an articulation not just of specific absences (hollowed stones and doorless doorways) but of absence itself. Indeed, the definition of a building as the creation of not just a space but an absence is very nearly realized when, later in the novel, the church at Caen is described as 'absolutely empty, the void being emphasized by its great coolness.' In this novel even the house of God is at odds with philosophy's traditional intuition of the house as a metaphor for presence. It is an intuition that Martin Heidegger has articulated in terms of 'the house of Being' and which Hardy himself seems to glance at in the sentence that begins 'Being a dwelling.'

A Laodicean does not, however, simply exchange absence for presence; for what most troubles presence is *re*presentation – that unruly realm of the copy, or image which lies (Laodicean-like) *between* presence and absence. The church in Caen, for instance, turns out *not* to be absolutely empty but occupied by a visiting painter; likewise, when Somerset takes Paula's hand to assist her exploration of the chapel's deep hollows it is almost as if her fingers were an artist's pencil: 'he seized her forefinger between his own finger and thumb, and *drew* it along the hollow.' In both cases, even as the house of architecture seems emptied of presence so the maker of *re*presentations emerges. Somerset's grandfather is a metaphysician, but his father, we note, is a painter; again, the castle, the very focus of the novel's architectural activity and debate, accommodates not only a temporary theatre but a whole gallery of portraits. In short, the novel complicates what Mark Wigley calls that 'general [and simple] opposition between an inner world of presence and outer world of representation,' which the house, 'as the traditional figure of interior[ity] is used to establish.' In *A Laodicean* the 'outer' world of representation (the world of theatre and portraits) is always already housed within the inner world of that house of houses, the castle. Indeed, the novel reminds us that a house is not just a dwelling but a semblance, a copy of other buildings and other styles – something that Victorian architecture, with its fascination for past forms, knew well. This point is made in the very first scene, where Somerset is copying a church which, with its 'battlemented parapet,' is already a copy, the copy of a castle. It is no accident that the architect should acknowledge that photography, the ultimate art of reproduction, is 'a shadow of his own pursuits.'

Photography/Telegraphy

There is, however, another sense in which photography is the shadow of architecture and, in particular, the house; for, as the novel reminds us, photography derives from the *camera obscura*, which literally means 'darkened room.' This optical instrument was so-called because it reproduced in a small, closed box the effect of light entering a minute hole in the wall of a darkened room and creating an inverted image of what is outside. The novel's first approximation to such a room is a castle turret which has only a 'slit' for the admission of 'a streak of fire as narrow as a corn-stalk'; the second is the railway tunnel 'in the darkness of [which Somerset] . . . could see th[e] . . . other end as a mere speck of light'; the third is the 'octagonal chamber . . . [with shutters closed and into which] only stray beams of light gleam'; and the fourth is a bizarre 'painting room' the 'overpowering gloom' of which is only offset, in curious mimicry of the photographer's 'arrangement of curtains and lenses,' by a 'complicated apparatus of lamps, candles and reflectors.' In so tracing the photographer's debt to the room (and thus to the house) the novel astutely places even this daring new medium under the ancient, domestic sign of philosophy.

The darkened room of photography is, of course, related to philosophy via Plato's cave, or rather his simile of the cave. I refer to that seminal simile of Western metaphysics in which man is compared to a prisoner in a cave and able to see nothing except the shadows projected by a fire on to the opposite wall; the visible world, argues Plato, is merely a projection of another, greater realm of essences and abstract forms. Photography and Platonism (albeit very much vulgarized) were, in fact, connected for the Victorians who, as Tom Gunning has argued, to some extent made imaginative sense of this new science by supposing all objects to have a phantasmatic double, or essence which exists in the atmosphere and is captured by the camera. What confirms, though, photography's implication in philosophy is that, as Eduardo Cadava points out, 'both take their life from light.' Photography depends, as its name suggests (*photos* meaning 'light'), on the chemical action of light on sensitive film, whilst philosophy has often taken the sun as a metaphor for a founding, or central principle. Sometimes this is explicit, as in Plato's use of the sun as the image of 'the absolute form of Good,' and sometimes implicit as in the eighteenth-century equation of reason with en*light*enment. In *A Laodicean*, however, Dare's trick photograph of Somerset (making him appear to be drunk) prompts the almost unthinkable thought that 'God's sun should bear false witness.' With this thought the novel throws into question not only the sun but the absolute Good or even God that, within philosophy, the sun has traditionally represented.

Victorian culture had, for some time, been marked by anxiety about the sun, from both scientific as well as poetic perspectives. The well-publicized fears of solar physicists that the sun was cooling were echoed in John Ruskin's declaration that 'I want to believe in Apollo [the god of the sun] but can't.' That *A Laodicean* touches upon the same anxiety is clear; the sunset with which the novel begins thereafter constantly repeats upon us, echoed as it is in 'Somerset' – the name of not only the chief male character but also the county in which the novel is, originally, located. So far, so Ruskin (as it were) since, for Ruskin, the Romantic myth of the sun-god, particularly as celebrated in the paintings of Turner, was best reinterpreted in terms of the myth of the sunset; this myth of death and decline was, he felt, more appropriate to his own, less confident generation. What, though, distinguishes *A Laodicean* is that its doubts about the sun finally focus not on a sunset but a trick photograph. For Hardy, the death of the sun is not redeemed by the sublime pathos of its setting; instead, it is implicated in the bathos of a trickery that was particularly popular among charlatan spiritualists keen to produce what were called 'spirit photographs.' As, then, *A Laodicean* throws the sun into question so we are introduced to a world in which the bizarre and improbable seem to take place: not only might ghosts appear but, as Mr Ray remarks, 'the German Emperor [might be] in a violent passion . . . the Prime Minister [might be] out of his mind . . . [and] the Pope . . . the worse for liquor.' Dare's photography represents not just the shadowy double of architecture but also the possibility of a shadowy inversion of the world itself. After all, as well as being 'a maker of negatives' (in which, of course, lights and shades are reversed) Dare is himself described as 'a complete negative'; he seems, that is, to occupy a space between all positive terms or categories. He is neither masculine or feminine ('his hair hung as a fringe . . . in the fashion [of] . . . the other sex'), old or young ('I can't think whether he is a boy or a man'), English or foreign ('he is a being of no nationality'), aristocrat or commoner (he is only an illegitimate De Stancy). In short, Dare, 'the complete negative,' alerts us to what Roland Barthes calls 'the profound madness of photography,' the madness of an art which, through inversion, offers the world an absolutely exact but monochrome double of itself – a kind of ghost, in fact.

So described, photography betrays something of its kinship to writing, that other 'black and white' art of duplication after which, of course, photo*graphy* is named – *graphos* meaning 'writing.' This line of descent is not forgotten in *A Laodicean*. In the first instance, a photograph of Dare is described as a 'transcript of . . . [his] features' and enclosed in an 'envelope' for Captain De Stancy to deliver, like a letter, to the police (though this he fails to do); in the second instance, Mr Ray refers to Dare's trick photography as 'libellous,' *libel* meaning 'book.' In both cases it is the sheer unreliability of writing that photography serves to foreground, its capacity (as Derrida would say) 'not to arrive' – not to arrive, that is, at either its addressee or, indeed, the truth. Dare's photography thus represents a shadow not only of architecture but of writing, not only Somerset's pursuits but Hardy's.

The whole novel, however, is almost a shadow or negative of what both contemporary and modern-day readers would recognize as a 'Hardy' novel. This is no Wessex tragedy of character and environment; remember, Hardy had already written both *Far from the Madding Crowd* (1874) and *The Return of the Native* (1878). Instead, it is an almost placeless novel of social comedy and improbable action which most Hardy critics have, until recently, considered dull if not disastrous. Moreover, the unique circumstances of the novel's very composition – Hardy dictated most of it to his first wife, Emma, from his sickbed – do themselves make strange, or unfamiliar the business of writing. Just as Somerset, when bedridden, is thereby rendered 'unarchitectural' so Hardy's illness effectively rendered him unauthorial; involving another in the act of composition necessarily disrupts the conventional nineteenth-century dream of the author-God as the single, undivided origin of the literary work.

The disruption of this metaphysical dream of authorship is not, however, most obviously reflected by photography (literally, 'light-writing') but rather telegraphy (literally, 'far-writing'). For whilst photography places writing beside the sign of light and, therefore, of metaphysics, telegraphy places it beside the sign of distance, *tele* meaning 'far off.' That photography represents the less radical model, or picture, of writing is underlined by its implication in patriarchy, the rule of the father. As the 'heliographic science' it is a masculine preserve both in name (the sun, *helios*, is traditionally male) and by implication: 'No *woman*,' we read, 'could have doubted . . . [Dare's trick] photograph.' By contrast, the telegraphic machine in the castle is dominated by Charlotte and Paula. Indeed, the only male who shares 'the trick of [the telegram] is . . . a page . . . called John' which is all we ever know about him. The trick, or joke of this 'page called John' is that the relatively new medium of telegraphy is marked by the name of the author of not only the biblical book of Revelation (from which, of course, the novel derives its very name) but also the famous biblical declaration 'In the beginning was the Word.' *A Laodicean* thus anticipates, in typically cryptic fashion, both the humour and seriousness of Derrida's claim that 'In the beginning was the tele-phone' (for Derrida, all communication, however direct it may appear, entails hidden distance). As Charlotte remarks, commenting on the long drama precipitated by the false telegram that Dare sends in Somerset's name, 'It was the telegram that began it.'

Of course, what begins the *whole* drama of the novel is Paula's refusal to be baptized and thus 'to fulfil the Word' or desire of both her heavenly and also her earthly father (it is his dying request). Paula's telegraphy, however, is part of this beginning in that it too is a refusal, albeit highly coded, of the father. For, in making possible the immediate to-and-fro of a dialogue, telegraphy very obviously departs from the monologic insis-tence of the 'Word' of her fathers. It is no accident that the novel's very first telegraphic exchange is between two women and wholly 'unintelli-gible' to Somerset. Indeed, telegraphy is so dialogic and so dominated by women as to help the novel, as a whole, give a new and cryptic meaning to 'mum's the word' – it's no longer 'dad,' as it were. After all, *A Laodicean* is not only about a woman but also, for the most part, actually *written* by a woman, Emma Hardy. Indeed, Seymour-Smith goes so far as to suggest that Emma had some part in the novel's composition.

Whether or not telegraphy takes writing out of the realm of the father, it certainly gestures, once more like Derrida, towards a 'writing [that] . . . is unattached to any house.' In this respect it again represents a more radical model of writing than photography with its dependency on the room that was the camera. It is telegraphy alone which finally contests that domestication of the space of literature which Henry James articulated (also in 1881) in his famous phrase 'the house of fiction.' This domestication is conspicuous throughout much of *A Laodicean*.

Note that Paula visits the house of Goethe. Note too how attention is drawn to the vocabulary common to both architecture and writing: 'the capitals in that letter were of the . . . semi-gothic type.' Indeed, the grave-stone epitaphs and the 'names . . . cut' into the castle's tower return writing to that moment in its own pre-history in which, as an act of cutting or engraving, it was a working with stone. Both this moment, and the larger writing/building analogy of which it is a part, find a cryptic summary when Dare (referring to the moment he no longer had time for reading) declares that 'literature went *to the wall.*' By contrast, Paula's telegrams, communicated along a wire that passes out of a loophole, suggest a writing that goes *through* the wall. These telegrams violate our sense of the homogenized space (and indeed time) of the house:

> the . . . message sped through the loophole of Stancy Castle, over the trees, along the railway, under bridges, across three counties from extreme antiquity . . . to sheer modernism and finally landed . . . in Somerset's chambers.

Though the telegram finally arrives, the sheer distance of its journey highlights the possibility that it might not, a possibility that is realized every time Somerset's telegrams to Paula are intercepted by her scheming uncle, Abner. Thus, even more than the novel's photographs, the telegrams draw attention to an indirection and frailty that seems to be a general characteristic of communications in *A Laodicean.* Here letters too are intercepted, a newspaper is read two days late, one invitation is never sent, another is sent to an old address, and a newspaper announces an engagement that has not taken place. In short, the novel's telegrams only make obvious what Derrida would argue is the non-homogenous space of all communication. To see it as also a non-domestic space means, in *A Laodicean*, that communication is always implicated in the world 'out there,' the world of forces and powers.

Powers

This non-domestic space of communication is never more vividly pictured than when Havill, having reluctantly written a self-damaging letter of conscience, stands in a 'deserted street' in the middle of the night hesitating for some time in front of a letter-box before eventually, upon hearing 'the footsteps of a solitary policeman,' he 'let[s] the letter go.' Far, as it were, from the freedom of home this letter occupies a literally policed space, a space controlled by the implied threat of force. However, any simple, oppositional model of 'peace within and violence without' is continually blurred by Paula's telegrams which pass through 'an arrow-slit' even as they go from inside to outside. In so doing, they suggest a more general complicity between the space (or rather spaces) of communication and the brutal fact of force. Indeed, philosophically speaking, force is inevitable even when thinking of literature as a house, as something homely and familiar; as both Heidegger and Derrida have stressed, the notion of 'the house [merely] represses the violation that made it possible' – namely, the exclusion of everything that is *un*familiar or *un*homely. There is, it seems, no space in which writing may be sheltered from the world of force.

This fate, in fact, is encoded in the very history of the word 'magazine,' a history to which *A Laodicean* bears tacit witness. Not only is it first published in *Harper's New Monthly Magazine* but, within the novel, we are reminded that the word has previously meant both a miscellaneous storehouse (Mr Ray, the shopkeeper, runs 'a magazine of old clothes') and, indeed, an ammunition store ('two [sentinels stand] at the magazine'). The house of writing that is today's 'magazine' leads directly, or at least etymologically, to the house of violence.

And this is nowhere more the case than in the writing that is *A Laodicean*. For even as it seems to narrow to the confines of domestic romance, a romance centred upon a heroine called 'Power,' so we are continually referred to the historical workings of force, if only because, as Paul de Man remarks, 'there is history from the moment that [the] word ...“power” ... emerge[s].' Indeed, the romantic plot surrounding William Dare's attempt to set up William De Stancy's marriage to Paula Power works, in effect, as an encoding of Nietzsche's famous contemporaneous slogan, 'Will to Power.' Written into the novel's domestic interior is the very dynamic of the battleground that is, for Nietzsche, history.

The novel's literal, domestic interior, the castle, is constant witness to such history; as well as being directly involved in the English Civil War, its crypts contain reminders of both the Wars of the Roses and the Crusades. Moreover, since it was built by the Normans, the castle owes its very existence to the violent enforcement of conquest. In a passage on Lyon, the narrator refers to 'some of the ghastliest atrocities . . . that the civilised world has beheld'; but the castle suggests that the civilized world might just be *founded* upon such atrocities. This irony is clearly signalled in that wry remark about its walls being 'of a thickness sufficient for the perpetuation of grand ideas.' The novel thus comes close to Walter Benjamin's claim that 'there is no document of civilisation which is not at the same time a document of barbarism.'

The classic proof of this claim is European colonialism, traces of which just occasionally pass across the pages of *A Laodicean*. Composed at the beginning of the 1880s, arguably *the* decade of imperialism, the novel traces its enforcement in the person of Captain De Stancy (just back from serving 'in the line' in India), its commercial exploitation in Abner's 'Anglo-South-American' trading station, and its 'civilising' spoils in passing references to: 'Greek . . . statues . . . in the British museum,' Paula's 'morocco case,' Dare's cigarettes, and even 'cotton thread.' The novel, it seems, is marked by the faintest intuition of what it is to occupy colonized space. It is an intuition most clearly articulated when De Stancy's discovery that Dare was in town is compared to Robinson Crusoe's discovery of 'the print of a man's foot in the sand' – the foot, of course, of a black native. This, though, is a rare moment in a novel whose focus is, quite literally, white; witness Paula's white baptismal robe and, later, her 'dress of ivory white,' the young Sir William De Stancy's 'white hat,' Somerset's 'white signal' of distress, the two white parasols, the 'white . . . fragment of swan's-down,' the 'white feather' of cowardice, and the 'watery white' of the final moon. In fact, for one cryptic moment, even that which is non-European is coloured white; note how, after refusing baptism, Paula moves off in her carriage leaving behind only a passing cat, and Somerset, we read, 'saw a white Persian standing forlorn where the carriage had been.'

One white object of attention is here replaced by another; and, indeed, the novel is so focused on the colour white that it almost becomes the very name for focus, or centre. Note how both the 'spot of white' that is Somerset's distress signal and 'the spot of watery white' that is the moon each repeat upon the novel in the phrase 'point-blank' (literally, 'white point'). Not only is Abner's revolver 'directed point-blank' at Dare but Paula, turning to Somerset's father, 'ask[s] . . . point-blank' after her suitor. However, and here is the twist, our heroine declines to 'tell him point-blank that [she is] in love with him.' For a moment, this romantic novel refuses not only its own romantic centre but also, and at the same time, its white centre, its point-blank.

And this is true of the whole novel, not only in the sense that it never finally erases the 'civilised' world's non-white margins but also in the sense that it never finally erases the dead. White, of course, is the colour that marks the end of Victorian mourning:

> Her black-and-white costume [of half-mourning] had finally disappeared, and in its place she had adopted a . . . dress of ivory white.

The novel itself may also be said to have discarded mourning clothes – the clothes, as it were, of earlier Victorian fiction; for here there are no death-scenes, and when death does take place it is curiously marginal. The deaths of Mr Wilkins and John Power, for instance, take place before the action of the novel, whilst that of Jack Ravensbury has absolutely no bearing on it. Moreover, De Stancy only learns of his father's death via a telegram, whilst Havill is not even told of his wife's death but merely 'overhears' the news. However, for all the novel's apparent determination to make death an irrelevance it is never beside the point, or at least never beside the 'point-blank,' if only because, originally, it refers to the white point at the centre of a target. Within the novel's white centre there is, as it were, a dead centre. This conceit, in fact, nearly becomes real when Somerset stands in the railway tunnel and sees a train entering at the far end: 'in the middle of the speck of light before him appeared a speck of black.'

Something very similar might, indeed, be said of the great fire with which the novel concludes. For here the very centre of the novel, the castle, becomes a kind of terrible sun ('here rose the light' 'in the meridian of its . . . splendours') within which an anonymous figure (presumably Dare) goes from door to door before ceasing to move and being 'seen no more.' Whether or not this disappearance is a death it is a black speck, as it were, in the very middle of this, the bright symbolic centre of the novel. As such, the disappearance is eerily suggestive of the death that so nearly overcame the literal centre of the novel: namely, its bedridden author who always knew his illness might be fatal. Paula's subsequent reference to 'a finished writer' has an obvious ironic significance. According to W. L. Phelps, Hardy remarked in 1900 that '*A Laodicean* contained more of the facts of his own life than anything else he had ever written'; as Dare, 'the author of. . . tricks,' disappears in the fire it is, for the modern reader, as if we also foresee one of the facts of *the* author's own death in 1928: namely, his cremation. Interest in cremation was certainly very high at the time of the novel's composition, peaking in 1884 with its legalization.

The uncanny, prescient force of this fire is not, however, exhausted by Hardy's eventual death. For what disappears in the flames is the ancestral home of a family who are clearly identified with (though not *as*) the 'house and lineage of Jacob,' the Jewish people. Given too an earlier reference to 'Nebuchadnezzar's furnace' into which were thrown three exiled Jews, the modern reader cannot but find herself momentarily mindful of those millions of Jews who perished in that latter-day version of Nebuchadnezzar's furnace, the Holocaust (literally, 'whole-burning'). The novel itself is, as we know, strangely mindful of the 'ghastliest atrocities the civilised world has beheld.'

The persecution of Jews, albeit on a much smaller scale, was of course a conspicuous feature of late nineteenth-century Europe; nevertheless, it is as if Dare, who earlier speaks of 'the map of the future,' has here contrived to draw it in fire. If so, then this conflagration, which begins with Dare setting fire to a heap of valuable paintings, echoes something of the prophetic force of Heinrich Heine's assertion in 1823 that 'Where men burn books / They will burn people also in the end.' We should not forget that Hardy is believed to have burnt the manuscript of *A Laodicean*.

And, of course, not even the published novel survives fire in the sense that Dare's conflagration is the final scene. Indeed, his scene seems almost to mark the end of the very medium of writing, for the fire is uncannily suggestive, even 'ere the art was known,' of the medium of cinema. As the flames play upon the portraits in the castle what we so nearly see are moving pictures:

> the framed gentleman in the lace collar seemed to open his eyes more widely; he with the flowing locks . . . to part his lips; he in the armour . . . to shake the plates of his mail with suppressed laughter; [and] the lady with the three-stringed pearl necklace . . . to nod with satisfaction.

The novel has already glanced towards the cinematic future with its reference to a 'phantasmagoria' (a device by which figures on a screen appear to move); moreover, according to one historian of photography, motion pictures were effectively born in 1880, the first year of the novel's composition. What, though, makes Hardy's fiery map of the visual future so peculiar, so haunting, is the sheer contentment and even mirth that is seen on the faces of these burning portraits. It is as if the future that is the cinema here gestures, like the trick photographs before it, towards an outrageous capacity to make almost anything happen, even to turn tragedy into comedy, Holocaust (dare we say it) into farce. Indeed, there is much about these four portraits which recalls the four figures that miraculously walk unharmed through the flames of Nebuchadnezzar's furnace, a fire in which three men are joined by a mysterious fourth who is compared to 'the Son of God.' If so, the farce, or comedy might just become a divine comedy. As De Stancy remarks, in another connection, 'Game? Call it Divine Comedy, rather!'

Pupils of His Eyes

(August 28th 2002)

On the death, from multiple sclerosis, of Martin York (b. 1961), a musician
and friend who, toward the end, when no longer able to speak,
communicated by moving the pupils of his eyes.

Yours became a still life,
and you its motionless
hero, a massive
monk in the foreground
of a
room that bent to listen.

Before you rested
two hands, long
and slender,
made for
another kind of
movement.

And
every now
and
then
we would touch
those hands
as if
to reply to
the
still moving eyes
as they did the work
of
speech,
the hard labour
of
breath;

breath, for you, un-
necessary.

MAY 2012

VIII
Leavis Spells Pianos
Coming Back to 'Life'
(2003)

'life' is a necessary word.
(F. R. Leavis)

To talk of 'life' after theory is, in a sense, to come *back* to life since we have been there before, before theory, with F. R. Leavis, the Cambridge critic who, from the 1940s to the 1960s, dominated literary criticism with his reverential and enigmatic talk of 'life.' According to Leavis, 'every creative writer of the greatest kind knows that in a major work he is developing thought – thought about life.' To this day, within literary criticism, 'life' means Leavis and Leavis means 'life'; if though, after theory, we may be allowed to invoke a clumsy and eccentric detail of Leavis' *own* life, we find that 'Leavis Spells Pianos,' that being the slogan with which Leavis's father used to advertise the pianos he both made and sold in Edwardian Cambridge.

Of course if, for literary criticism, 'life' is a necessary word, 'piano' is a supremely *un*necessary word, a word that does not follow; but it is for that very reason that it *is* necessary in that it recalls us to the simple fact that our thinking about a text does not always make sense, or at least common sense, and yet in so doing immediately makes *un*common sense; for criticism or theory does (if we think about it) have a fragile but curious relationship to the piano. On the front cover of a recent Derrida text the theorist appears, almost ironically, seated with his back to an upright drawing-room piano. Again, in a piece called 'Circumfession' (1991), where he comments upon being seated at his computer, Derrida talks knowingly of 'playing the keyboard.' Almost twenty years before, Derrida's friend Roland Barthes glances at the 'history of the piano' and declares:

we know that today post-serial music has radically altered the role of the 'interpreter,' who is called on to be . . . the co-author of the score. The text is very much a score of this new kind: it asks of the reader a practical collaboration.

There is, it seems, something about the twentieth-century piano that lends itself to a radical or writerly account of the reader as player, or improviser. As Valentine Cunningham says, there is a tacit relationship between poststructuralism and jazz; it is no accident that Derrida did, on one occasion, write a text for accompaniment on jazz-piano. Theorists and critics did not, though, need to wait for jazz, or even post-serial music, before they first thought of themselves as artists; all they needed was a piano. As early as 1890 Oscar Wilde gave us the 'The Critic as Artist,' a comic Socratic dialogue between two characters or voices called Earnest and Gilbert; if Barthes is a theorist *on* the piano then Gilbert is the theorist *at* the piano: the dialogue opens with the splendid Gilbert seated, quite literally, 'at the piano.' As the dialogue proceeds Gilbert, when not offering to 'play Chopin . . . or Dvořák,' advances an effortless and paradoxical overturning of Matthew Arnold's famous essay 'The Function of Criticism at the Present Time' (1864). While, for the commonsensical Arnold, the critic is famously secondary to the author, for Gilbert it is the critic who is the true artist; moreover, while for Arnold the true function of criticism is 'to see the object as in itself it really is,' for Gilbert it is, naturally, 'to see the object as in itself it really is *not*.'

The view from the piano is, as one might expect, no view at all; it is more about the art of *not* seeing, of *mis*-reading, of not doing 'proper' literary criticism at all. Gilbert, we sense, would rather be playing Chopin. And the possibility of *not* doing literary criticism, of giving it up, was in fact presented to Leavis himself when, in 1929, he received a visit from the philosopher Wittgenstein, a man who, as it happens, had grown up in a house of seven pianos; apropos absolutely nothing, or 'without prelude,' as Leavis notes, Wittgenstein declared: 'Give up literary criticism!' Academic literary criticism thus no sooner begins than it is told to give up; it is, from the beginning, marked with what Kermode has taught us to call a 'sense of an ending,' its *own* ending.

Literary theory has in very various ways renewed this sense of crisis; at times, it too implies there may be better things to do than literary criticism. The deconstructionist, one senses, would rather be doing philosophy, which takes us back to Gilbert who spends a whole night theorizing about criticism but never actually does any. Again, the new historicist or cultural materialist, one senses, would rather be doing history, *doing life*, as it were, or *the real*. This, curiously, might just take us back to that would-be 'Professor of Life' (as Woolf called him), Sir Walter Raleigh, the Oxford Professor of English Literature who was quite open about the fact that he could not wait to give up literary criticism for something more active, or vital – an ambition that he finally realized with the onset of the First World War. To make fun of Raleigh is easy (and indeed fun) but, after theory, we may just share, almost without knowing it, something of his conviction that there is more to life than 'English Literature.' It is true that Leavis protected us from this sense, convincing many both inside and outside universities that academic English almost *is* life; as Eagleton writes, 'by the early 1930s . . . English [Literature] was . . . [considered] the supremely civilizing pursuit.' Now, of course, like Raleigh, we are not so sure; partly because, after Auschwitz, we are not sure what civilization is and partly because theory is, above all, an opening of English to other disciplines. Theory is, in a sense, a way of taking Wittgenstein's advice; quite literally, in the case of Christopher Norris – 'Mr Norris,' as William Empson once called him, recently changed not trains but departments, Philosophy for English.

Others, though, cannot give up; after 50 years of literary criticism, Frank Kermode is still, as he says, 'doing this kind of thing.' Likewise, Derrida has never wholly given up literature for philosophy; his recent essay 'Le Parjure,' for instance, is primarily a reading of a single novel. T. S. Eliot once wrote that 'criticism is as inevitable as breathing'; it is for life, as it were, and so it seems even after theory. What may have changed, however, is that theory has reminded us that life in fact means death, that living is a form of dying. This has much to do with the turn to Freud for whom 'the end of all life is death.' It also has much to do with Derrida who often seems to recall the medieval *memento mori* tradition; for Derrida, that is, life and death constitute an impossible binary: 'it is, already, *life death*,' he writes. Or, as very different theorists would say, life for one often comes at the expense of death for another, *the* other.

Indeed, it is the argument of Paul de Man *et al.*, that such killing is carried out in the *name* of Life, that at the dead centre of ideology, at the dead centre of all the ways in which we blind ourselves to the difference, or otherness of the other, is the myth of the organic whole. To dream of the One, of the whole, has often meant drawing on notions of organic unity; as Derrida observes, in Hegel

> the absolute Idea in its infinite truth is still determined as Life, true life, absolute life, life without death, imperishable life, the life of truth.

The dangers of such absolute, or total Life are obvious; we cannot forget that Leavis was not the only one to talk of 'life' in the 1930s. When Nazi Germany invaded Eastern Europe they did so because Hitler had developed the theory of *Lebensraum*, meaning 'life-space,' or 'living-room' for a greater Germany. This is not, of course, to suggest that Leavis was drawing on Hegel or was complicit with the extreme nationalism of his day; it is simply that theory has made us wary of the idea of Life, or indeed any other organicist master-word. The organic, though, need not always serve Hegelian ends; as Kermode points out, when the German Romantics thought of the work of art in organic terms it entailed a sense of the inevitable decay and dissolution within nature.

Life is not necessarily whole; this, in fact, is Derrida's point when, in *Glas* (1974), he looks at the divided 'structure of the flower,' at what the botanists call dehiscence, and remarks that 'life and division go together.' Theory, it is often said, 'murders to dissect' but, for the Derrida of *Glas*, it is life that does the dissecting: 'deconstruction of the transcendental effect,' he writes, 'is at work in the structure of the flower.' Strangely, in Derrida the familiar poststructural stress on difference arises from not only linguistics but botany, not only the library but the garden. In this respect deconstruction is a kind of life-writing; it is, though, life implicated in death, or *thanatos* – hence Derrida's conceitful talk of his 'auto*biothanato*heterographical opus.'

This outrageous neologism comes from Derrida's 'Circumfession,' a strange mix of memoir and meditation, where theory becomes life-writing in the sense of autobiography. Theory, though, has often had a secret autobiographical life; the very people who brought us 'The Death of the Author' have, for some time, also had the nerve to bring us, in effect, The Life of the Theorist; witness, not only 'Circumfession' but also *Roland Barthes by Roland Barthes* (1975), and Althusser's *The Future Lasts a Long Time* (1992). This irony would not surprise Gilbert, the paradoxical theorist at the piano; for, with unswerving hyperbole, Gilbert announces that 'Criticism . . . is the only civilized form of autobiography.' And this is so, it seems, even when the criticism itself disavows the personal; take the case of Foucault, who declares that he 'writes in order to have no face' and yet admits that 'I have always wanted my books to be fragments from an autobiography.' Note that Foucault does not say *whose* autobiography; perhaps, it is 'everybody's autobiography,' a phrase of Gertrude Stein's that fascinates Derrida; and Derrida it is who, with a perversity worthy of Gilbert, coolly remarks that '"autobiography" is perhaps the least inadequate name' for 'what interests me.'

This may come as something of a surprise and, if true, deconstruction is life but not as we know it, not as we know it from conventional life-writing; for deconstruction is hardly 'a civilized form of autobiography.' Instead, it is life as Derrida knows it from Walter Benjamin, life as something resistant to the smooth continuities of civilization; Benjamin is the German-Jewish refugee who, in 1940, just months before killing himself to avoid a still worse fate at the hands of the Nazis, writes that in order to 'blast open the continuum of history' one must 'blast . . . a specific life out of the era.' Thirty years later Benjamin's blasted life is echoed by de Man when he writes that 'any attempt at a total understanding of our being (*Wesen*) will stand in contrast to actual . . . fragmentary, particular and unfulfilled life (*Leben*).' There is, though, an obvious irony here; for de Man's own life – one part a columnist for a collaborationist newspaper in occupied Belgium, another part an arch-theorist at Yale – was so fragmented, so divided as to disrupt a total understanding of not just 'being' but deconstruction. De Man's double life blasts open not just the continuum of history but the continuum of theory; the dramatic discovery in 1987 of de Man's wartime journalism rudely interrupted the American dream of deconstruction as 'the joyous affirmation of the play of the world and of the innocence of becoming.' These words come from Derrida at Baltimore, way back in 1966 when describing what he calls the Nietzschean 'side of the thinking of play'; after the de Man affair, twenty years later, never again such innocence. Almost overnight, or so it now seems, theory discovered itself to be, in a sense, a post-war event, or trauma – an attempt to deal with dark European memories. Admittedly, this had already been hinted at; as early as 1984 Eagleton spoke better than he knew when he remarked, of deconstruction's absolute scepticism, that

> behind the . . . Yale School would seem to loom . . . [the] shadow of the holocaust. Harold Bloom is a Jew, Geoffrey Hartman is of central European Jewish provenance; de Man's uncle . . . was politically involved in the Second World War period.

Once de Man's own political involvement was known there was certainly no escaping the Second World War; indeed, in Derrida's work we seem still to be at war, even when in California, where in 1993 he remarked: 'it is still evening, it is always nightfall along the "ramparts," on the battlements of an old Europe at war.'

I. A. Richards once suggested that Leavis' veneration for 'Life' was shared by many of those who, like Leavis himself, witnessed first-hand the horrors of the First Word War. To suggest that theory is, in its turn, a response to the Second World War is, in fact, to say that theory is 'life' in the strict etymological sense of the word; for the word 'life' comes from the prehistoric German *lib* meaning 'remain' or 'be left' and, as one dictionary puts it, 'the semantic connection between "remaining" and *life* . . . is thought to lie in the notion of being "left alive after a battle."' If life is, necessarily, *after*-life; if all living is a form of 'living-*on*,' in particular living-on after war, then poststructuralism is very much a form of life in the simple sense that so many of the major poststructuralists *are* survivors, those who have lived on. Not only do Bloom, Hartman and Derrida all belong to a generation of Jews that was ravaged by the Holocaust but when Lacan's wife declared herself Jewish he went personally to the Gestapo to retrieve her dossier, thereby almost certainly saving her life. There is also Louis Althusser, he who never forgot the experience of being a prisoner of war, not to mention Foucault who once invoked the 'sight[s] we had known during the German occupation.'

If the generation of post-war French intellectuals that gave us post-structuralist theory are, by definition, survivors then Derrida is a survivor *of the survivors* since he has lived to see life after theory. In the last twenty years Derrida has on at least fourteen occasions written texts in memory of dead colleagues: from Barthes in 1980 to Lyotard in 1998; enough writing to fill, quite literally, a whole book, or work of mourning. At Lyotard's funeral Derrida remarks,

> I seem to recall having [recently] said that . . . Jean-François . . and I [are] the sole survivors of . . . a 'generation' of which I am the last born, and, no doubt, the most melancholic. . . . What can I say today, then? That I love Jean-François, that I miss him.

Derrida, it seems, could almost be speaking of himself when, in 'Le Parjure,' first he dwells on what grammatarians call the anacoluthon (their name for a syntactical break or discontinuity) and then he proceeds to cite one particular definition of the anacoluthon, a definition he describes as 'pathetic and human'; the definition is composed by Pierre Fontanier and reads as follows:

> letting stand alone a word that calls out for another as companion. . . .

Theory, if personified by Derrida, is a 'wanting sentence'; life after theory, or at the end of theory, thus answers to a grammatical definition. The last laugh, or last sigh, belongs perhaps to de Man, he who (in)famously declared that 'death is a displaced name for a linguistic predicament.' If so, de Man returns even as he departs.

This, as it happens, is very nearly the logic of Derrida's recent remark that 'Paul de Man *was* my friend. Paul de Man *is* my friend.' Here, though, de Man does not quite return as he left: Paul de Man the new, posthumous friend is not the same as Paul de Man the old, living friend; the posthumous friend has a guilty past and is, therefore, someone whom Derrida never quite knew while alive. This coming and going – or rather going and coming – is, in fact, inscribed in Derrida's extended account of 'anacoluthonic discontinuity'; for although it leaves you lacking the companion you expect it also gives you a companion you did not expect – to quote 'Le Parjure':

> In life . . . I [cannot] foresee change . . . I [can]not foresee who, the other who has arrived in the interval.

For Derrida, the anacoluthon entails the possibility of a *new* companion, 'the sudden arrival of another person.' But then we should know this, for the most famously interrupted text in English Literature is, of course, Coleridge's 'Kubla Khan,' a transcription of a dream that is forever abandoned following the strange and sudden arrival of an unidentified 'person on business from Porlock.' There is, then, more to anacoluthon than simply lack, and this secret is buried within the very word 'companion,' the word on which both Fontanier and Derrida insist and which, if broken open, reveals *companis* meaning 'with-bread.' A companion is, literally, one with whom you share bread; and, of course, the most famous sharer of bread is Christ, he who, on returning to life, appeared to two friends on a road who only recognized him when he broke and shared bread – in that instant he immediately disappeared:

> And it came to pass, as he sat at meat with them, he took bread, and blessed it, and brake, and gave to them. And their eyes were opened, and they knew him; and he vanished out of their sight.

Here, in the very moment of becoming a com-panion, Jesus not only plays the interruptive, anacoluthonic role of leaving others alone but he also, and at the same time, reveals himself; he both comes and goes in the same moment of com-panionship. The expected, predictable, figure (the man they had met on the road) has gone and a wholly unexpected figure arrives, the man they would call God.

All this recalls Kermode's observation, apropos theory, that 'the door that was opened in the late 1960s let in many unexpected visitors'; and perhaps the most unexpected visitor has been, as for those men on the road, the enigmatic and almost embarrassing figure of God. 'Leave the door open to . . . Elijah,' suggests Derrida in 1977. For Lacan, indeed, writing in 1975, 'God has [never] . . . made his exit.' Cixous, Irigaray and Kristeva have also all made major and obvious contributions to theory's theological turn, a turn that has been both dramatic and conspicuous. It is, though, for many a turn for the worse; this is certainly the case for Christopher Norris who has expressed a disquiet that is shared, perhaps, by a number of theory's early enthusiasts. Many of these belonged to a profoundly secular, even secularist, generation, particularly in the UK where the greatest impetus for theory came, as Toril Moi has observed, from the Left, from critics committed to materialist, or empiricist modes of thought.

It is true, of course, that Anglo-American criticism has traditionally styled itself as a would-be religion, as a discipline that only just falls short of the realm of the spirit; as late as 1982 Kermode could write that

> the history of criticism . . . is a history of . . . attempts to earn the privi-lege of access to that kingdom of the larger existence which is in our time the secular surrogate of another kingdom whose existence is no longer within our range.

This is, of course, not far from many a remark in Derrida's more recent work, his work on the question of spirit; but what distinguishes the two is Kermode's insistence on the secular/sacred opposition. Elsewhere Kermode expands on this, arguing that 'secularization multiplies the world's structures of probability'; with secularization, Kermode suggests, there are more stories rather than less, but he may also be saying that the secularized world is not, as we usually think, a more contingent and anarchic place but rather a place *full of probabilities* – in short, a *more* predictable place. This is nowhere more obvious than in Anglo-American literary criticism whose characteristic empiricism has very obviously made for more probability, pattern and rule than in the texts of high and, as it were, high-Spirited French theory. Empiricist criticism, we might say, tends not to expect the unexpected, is less expectant of surprise; however, ironically, it is for precisely this reason that such criticism is all the more *vulnerable* to surprise, in particular to the surprise of the spirit. It is not Derrida but Kermode who describes reading as 'the blindman's bluff of the spirit,' and it is Anglo-American criticism rather than French theory that has been most consistently marked by the true surprise of the spirit, which is not so much to be (as Wordsworth would have it) 'surprised by joy' but rather (as Stanley Fish would have it) 'surprised by sin,' or injustice. For some thirty years English Studies has at least heard (if not heeded) the very various critiques of feminists, Marxists, postcolonialists and queer theorists; these critiques, though once informed by such as Foucault and Althusser, have increasingly returned to the moral and political roots of English Studies to read much literature and indeed criticism as ideological, as silently complicit with the operation of power and privilege. What has been at work is a hermeneutics of suspicion in which the object of suspicion is, in part, hermeneutics itself, or rather the institutionalisation of hermeneutics that is academic English. The criticism that has raged against this establishment has been, at best, a form of institutional confession, an admission of collective, and structural guilt.

We are not, perhaps, accustomed to think of criticism as confessional; however, one of the surprises of theory is its intuition that *all* criticism entails an admission of guilt. After all, if no one can ever mean exactly what they say then the critic is doomed to a kind of perjury: 'one always asks for pardon when one writes,' writes Derrida. Again, if everything is always already written then all writing is a form of theft: 'I didn't earn my book by the sweat of my brow . . . I stole [it],' writes Cixous. And, yet again, if the birth of the reader requires the death of the author then all reading is a form of murder: 'right here I kill you,' writes Derrida. 'We are,' he also writes, 'the worst criminals in history,' and so we are if we accept his Levinasian account of ethics as a responsibility to the other: 'in ethics,' writes Derrida, 'responsibility . . . is infinite . . . that's why I always feel guilty.'

Back in 1971, at the beginning of theory, Barthes declared that 'the Text cannot stop,' a phrase that for many announced the endless and unbounded play of meaning; however, by the end of theory it seems as if *responsibility* cannot stop. This logic, or illogic, is pushed to its hyperbolic extreme when Derrida, in 1992, remarks that

> by preferring my work . . . as a . . . philosopher . . . I am sacrificing and
> betraying at every moment all my other obligations: my obligations to
> the other others . . . the billions of my fellows, my fellows who are dying
> of starvation and disease.

This, of course, is easy to say and yet impossible to mean; it is, though,
also difficult to forget, the reality of 'third-world' starvation being so
absolute in its awfulness that if the activity of reading and writing about
books is to mean anything, is to be in any sense a responsible activity, then
it must somehow connect with that starving. In the instant we recognize
this we are alerted to the unbearable heaviness of being a reader.

In the very same instant, however, we are also alerted to the unbearable *lightness* of being a reader; for if we are persuaded, albeit only for
a moment, by Derrida's sense of infinite responsibility, by this ethical
version of Freud's conviction that 'everything is related to everything,'
then we might also be persuaded (or at least infected) by Barthes' sense
of infinite textual play, or freedom. As usual, responsibility and freedom
are related; as Derrida writes, 'There are ethics [in reading] *because* there
is no rule . . . because I don't know what to do'; reading is weighed
down with responsibility because it is so free. Reading's heaviness is also
its lightness; responsibility does not stop because the text does not stop.
If this is so, if every text is indeed related to every other text, then my
interpretative choices are forever haunted by the possibility that they
could be otherwise, that they are, in some sense, contingent or arbitrary.
In this connection, Kermode once asked the question 'Can We Say
Absolutely Anything We Like?' and in a sense, or in theory, perhaps we
can. As Derrida argues, 'the space of literature . . . in principle allows
one to say everything/anything [*tout dire*]' – that is, in part, the point of
literature. Again, this is no weightless freedom since, for Derrida, it is
'inseparable . . . from what calls forth a democracy'; this freedom, however, is also inseparable from what Derrida describes as 'bewilderment,'
or 'a feeling of existence as excess, "being superfluous."' Tellingly,
Derrida here quotes Sartre and he too, back in 1947, saw literature as
freedom: 'the work of art,' writes Sartre, 'from whichever side you
approach it, is an act of confidence in the freedom of men.' For Sartre,
though, this freedom is *too much*; with neither God, nor even human
nature to determine existence Man is too free, 'he . . . is *condemned* to
be free.' Looking back to Sartre, Derrida sees the freedom that is literature as not only blessing but curse, an aspect of the nauseous lightness
of reading.

This lightness is never felt more than whenever I find that my mind has
wandered in the very act of reading; I am still 'reading' (in an automatic,
senseless sense) but I am not thinking about it. To echo a refrain of
Derrida's: 'Just imagine, I was not thinking about it,' or at least not
always. And that, argues Derrida, is our fate even when we *think* we are

thinking about it; for Derrida, there is always 'the possibility . . . threat or chance of . . . forgetting, the effects of an irreducible distraction at the heart of finite thought.' It is true, as Kermode observes, that much theory is thinking about thinking about books, but sometimes theory is thinking about *not* thinking about books. Hence Derrida's question 'What is called not thinking?' and, if you like, Lacan's answer which is, quite simply: *Being, being* human, for Lacan declares, 'I think where I am not, therefore I am where I do not think.' Lacan, of course, is inverting that most fundamental philosophical axiom: Descartes' 'I think therefore I am'; and, in much the same anti-philosophical way, Derrida's question is a disruption of the title of Heidegger's essay, 'What is Called Thinking?' But then the title disrupts itself in the sense that the original German, *Was Heisst Denken?* can also mean 'What Calls for Thinking?' implying that something prior to thinking lies beyond, or ahead of thinking, a something that thinking is after, or in pursuit of. For theory, it seems, this something is '*not* thinking'; *that* is what theory is after. Hence Derrida's concern to 'bring back non-memory to memory,' or Pierre Macherey's pursuit of 'the unconscious' of the text.

Other theorists have reflected this same concern with *not* thinking by attempting to think that which can*not* be thought, or indeed by thinking that which simply *is not*. Witness Foucault's fascination with 'the madman's speech . . . [that does] not exist'; Irigaray's riddling account of 'the second sex' as 'this sex which is not one'; and Lacan's claim that, in language, 'Nothing exists except in so far it does not exist.' If all these negatives have a single 'origin' it is, of course, the structuralist claim that a word only signifies by virtue of its difference from every other word. As Ferdinand de Saussure argues, 'what characterizes each [sign] most exactly is being whatever the others are not'; or, as Eagleton puts it, 'every sign is what it is because it is not all the other signs.' Each word, we might say, is haunted by every other word, by all that it is not; it is haunted, in other words, *by everything else*. This being the case, the sombre 'not,' or 'no' of Saussure's differential account of language entails the wild 'yes' of everything else. And that is precisely what poststructuralism picks up on; as Derrida demonstrates when he writes, 'What deconstruction is not? Everything of course!'

This returns us, of course, to the theorist at the piano, to Gilbert's perverse insistence that the task of criticism is 'to see the thing in itself as it really is not'; after theory we might, though, say that the task is to see the thing in itself as *everything else* it is not. And that is precisely what Lacan does when he finds, in Saussure's text, the diagram of a tree and, in a self-parodic *tour de force* (or farce) of quite spectacular over-reading, sees not the poor tree but instead:

> the cross . . . the capital Y . . . the sign of dichotomy . . . [the] circulatory tree, [the] tree of life of the cerebellum, tree of Saturn, tree of Diana, crys-

tals formed in a tree struck by lightning, is it your figure that traces our
destiny for us in the tortoiseshell cracked by the fire, or your lightning
that causes that slow shift in the axis of being to surge up from an
unnameable night into the 'Εϋπάντα' [one in all] of language:

> No! says the Tree, it says No! in the shower of sparks
> Of its superb head

Paul-Ambroise Valéry

The protest of Valery's tree is, in a sense, the protest of the thing in itself
as it really is; and the protest is telling, resonant, even tragic – Lacan allows
it and hears it but it is, finally, ignored. But Lacan is by no means the first
to ignore it. Even I.A. Richards, that most scientific of critics, insisted that
a tree in a poem 'is *not* a tree'; but then this was in 1924 at the height of
literary modernism, a movement that was determined to 'make it new,' to
see the thing *not* as it is in a mirror or a realist novel. In this sense, much
theory is *belated* modernism; indeed, Gregory Ulmer argues that poststructuralism is to the history of literary criticism what modernism is to
the history of art:

> the break with 'mimesis,' with the values and assumptions of 'realism,'
> which revolutionised the modernist arts, is now underway (belatedly) in
> criticism.

As we know, Lacan drew very deliberately on one particular school of
modernism: namely, surrealism; and there is a sense in which the true
legacy of theory is, in part, surrealist. Hence Hayden White's immodest
proposal that literary historians might pursue 'the possibility of using
. . . surrealists' modes of representation.'

   To do so, of course, would entail the possibility of laughter, but if theory has taught us anything it is that critical thought, however sublime,
may never be far from the ridiculous. Witness not only Lacan's
hermeneutic over-killing of Saussure's poor tree but also Derrida's *Spurs*,
in which Derrida offers, with almost exaggerated seriousness, a profound philosophic meditation upon the words, 'I forgot my umbrella.'
Paul de Man once wrote that 'the impossibility of reading should not be
taken too lightly' but he forgot to add that it should also not be taken
too seriously. At its best, theory makes us profoundly aware of the gravity of reading without our mistaking gravity for seriousness. In 'Envois,'
in defence of Oxford scholasticism, Derrida writes, 'it's . . . grave and
dangerous . . . but not serious' – that is why he likes it; a little further
on in 'Envois,' apropos something else (but just imagine it is theory),
Derrida writes, 'it is [still] the sacred, for me . . . but as such it also
makes me laugh, it does leave us laughter, thank God.' It also leaves us
Oscar Wilde, thank God; for part of 'Envois,' an epistolary essay centred
on Oxford, is 'thought for Oscar Wilde,' that tragi-comic Oxonian who

was so often grave and dangerous but never serious. What theory leaves behind may yet prove to be comedy, an appreciation of what Kierkegaard called 'the strength of the absurd.' If so, Wilde is a key figure. It is no accident that in the 1970s Eagleton was working towards a Machereyean 'science of the text' but by the late 1980s was writing a comic stage-play on the life and death of one he calls 'St Oscar.' After theory *is*, in a sense, Gilbert; here is not so much the critic as artist but what Eagleton elsewhere calls 'the critic as clown,' or even *piss* artist, for though Gilbert sits at the piano offering to play Chopin he scarcely seems to touch the piano.

In this respect Gilbert comes closer to playing John Cage's infamous *4 minutes and 33 seconds* in which the pianist sits solemnly before a closed piano while the audience hears *everything but the piano*. Cage's pianist demonstrates, in a sense, what Gilbert believes is the 'importance of doing nothing'; for Gilbert, it seems, unless we do nothing with the text, unless we are distracted from it, see it as it really is *not*, we cannot hear the roar of everything else – or what Lacan calls 'the real,' that 'noise in which everything can be heard.'

If Matthew Arnold was concerned with what he calls 'the function of criticism' then Gilbert, we might say, is concerned with the criticism of function. He teaches us a lesson also taught by theory: namely, that if the text (like the sign) is what it is *not* then in order to read the text we should read everything but the text . We might well call this 'new historicism,' or doing cultural history; whatever, it is patently absurd, not serious. It is, though, both grave and dangerous for it involves a gamble or risk, the risk of losing not just the text but ourselves. This, of course, is the existential condition, what Heidegger calls 'the high and dangerous game and gamble in which, by the essence of language, *we* are the stakes.' And so we are, or should be; for if we really are to read the text as the everything it is not then we might just become, in a sense, *everybody* we are not. Witness Cixous' vision of the woman that 'is . . . capable of others, of the other woman that she will be, of the other woman she isn't, of him, of you.' Note too that Derrida, echoing James Joyce, cries 'Here Comes Everybody' and dreams, as we know, of writing 'Everybody's Autobiography.'

If to read after theory is to be left with everybody but ourselves then we may just be nearer to something we would call truth; as Derrida remarks, 'when *we* are present, the truth is not there' – we frighten it away. This, for Derrida, is part of the illogic of the anacoluthon, according to which we can never be in the company of the truth about ourselves; we are always, in Fontanier's words, 'left standing alone without companion.' But, of course, to be without com-panion, without one-to-share-bread-with, is to discover as new companion (or rather, new double or demon) anyone who has no bread to share simply because *they have no bread at all*. This, in a sense, is what Derrida calls 'the *companionship* . . . of ghosts.' We may yet be alarmed by what comes back to life after theory.

> Like ghosts amid your palaces
> Thoughts of poor men force their way
>
> Ernest Jones, 'We are Silent' (1851).

EMPEROR AND DOLL

(JULY 31ST 2004)

*On the birth of one delivered in caesarean style to one
who was also born a caesarean.*

It is whispered
that Caesar was born
just
like you
and her, she who's
mine
and yours.
For her,
you see,
they also came with knives.

So
now
she
my Russian doll
she
is herself
the doll's house;
until
inside and upside
down
you
from lonely
carnival
are seized
and
turned the
Right Way Up,
the way, the way
that most of us must come
and

go
as
once more
the knives are out.

Ask the Emperor who bleeds.

MAY 2012

IX

Someone Called Derrida

An Oxford Mystery

(2007)

Preface

What follows is the opening section of a book-long mystery of the same name that I published in 2007. The book is an experiment in which I am often attempting a style that is, in many ways, novelistic; however, I am also attempting that equally difficult thing – to tell the truth. To be more precise, every factual detail is, as I far as I can tell, correct. The same applies to every quotation; on the few occasions when I adapt a quote it is made clear in the notes. Just occasionally I invent some dialogue but the context makes clear, I hope, that this is invention rather than quotation.

As you will see, I quote extensively from Jacques Derrida; his words are always italicised and the vast majority are from a book called *The Post Card: From Socrates to Freud and Beyond* [1980]. I also quote my father throughout; most of his words come from a transcript that is included as an appendix in the full, book-length version of 'Someone Called Derrida.'

It is late, later than I think, and I am reading; but even while reading I keep drowsing and dreaming, and often I am dreaming that I am still reading. The book in question, the one I am supposed to be reading, was written by someone called Jacques Derrida, a philosopher, a strange one. And his book is also strange – strange, I would say, in about a thousand ways; in fact it is, says the philosopher, a book of *inaudible murmurs . . . deformed names, displaced events [and] real catastrophes.* One particular catastrophe, or strangeness, is that this philosopher does not seem to know the someone of whom he somehow writes. He murmurs, *I truly believe that I am singing someone who is dead and that I did not know.* Still more strange is that, as I read this book (and as, from time to time, I drowse), I have become persuaded that this someone is my father. After all, he is dead and the philosopher did not know him.

This, I know, is absurd. But I simply cannot help dreaming that the philosopher's book has me in mind. *Suppose that at the end of reading something, one of the voices of the book murmurs to you . . . I was thinking of you.* And that's what it's like when I read this book; the philosopher, I do think he sees me coming, knows how I will read. *'That's me.' I can hear it said by so and so who by chance falls upon this letter.* I am not, I suppose, quite saying 'That's me' but I am saying, *Why am I thinking . . . of my father?* These too are words stolen from the philosopher's book.

So, why *am* I thinking of my father while reading a book by someone called Derrida? They are, or were, so very different. Jacques Derrida was famous and even glamorous, a celebrated Parisian intellectual; my father, John Richard, was a minister of religion who lived and worked on a council estate near Watford. He is, though, most definitely dead, and Derrida most certainly did not know him. *They did not know each other, but according to me, they form a couple . . . just because of that.* Philosopher and pastor, *an odd couple*, it is true; but the philosopher says that *haunting has no limit*, that we may all (all of us) be haunted by each other. I shall, therefore, clutch at straws and point to anything that might just possibly link the two men. I shall say, firstly, that they were both born in 1930; secondly, that both were known to me – albeit, not very well; and thirdly, that both died on a Friday somewhere in October. I consider it no accident that, way back in October 1978, the philosopher should whisper: *I hadn't noticed it was a Friday.*

Still clutching at straws, at *these interlaced lines of life*, I shall also point, like a mute, to the fact or facts that both pastor and philosopher had sons called John or Jean, were related to a woman called Esther, and wrote censored love letters from somewhere called Oxford. Finally, I must add this: that both suffered, or seemed to have suffered, some kind of childhood calamity in the middle of the Second World War.

Allow me to explain, or begin to explain. In September 1942, on the very first day of the new school year, someone called Derrida into his study. *The only school official whose name I remember today, he has me come into his office: 'you are going to go home, my little friend, your parents will get a note.'* The boy, just twelve years old, is told he will be leaving his school because he is Jewish; after all, this is French Algeria, a place where (the boy must understand) Nazi writ now runs, runs in jackboots. No Germans have walked on the Algerian earth, but they occupy most of France and that is enough. So the Jewish boy leaves school for home.

Exactly one year later, in England, another boy goes the other way, leaving home for school. He is, or will be, my father. He is thirteen, has finished preparatory school, and is beginning at boarding-school, in Sussex. Here, at some early stage, something happens, something quite terrible; or rather, it may have happened. We don't know. Or at least not yet.

All we have to go on is that, at around the age of sixty, after several

years of a cruel, premature and mysterious dementia (it was never diag-
nosed) my father slowly disappeared. He took the slowest possible train
out into the dark, into a dark room of his own. In the black-out that
followed he was like a man dispossessed, a kind of beggar. Every day he
simply sat, folded in a chair or, worse still, poised precariously on the very
edge of a bed that had been brought downstairs, into the living room; he
could no longer climb the carpeted Alp that the rest of us mistook for a
staircase.

He would hang his head, his face would be agitated, and his thinning
body would be afflicted with a whole school of alien pains, both real and
phantom. My father seemed to understand almost nothing that we said,
just as we understood almost nothing that he said; but then, we did not
really want to understand, since his words and cries seemed to describe a
series of appalling events.

Well, perhaps not events. Perhaps I should purloin yet more of the
philosopher's words and ask: *Disaster – we have dreamed of it, no?* My
father, he may have dreamed of it. In the living room. If so, he was
dreaming of it every day and every night for the last five or six years of
his life, his death; in the living room.

Perhaps his dream was what those Freudians love to call 'false
memory.' I see the philosopher nods at this, as if to say 'yes'; he then asks,
very gently: *Is it what the child says or is it what says the child?* The
philosopher is right, there may have been something scripting my father,
working him like a ventriloquist's doll. It is, I accept, quite possible that
my father was duped by the memory of something that never happened;
but if so, that is still more alarming, a memory from somewhere called
nowhere or nowhere called somewhere.

It certainly seemed to come from nowhere, my father having never
spoken like this before. It is true that he had, from time to time, talked of
not being particularly happy at school, but there had been no prologue to
the dramatic monologue of his final years. I heard much of it myself, but
my mother, she heard it all, and set it down, even as he spoke.

For instance, he said and she wrote: 'Tell my mother about the teacher.
Don't make me go back mother. It was lethal . . . . He was hanging there,
they were kicking him . . . at school.'

Another time, he said and she wrote: 'Hanging. I said "Turn on the
light you can't see anything." They were just kicking him. Just shut the
door. 666.'

Yet another time (I recall) he said and she wrote: 'I must telephone. He
is murdering me.'

The boy did, finally, telephone. I think he meant to make the call in or
soon after 1943, but it took him fifty years to do so, fifty years before he
could get through. (*I tried to call you but it was busy, then no answer, you
must have gone out*). When he did get through it was not just my mother
who picked up the phone; anyone who sat with my father would have

heard him. I did. And I am now beginning to think that the philosopher heard as well, that he too heard what (and I quote) *my 'poor father' said.*

I should perhaps explain that the philosopher was well used to peculiar phone calls, calls even from the dead. For example, in the summer of 1979 someone called Derrida, someone called Martin Heidegger, even though he, Heidegger, had died three years before.

On the morning of 22 August 1979, 10 a.m. while typing [the words, 'from Freud and from Heidegger'] . . . *the telephone rings* . . . . *The American operator asks me if I accept a* . . . *'call' from Martin* . . . *Heidegger* . . . . *I know that I will be suspected of making it all up, since it is too good to be true. But what can I do? It is true, rigorously, from start to finish, the date, the time, the content etc.* . . . . . *All this must not lead you to believe that no telephonic communication links me to Heidegger's ghost, as to more than one other. Quite the contrary, the network of my hook-ups* . . . *is on the burdensome side, and more than one switchboard is necessary in order to digest the overload.*

With messages coming in from the dead as well as the living, the philosopher's switchboards are overloaded, burdened with crossed-wires, interference, noises off. And these are terrible noises: the noise of *all the cruelty in the world,* even (he says) *the worst concentration of evil.* Indeed, this concentration is itself concentrated when the philosopher begins to curse and to damn: *To the devil with the child* . . . *the child, the child.* You can, perhaps, see why I have thought that the philosopher got my father's call, my father's 666 call. I am now thinking all this again as, of a sudden, the philosopher pauses, looks round, and tenderly asks: *Who is he afraid of, this child?*

This, I guess, is an inquiry worthy of Dr Freud, but it is also a detective's question. *The police,* you know, *are not far off*; and they are never far off, not as long as there is what you call 'literature.' As our philosopher insists, *in literature everything* . . . *is a* . . . *police affair.* The philosopher would like to evade the police but he can't, he is too much in love with literature, particularly detective literature. That is why he is forever pursued by *all those cops always on my path*, even cops and detectives from far-away books, from his reading as a boy. Hence, from nowhere, his long-ago friends *Dupont and Dupond* whom you may remember as 'Thomson and Thompson,' the hapless bowler-hatted sleuths from Hergé's *Amazing Adventures of Tintin.* These two resemble, it is said, 'twins who are constantly lost, running to catch up, beside the question, always on the wrong trail.' What on earth they are doing here, in the philosopher's open and wounded book, heaven only knows; but even more unlikely detectives appear to the philosopher as, in 1979, he drowses in his hotel room whilst watching the television: *I have just fallen asleep, as I do every day, watching* . . . *Charley's Angels (four female private detectives).*

Hold it there. Charley (or rather Charlie) has only *three* angels; the nodding philosopher must have dreamt a fourth into existence, a fourth and phantom angel. This fourth TV detective is, I think, the philosopher himself. And, in fact, I have a friend who has always insisted that Jacques Derrida was, in reality, none other than Peter Falk in the part of that celebrated seventies TV cop, 'Columbo.' I can see the physical resemblance but I think it unlikely that they are one and the same person, or detective, if only because the philosopher receives his calls from the dead. *Charley's Angels*, he observes, get *their orders . . . on the telephone, . . . and [as I watched on TV] in passing I caught this: ' . . . the dead don't talk.'* This, though, is folly (thinks the philosopher) who immediately shouts at his hotel television, bellowing: *That's what you think! They are the most talkative . . . .* And he should know; with the late Martin Heidegger on the line, our philosopher's case opens with a phone-call from a dead man.

He said and she wrote: 'I must telephone, he's murdering me.' And the philosopher does seem to get this call too, this call from my father as a child. I know this, because his book is stuffed full with dead children, hundreds of thousands of them. *For the children*, he writes, *the holocaust has already begun . . . Holocaust of the children.* As if this, or they, were not enough, there is also *Norbert, my dead younger brother*, he who died in March 1940 of tubercular meningitis at the age of two. And as if *he* were not enough, there is also *Paul . . . the little brother dead before me, a year before I think, and they have never wanted to know or to say of what.*

He said and she wrote: 'Poor boy, dead boy . . . .' But *which* boy is this now? Which boy are we mourning? The boy erased by meningitis? The boy they had called Paul? The boy expelled for being a Jew? The thousands of boys that were lost in the Holocaust? Or simply the boy that was my father? Or, perhaps, the boy my father says he saw being killed; if there ever was such a boy, such a never never boy.

He said and she wrote: 'The last time. This is the place where . . . . Poor lad . . . only one little lad . . . . He's dead! That poor little boy . . . I saw them bring him out screaming. His poor mum. . . . He was hanging . . . chairs and a plank. I had to get him down.'

The boy, if ever he was, did he survive? Did he live? This question, it happens, is a question our philosopher asks; or rather it is a question which confronts him in a book from the thirteenth century, a book called *Prognostica Socratis basilei.* The philosopher found it one day in Oxford's Bodleian Library. It is a mysterious fortune-telling book that includes a series of thirty-six questions, or half-questions, and each time you open the book you are invited to choose one. I do not know why, but the philosopher chose: *Si puer vivet* – 'If the boy lives.'

Once you have chosen your question you are then referred to a bird: a Goose, a Peacock, a Quail, and so on. Beside the name and picture of each bird is a different text, with each text including an answer to your question. And if you are asking about the boy, you are advised to see the Dove,

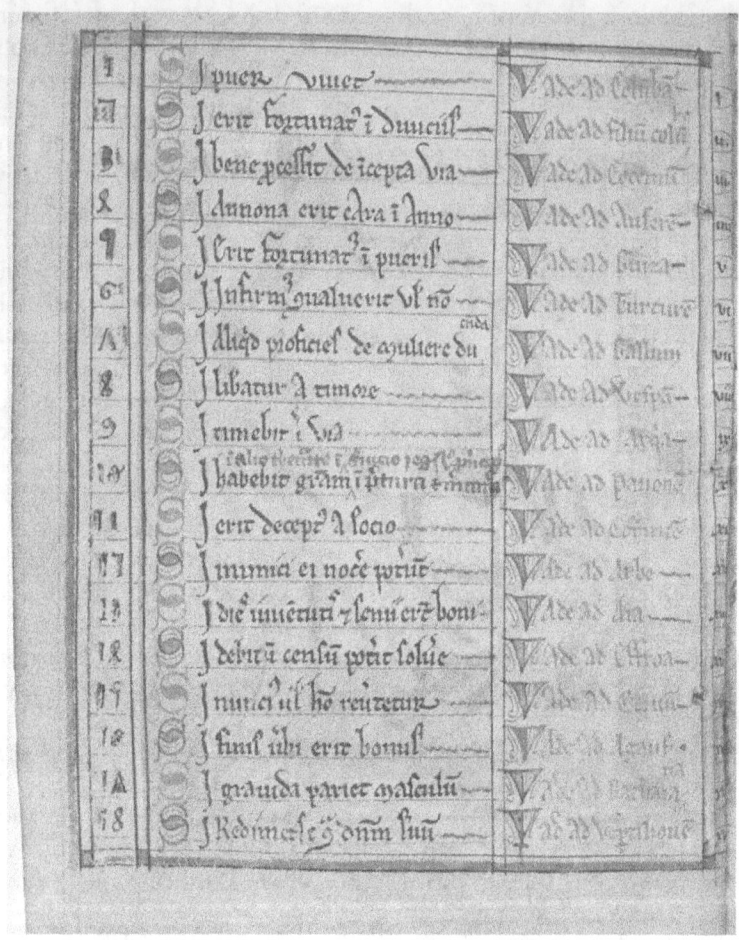

Si puer vivet (MS Ashmole 304, fol. 42 v).

Columba. The Dove gives the answer of an unnamed judge, but the philosopher does not tell us the answer. Or rather, the answer is censored.

Forgive me, I forgot (as I do these days) to explain something. I forgot to explain that the philosopher's book consists of a vast collection of messages written to an unnamed 'you,' a far-away lover that is someone close: *give ear closely, come near to my lips*. This lover may be someone best called no-one, but whoever she is (or *whoever you are, my love*) the philosopher does not want us to see all he has written. Whole passages have completely disappeared, many words have gone as if *destroyed by fire*, and *whatever their original length, the passages that have disappeared are indicated, at the very place of their incineration, by a blank of*

52 signs. And here, here at the very point at which we are referred to the bird that is the Dove, the bird that gives us the judge's answer to the question of the boy, the question 'does he live?', what we have is: . . . nothing, or rather 52 nothings, a blank of 52 no-signs, one for each week of your year.

To find the answer you must, therefore, take the last train to Oxford, a city that is home (as someone once said) to lost causes, forsaken beliefs, unpopular names, and impossible loyalties. Once in Oxford, amongst the lost, forsaken, unpopular and impossible, you must descend into that *labyrinth between the . . . colleges.* At last, you must follow the philosopher to the dead centre of the labyrinth. There you will find the oldest part of the Bodleian Library, a room they call the Duke Humfrey Room, *sanctuary of the most precious manuscripts.* The philosopher asks, *Are you following?* Perhaps not, but you should. You owe it to a boy, and perhaps even to a philosopher. So, listen well as he tells your future, as he says:

One day I will be dead, [and] you will come all by yourself into the Duke Humfrey Room . . . [to] look for the answer in this book [and] . . . you will find a sign that I am leaving in it.

The philosopher *is* now dead. He died on Friday, October the 8th 2004; I heard it on the radio, a day later, a day late (*the radio transmits . . . no one understands*); but the philosopher is now dead, of that I am certain. It is, then, time for you to go, at last, *all by yourself,* into the Duke Humfrey Room *to look for the answer.* Before you do, however, you must take the Bodleian oath.

Did I tell you, the oath that I had to swear out loud . . . stipulated . . . that I introduce neither fire nor flame into the premises: 'I hereby undertake . . . not to bring into the Library or kindle therein any fire or flame.' . . . The librarian seemed to know me . . . but this did not get me out of the oath. . . . Therefore I read it and handed her back the cardboard covered with transparent paper that she had tendered me. At his point she starts to insist that I had not understood: no, you have to read it out loud. I did so, with the accent you make fun of all the time, you can see the scene.

The Duke Humfrey Room is an ancient, T-shaped library, almost cruciform; it is, though, a room shaped not so much by prayer as concentration, the concentration of all the knowing world. *Letters, knowledge wall them up in their crypt.* The ceiling of the crypt is like an inverted chess-board, each square a coat of arms; history in code borne up by history in wood, a frozen procession of ornate oak beams. And here everything seems to be made of oak, not just the beams but the desks, the book-cases, even the books and, above all, the light – what once was fire here takes on the pale aspect of all this oak and all these books. Or so it seemed on the day

I visited the Room. As I stood there I thought the books so splendid, so imperious, that they seemed not to need the light any more than they needed readers – certainly not this rough reader. With my head stuffed full of sleep and distraction I knew I did not belong here, in this concentration room.

As for the philosopher, he remarks, of his visit that, *I felt myself watched*; and so he too just stood there. This I was told by a man who had emerged, like a holy father, from the latticed confessional box that they call 'The Reserve.' The man, himself reserved, was an archivist, and explained that it was he who, twenty-six years before, had assisted the philosopher. The archivist was French, and the very last person I had expected to meet in such a place, for he looked at once too savage and too noble to be an archivist. He was not, I felt, one of those *archivists [who] . . . with . . . their imperturbable assurance . . . will kill us with their taste.* No, this man was more anarchist than archivist. His ungovernable hair was a Paris revolt and his beard an outrage, whilst his loose-fitting shirt was un-tucked, open-necked and collarless. And if he did not look like an archivist neither did he walk like one, his gait seeming almost recalcitrant – as if, after all these years, he was still ever so slightly at odds with his wooden prison. It is true he spoke with the diffidence and care of one who had lived forever among precious books, but even as he spoke he seemed to nod to himself at almost every word, as if to check each one for fire or flame, as if, just occasionally, he suspected himself of wanting to burn the whole place down.

After all, this is the kind of thing that the French will do, at least when in Paris. As in 1970, when rioting students, infuriated at being too late for the famous events of May '68, set fire to part of the library at the École Normal Supérieure, the philosopher's own institution at that time. As it happens, this belated storm brought to a fiery end a series of academic exchanges between Oxford and the ENS, a series that had, more than once, smuggled our philosopher across the Channel and into England. It is said that the funds which had once supported this human contraband were now consumed by the need to replenish the fired Parisian library. However, if the Bodleian's noble anarchist was to be believed, there were some in Oxford who felt that 1970 was not quite the right time to be sharing fine wines with French Structuralists. In the late-sixties anyone suspected of being a radical Parisian philosopher was also suspected of being more interested in sedition than sherry; inspired by near-revolution in Paris, there was considerable student activism in Oxford and much fear as to 'Where It Would All Lead.'

My noble friend was very keen that I should be aware of this historical tension, even hostility. At times, as we stood half-hidden in an alcove, he seemed to be looking over his shoulder, as if ever-so-slightly afraid to be seen talking with me. The more we talked the more I dreamt that within this kind and learned man I could see a mute Parisian rage. Indeed, I begin now to think that he was himself the sign that the philosopher had left, a sign of nameless anger, a sense that even here, in the Bodleian, something is wrong, or someone is dead.

So: does the boy live? The omens are not good. I am beginning to suspect there may be a body in the library. Any reader of detective fiction would feel the same, and that includes the philosopher. I say this because another Bodleian archivist kindly showed me what the philosopher had hand-written, using bold and blue ink, in a special copy of his book, a copy which he had sent to old Duke Humfrey way back in 1980; there, on the frontispiece, I read *To the soul and body of the Bodleian* ('à l'âme et au corps de la Bodleian'). For some reason, my quiet French anarchist had never seen this inscription before, but he immediately got the long-delayed message, the inter-linguistic news: '*I*,' he announced, 'am the *corpse* of the Bodleian.'

And he is right, there *is* a stiff in Jacques Derrida's Bodleian; however (and this must be stressed) it has not yet been finally identified. *I arrived [at the Room] at opening time, just now, still dragging along with me a dream: all around someone sick and visibly in danger of death, several doctors. The patient . . . is stretched out, passive, immobile. . . . The death sentence won't be long now, everyone appears to be waiting for it. The disease is visibly at chest level (my father). . . .*

If there is a body in the Room then, at first glance, it is (the philosopher dreams) *my father.* Several years before, the philosopher's father, someone called Aimé (*he was well loved*) had died of cancer at the age of seventy-four. One day, the philosopher would also die of cancer at seventy-four, in hospital, during an operation. The passive and immobile patient is, I now fear, Jacques as well as Aimé, son as well as father. The philosopher, I think, is addressing himself when he writes: *You are my fortune teller, the seer and indicator of my [own] death.* The body in the Bodleian may yet turn out to be the philosopher's.

Six months before, in January 1979, he had declared: *I intend to go back to Oxford, to take [the] investigation to its end.* The philosopher's investigation is, ostensibly, into that book from the thirteenth-century, but I have always believed that it secretly doubles as an enquiry into his own death. In his late 40s, his own middle-ages, the philosopher has come to Oxford in order to die. *It would be good,* he breathes, *if I died tonight, in the college.*

The college is Balliol. And it is a place where the thought of the philosopher's death has, in fact, already been entertained, even proposed:

June 6th 1977 . . . seminar (at Balliol) . . . . Afterward, on the lawn where the discussion continued . . . a young student (very handsome) thought he could provoke me and, I think, seduce me . . . by asking why I didn't kill myself. In his eyes this was the only way to 'forward' (his word) my 'theoretical discourse.' . . . Instead of arguing . . . I answered with a pirouette.

If, two years later, when the philosopher returned to pirouette once more on the lawn he had then died overnight (as was his morbid fancy) the handsome student may himself have faced some awkward questions; the pirouettist's Balliol death might have looked somewhat suspicious.

Balliol, you see, is particularly adept at murder. I first learnt this valuable lesson when, about three hundred years ago, I came across an old issue of *The Spectator*. Here I read a letter from Oxford that had somehow been intercepted by the magazine's editor. The letter was written by an Oxford don who went by the name, or pseudonym, of 'Mercurius Oxoniensis' and seemed, by his diction, to be living deep in the seventeenth century. The letter was, nevertheless, somehow concerned with student activism in 1970, and revealed that the Master of Balliol was now dead. According to Mercurius, whom I have no reason to doubt, 'The late Master was hustled to his grave at midnight very obscurely . . . . The Proctors have, though, forgiven the young men who hanged their Master, as they were doubtless ignorant of the statutes against murther.'

You or I might find this somewhat alarming, but not Oxford; for the Master in question was Christopher Hill, the Marxist historian, and Oxford tends to overlook the murther of Marxists, or indeed trouble-makers of any hue. If our trouble-making philosopher from trouble-making Paris were aware of this (which is possible, since he returned to Balliol in 1970) he must have slept uneasily in his college bed.

He would, in fact, have barely slept at all if had ever read Thomas de Quincey's famously famous essay, 'On Murder Considered as one of the Fine Arts,' written one day in 1827. 'Gentlemen,' de Q. declares, 'it is a fact that every philosopher of eminence . . . has either been murdered or at least been very near it, – insomuch that, if a man calls himself a philosopher and never had his life attempted, rest assured there is nothing in him. . . .'

Quite so. A sentiment shared, one feels, by our philosopher, particularly whenever in Balliol. But then, where better to be murdered than glorious Oxford? Indeed, where else are you so likely to have your murderer identified than in a city which, despite all its lost causes and forsaken beliefs, also boasts a host of brilliant detectives. Who could ever forget such as Gervase Fen, sometime Professor of English Literature, or Lord Peter Wimsey the Balliol alumnus, or indeed our beloved Inspector Morse? I do realise that all three, even Morse, are dead now, but perhaps that helps when it comes to solving a murder.

I was, in fact, reminded of dear Morse even whilst researching this book of mine. I was slouching along Catte Street roughly heading for the Bodleian, when who should I see plodding toward me but Morse's doughty assistant, Lewis. However, I scuttled past, head down, clutching my brief-case, all the while pretending not to recognise this latter-day Dr Watson. I did not, you see, wish to inflate still further the ego of the celebrity sleuth. But it was also, I must confess, that I did not wish to involve the police in my investigation. It is true that my desperate father once said, 'We must tell the police,' but I would really rather not. I might, now and then, make as if to call them, but it will only be a ruse.

That is, by the way, exactly what the amateur detective does in a wonderful novel I once read called *Which Way Came Death?* I love this book; it's a 1936 murder-mystery that is set in (of all places) my father's school. As ever, this is true. The novel was written by one Faith Wolseley, the *nom-de-plume* of the then-Headmaster's wife. At the novel's climax, a scene set in her study, the Headmaster's wife (the fictional one, that is) confronts the murderer, or at least the man who thinks he is the murderer. This man (he is called 'Floyd Burney') was, until fired, a master at the school; he is, though, described by a fellow master as 'that bounder with the Homburg hat, Bohemian tie and Nazi manner'- a somewhat conspic-uous figure, one might feel, in an English public school; but then again, perhaps not. Whatever, the Headmaster's wife (one 'Petronella Cary') threatens to call the police unless Burney persuades a certain benefactor to endow the school.

'"I see – blackmail," said Burney, with a sudden sneer.
"Exactly," she replied, looking at her clock.
"I can't," he said.
"Then you'll hang," retorted Petronella, as she put out a tentative hand towards the telephone. Burney was silent, there were beads of sweat on his forehead.'

So, what will the master with the Nazi manner do? Will he give in to Petronella's blackmail or will he call her bluff? As the Headmaster him-self observes, 'No school could stand up against the sort of scandal a prosecution for murder would bring. . . . Death from natural causes is bad for a school, but, if a suspicion of unnatural causes leaks out, it's – damnation.'

He has a point, any school, any college, would be tempted to keep a murder silent, mute; a pale hand may reach towards the telephone but the police may not, in the end, be called. Yes, let us keep this in-house, in-school, within the academy; we must, like weary caryatids, bear this heavy load ourselves. Let us return to our libraries, our learning, and our books to help us deal with the very worst things we could possibly imagine, or even do. Some things are just too strange for the police. Let us see what books can tell us, what books might know, or even fore-know.

This, perhaps, is madness, or even dementia; but if so, it is shared by the philosopher. *I will look up*, he says, *what has happened to us . . . in this . . . book from the 13th century.* He is, for some reason, certain that this fragile book *secretly recounts . . . our history.* And that is precisely why I must find the fading page that will tell me, once and for all, if the boy lives, *Si puer vivet.* It is also why I turn, and return, to this murder-mystery called *Which Way Came Death?* It too whispers our history. And what it first whispers is that the one who investigates murder must himself be a suspect. You see, the headmaster's wife might herself be the murderer; after all, she is the first to discover the body, she has a motive, and she is (remember?) reluctant to call the police. The detective must always be a suspect. He must even suspect himself.

My father certainly suspected himself, suspected that he was in some way complicit in the beating and killing of which he spoke, in particular the beating and killing of a girl and her child.

'The girl . . . I had to hold her head . . . . They took turns . . . . I could not kill her . . . . I had to drag her. She gave birth. I had to see the dead boy. I could not kill him. . . . I didn't kill the girl. I never hurt her. Kill her. . . . My gun. . . . Shoot!'

So, which way came this particular death? Did my father shoot the girl? Was it his gun that killed her? The philosopher, he cries: *It's a firing squad . . . someone gives the order to fire, and . . . everyone goes to it.*

I now remember how, one day, my mother told my father, 'You didn't kill her'; to which my father, who hardly ever responded, astonished us by replying (after the longest possible sigh of relief) 'Oh good.'

This 'good' moment means much to my mother; but the trouble is, when you're shooting in the dark it's difficult to know who shot whom. Friendly fire, you call it. The point is made in the school magazine, in a report on an army cadet camp of August 1947, a camp my father attended. As the boys themselves recall, 'We had the thrill of night ops on the Saturday; blackened faces and lowered voices helped towards realism, but the problem of "who shot whom" was never solved.'

It may never be. Not that it matters; I do realise that these were only operations, that the cadets were only play-shooting. Bang-bang, he is dead. It's like when, as children, we would go to the fair, and my father would so impress us at the shooting-booth and say that he'd learnt to shoot at school. Fitting, then, that at school he should have played the part of a character called Pistol in Shakespeare's *Henry V*. That was June 1947, just a couple of months before the cadet camp.

So, to resume, to summarise: Whom did Pistol shoot? And if it wasn't Pistol that did the killing, who was it? It is, I think, too early to say, and too late; but no-one can be ruled out. Everyone of us is a suspect; not just the school-master, the Headmaster's wife and the army cadet but also the scholar, even the philosopher.

I say this because Jacques Derrida openly confesses to murder; he says, with blackened voice and lowered face, *Right here I kill you . . . there is someone in me who kills*. Bang-bang, you are dead.

I accept that confession is not proof, but it is evidence; as is the philosopher's astonishing claim that Socrates had (and I quote) a *revolver-pocket*. This pocket is detected by the philosopher as he stares at the picture of Socrates that he finds in the fortune-telling book. Have a look for yourself – it is the figure that follows.

Plato and Socrates (MS Ashmole 304, fol. 31 v).

Can you see it, the revolver-pocket? Can you? . . . No, neither can I. But perhaps anything is possible in a picture that reverses the one thing everybody knows about Socrates: namely, that he spoke and Plato wrote. Here, in this Oxford looking-glass, Socrates is no longer the dictator, the great dictator; here it is the finger-pointing Plato who dictates and Socrates (the one in the ludicrous hat) who is busy transcribing.

I should perhaps add that our philosopher, who may yet emerge as something of a milliner, once remarked that Socrates' hat is *rather like a condom*. This I do see; though I should not say it to Socrates' face lest he really does have a gun in his pocket. Or, perhaps, he is just glad to see someone? Mind you, I get from our philosopher the impression that Socrates would know how to use a gun.

. . . you know the end of the detective story: Socrates knocks off all of them . . . he remains alone, the gangbusters take over the locale, he sprays gas everywhere, it's all ablaze in a second, and behind the cops the crowd presses forward somewhat disappointed that they didn't get him alive.

I knew that Socrates was tried and found guilty of perverting the youth of Athens, and I knew he was condemned to take hemlock, but what I did not know was that, like Samson, he took everyone else down with him. Again, we are in the dark as to who shot whom, but I have now learnt that the first-man of Western philosophy is not so much a martyr as a suicide-bomber with a condom on his head.

This particular Socrates is funny, even dead funny. But I guess that's because he writes, and writing, as every philosopher knows, is odd, or queer, and fatally so. St Paul once said that 'The letter killeth,' but so too do all philosophers, for philosophers (I have learnt) are always writing, always killing, even when just thinking, just using their brains. 'The brains, kill, quick!' said my father. 'The brains, kill, quick!' The brain, I think, is another unusual suspect. Let it be noted: thinking may not be trusted.

'Think! Think!' cried my father, 'Think! Think!' And think-think is exactly what Socrates does, *that devil of a Socrates*, that perverter of youth, that philosophical celebrant of the beautiful boy. Everyone knows that the father of metaphysics cannot be trusted with boys, or at least not his thinking, his brains, his mind. Indeed, I shall here insist that if philosophy were personified, were someone (as she so often is), she might well be saying, 'Hell is in my father's head.'

'Hell is in my father's head.' These are words that my own father heard, in Oxford, at the University Church, on April 23rd 1951, in the first-ever production of Christopher Fry's play *A Sleep of Prisoners*. It is, I have found, a verse-drama about four British soldiers held in a church that has been turned into a prison camp. I am not sure why they are prisoners, or who is holding them, or even where they are, but their hell somehow mirrors the hell that, one day, would be in my father's head.

He said and she wrote: 'Oh, someone take me out. . . . The door, smash it. . . . He came back. To get to church. . . . I know where to get blessed, the cross. A little church. . . . I don't want to go and sing. . . . It was the

Sergeant. . . . He was wearing uniform. . . . In the army . . . You're coming with me. . . . Trapped.'

The boy that was my father is trapped in a church with men who look like soldiers. Or so his blackened story goes. If the boy then lives, lives to become a young man who, in 1951, watches a play about soldiers caught in a church, what happens in the young man's lowered head? Did the play awaken a memory, or create a memory? 'The boy's dead. / You might as well be told: I say / The boy's dead' – these are words from the play, first spoken forty years before it is staged within my father's head.

Writing at the time, my father remarks: 'It was a very fine play.' And so it is. In fact, it is a fine play finely entangled with the history of my father's school; and this is despite Christopher Fry himself having no known connection with the school. The play was, though, performed by the school in 1960 – a highly improbable choice I would have thought, except perhaps that the play opens with one of the imprisoned soldiers playing, at the organ, the opening bars of 'Now the Day is Over,' a hymn that happens to have been written by a long-dead master at the school.

Strange this, or these, these coincidences; but perhaps they begin to explain why my father remarks that 'the play, though fine, was rather too mystical, by which I mean that I found it rather hard to get hold of the meaning and the moral.'

I should like now to shake him and say: 'Think! Think! Is not the meaning and moral what you suffered as a boy, whilst away at school? Don't you recall – the church? the soldiers? being trapped?'

But he would not listen. He was never one to look back and, besides, April 1951 was no time to look back. This was Oxford in springtime and he is in love, has just turned twenty-one, and is busy finding ways not to revise for Schools. His letters, at this time, speak of choirs and cocktails, of dancing like the Scottish and playing canasta like the smart set, of chasing the college eight on the river and singing madrigals from a punt in the evenings. The philosopher whispers: *madrigal . . . a song with 4,5,6, 7 voices.*

My father's Oxford letters transcribe, I suppose, a *dream* of Oxford, a dream of Oxford-past. But it is also a dream of Oxford-future. For in March 1951, he declares, 'Somehow I am sure that the summer is going to be a fine one.' And it was. The young woman who would become his wife will return from a year of America; and, once Schools are over, she will go up to Oxford for a Commemoration Ball, and that night, at Christ Church, within the Dean's garden, he will propose to her. She will answer with a pirouette and, come the dawn, they will drive in a 1926 Morris Cowley to Woodstock for breakfast. The summer is going to be fine, and so too the world.

The philosopher, he pleads, *Promise me that one day there will be a world*; but he need not worry, the young Oxonian will make sure that there is. In February 1951 he writes, 'Though I haven't become a socialist

yet, I am very much in sympathy with pacifist ideals.' Just a month later
he has become a socialist, and is already impatient for the millennium: 'I
have now swallowed socialist clap-trap hook, line and sinker; however, it
does not seem to make our meat rations any larger.' War was slow to leave
hungry Oxford, but Pistol-the-pacifist will still set down his gun, declaring
himself a conscientious objector to National Service. He once said (and
she wrote): 'We don't fight . . . '

In *Henry V,* when Pistol exits stage-right, a character simply known as
'Boy' is left, all alone; looking around at the deserted English camp, he
declares that 'there is none to guard it but boys.' In 1951 there is one boy
less to guard camp England. ('We don't fight,' he says). Not that England
needs saving any more: war is finally over, the summer will be fine, so too
England; and my father is sure of this, for his world is one of pure predic-
tion, pure prognostication. In the summer of 1951 his world is the world
of the Oxford fortune-telling book.

Time then to turn, at last, to the page to which the philosopher points,
Columba's page (opposite), the page that will reveal if the boy lives, *Si
puer vivet*

Like the headmaster's wife, I put out a tentative telephonic hand, and
hesitate. A moment later and the page is turned, another page from our
thirteenth century, but I cannot read it, *I have to get some help*. Then,
someone transcribes, someone translates, and what is transmuted is:
someone familiar; for the text before me reads like a dream-text that has
somehow come straight from my father, the post-war, pacifist man-boy
who was so much in love. It reads:

> That boy will live long in the land . . .
> Wars initiated will be rendered peaceful . . .
> You will have good sleep by the side of your heart's desire.

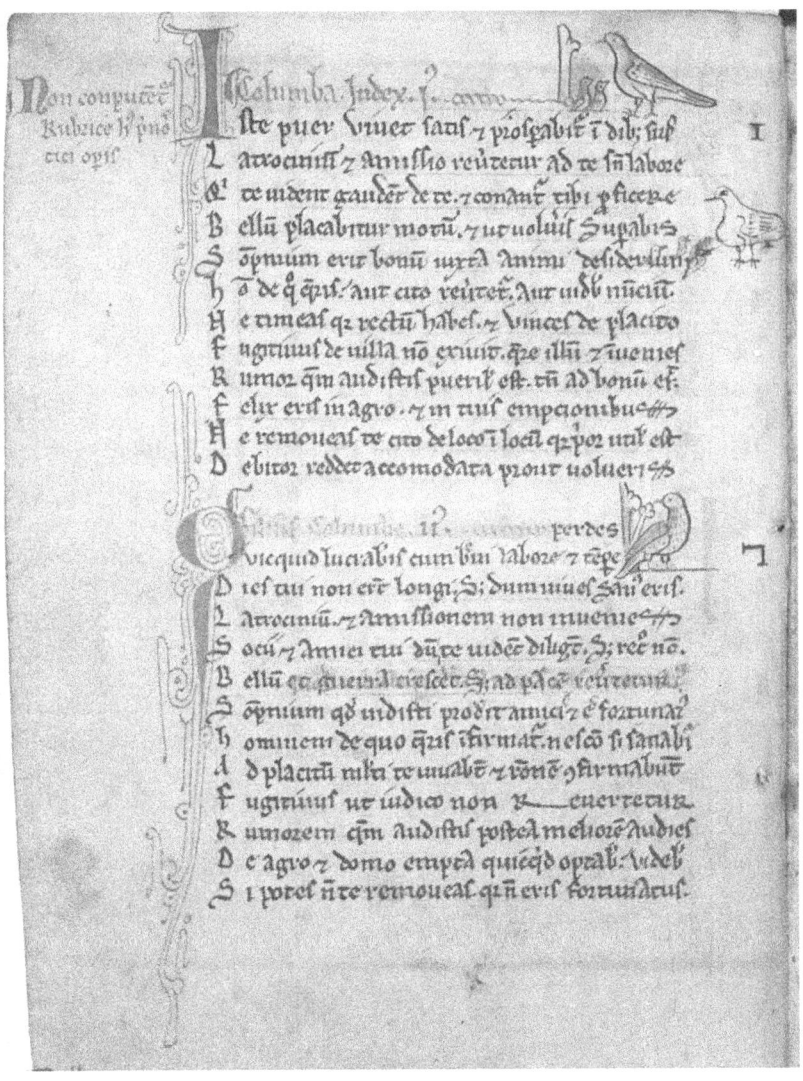

Columba (MS Ashmole 304, fol. 43 v).

X
Our Lives, Mrs Dalloway
(2012)

Preface

The narrative that follows is largely imagined; however, all the texts – some legal, some historical, some literary, some philosophical – that are here investigated, or decoded, are real. The action takes place in the West End of London in 1924, just a year after the events that take place in the very same quarter of London in Virginia Woolf's *Mrs Dalloway* (1925). All quotations from Virginia Woolf (some from *Mrs Dalloway*, some from her diaries and letters) are italicised.

Part One
(JULY 4TH 1905)

Minutes of Acts of Marriage
17th Arrondissement, Paris, 1905

On the Fourth of July, at noon, Johannes Schad, clerk, born at Basel, Switzerland married Marie Anne Wheeler, dentist, born in Paris.

Johannes Schad (1880–1961)

Part Two
(APRIL 7TH 1924)

Marie said she would buy some flowers, and the trams, the pigeons and the motor cars all murmured 'yes.' (*Mrs Dalloway said she would buy the flowers herself*). Marie was light upon her feet; quick, careful, lest she should brush against another. None, she thought; there would be none who would know her, though some had smiled. (*Odd affinities she had with people she had never spoken to, some woman in the street*). She would buy the flowers on her way back, and as she walked her head was set low. (*I want to gather material for the Lives of the Obscure*).

She paused to allow a file of children, two-by-two, to pass in front of her. Nineteen, she counted. One, a girl, turned and looked. It was her hat, she thought; Johannes had bought it in Russia. But she should quicken her step. *She . . . never tired of walking for all her delicacy*. On she walked. On. '*I love walking in London,' said Mrs Dalloway*.

Marie wondered if Johannes came this way to his office. Taking a cab was, he said, beyond their means. Besides, walking was more natural than talking, he would say, quoting their friend, 'the eminent linguist Mr X,' as he had been introduced the night they had first met. He was an elegant man with a fine moustache, the points of which seemed to quiver as if receiving messages from the air. Some said his name was Ferdinand de Saussure, Professor Ferdinand de Saussure. He certainly spoke with authority; though was inclined, Johannes would say, to mistake language for Switzerland. 'A panorama of the Alps,' the linguist had said, 'must be taken from just one point. The same,' he had added, 'is true of a language.' The linguist's great-grandfather, she had heard, was a mountaineer, among the first to ascend Mont Blanc.

Was it not, she thought, the poet Shelley, who had called Mont Blanc 'a city of death'? Strange thing to write, whatever the light; but then Shelley had been an unbeliever, even among the mountains. Especially among the mountains, Johannes said. The poet, he said, had written the words, 'Percy Bysshe Shelley, Atheist,' when, upon visiting Chamonix, he had signed the guest-book. And here, she thought, right here is Somerset House. *Over the Strand . . . the clouds were of mountainous white*.

Perhaps, perhaps she should not read so much. After all, there were, these days, so many peculiar books, and so many peculiar authors, such as that Mrs Woolf or Mr Eliot, Eliot-the-Clerk, as Johannes would say. Mr Eliot, however, she could not help but like, seeing that he had written about a woman called Marie. Moreover *his* Marie, Mr Eliot's, was also inclined to read through the night, and fly down the mountains upon a sledge, whilst exhorted to hold on, to hold on for dearest life. She thought of Miss Emily Dickinson, the hermit of Amherst. 'Our lives,' she had written, 'are Swiss – / So still – so cool – / Till some odd afternoon / The Alps neglect their Curtains / And we look further on.'

She paused, a little faint, and glimpsed a poster in the window of a shop. The British Empire Exhibition, it said. Wembley Stadium. Yes, the crowds, she thought. The poster portrayed 'London' as a woman in bronze, naked and slim. Marie shivered. April was indeed a cruel month, just as Mr Eliot had thought. And, now, a shower was upon them. Rain, rain all over London, she should not wonder, even at the Exhibition. (*It is nature that is the ruin of Wembley. The problem of the sky remains . . . . Is it, one wonders, part of the exhibition?*). Marie put up her umbrella and thought of the mountainous clouds.

Vectia. A Banned Play (1916), by Marie Stopes
The curtain rises on a comfortable living room. Vectia is discovered. The telephone rings. Vectia takes up the receiver.
VECTIA: Hullo hullo! . . . No . . . . My husband can't be back for about
    half an hour . . . the Continental trains are often late.

Johannes had been travelling again. He had mastered several languages. French, German, even Russian. Quite how he had learnt Russian she was not sure, but the rubber-trade took him to so many places.

Metropolitan Police
January 7th 1925
Johannes Schad has paid periodical visits to the Continent on business and pleasure, and intends doing so in the future.

She did not, herself, like to travel by train; it was not, she had heard, altogether safe. (*Villains there must be . . . battering the brains of a girl out in a train*). The trains on the continent were very different, as she had once said to the linguist. He, though, had muttered something about trains in general, about how no two trains, whatever we think, are exactly the same. 'We assign identity to two trains,' he had said, 'for instance, "The 8.45 from Geneva to Paris," one of which leaves twenty-four hours after the other. We treat it as the "same" train even though probably the loco-motive, the carriages, staff etc. are not the same.'

Trafalgar Square was stirring. People of all nations and none, she thought. She had not intended to come this way, but paused to open her purse for a man without legs, his upturned cap begging beside him. He stared for a moment. (*Every man fell in love with her*). 'The bride is beau-tiful,' as Johannes would say. It is true he would sometimes add: 'but she is married to another man'; this, though, had been a jest of his. 'The bride is beautiful, but she is married to another man' were, he would add, the famous words of a famous telegram. This cable, he would say, had been wired from Palestine by two of Vienna's wisest rabbis, both hot-foot from the world's first Zionist Congress, a gathering held, strange to say, in

Basel; the rabbis had gone off in vainest search of Israel and found her to be beautiful but, also, to be another's. True, all true, he would say.

She enjoyed the gaze of the invalid. It was a feeling that *lifted her up and up when – oh! a pistol shot in the street outside!*

'Dear, those motorcars,' said Miss Pym, going to the window to look, and coming back and smiling apologetically as if those motorcars, these tyres of motorcars, were all her fault.

Marie also smiled, though to herself, and to apologise. It was, she knew, *her* fault, for Johannes and she had grown comfortable from the tyres that rubber made, and indeed from all that rubber made. The disturbance in the street, it *was* all her fault. But she could not stop, for she was expected at noon. ('My husband,' whispers Vectia, 'can't be back for about half an hour').

Her shoes worried her; the heels, modest yet fragile, were about to give way, and the points of her shoes were worn. Better not to look down; best look up, right up. *All down the Mall people were . . . looking up into the sky. See, an aeroplane! There it was coming over the trees, letting out white smoke behind, which curled and twisted, actually writing something!* She thought of the linguist and of how he would have loved these letters. *'C was it? And an E? Then an L?'* There was, she saw, no 'A' in the sky. The linguist would have been dismayed, for he had loved the French letter-sound *a*, handling it like the most fragile shell. 'In its consistency,' he had once said, 'it is something solid, but thin, that cracks easily if struck; like, for example, a sheet of paper (yellowed with age).'

The aeroplane overhead breathed several more letters into the sky. *'K . . . R . . . ,' said the nursemaid.* And Marie remembered a dazzling day in Palmers Green; 'Honeymoon Land' it was known as – new-minted suburbia, modern houses for the modern couple. This dazzling day was in December 1912, when an Italian airmen, heading for Hendon Aerodrome, found his engine faltering high over Honeymoon Land and, seeing Broomfield Park, had attempted to effect a landing; the aeroplane was, though, by now flying so low that its wings touched first one roof and then another before finally settling, with a murmur, upon the slates of 75 Derwent Road. She recalled that Mrs Woolf, Mrs Virginia Woolf, had written that 'In or about December, 1910, human character changed,' but in Palmers Green it changed two years later, she thought, changed with an aeroplane upon a slated roof and a stranded aviator, a continental traveller emerging from a wounded butterfly. He had waved, they said, waved to the Honeymooners below, waved from his suburban Alp, waved as if he had something to communicate, just like, so like, the aeroplane even now assaulting *the ears of all the people . . . in Piccadilly.* But what was it? What was it? What had he been trying to say? *What word was it writing?*

The traffic stammered an answer, and Marie strained to listen; but here, now, were *boys in uniform, carrying guns . . . and the wreath which they had fetched from Finsbury Pavement to the empty tomb.* The Cenotaph, thought Marie, they are marching to the Cenotaph. Greek for 'empty tomb,' she thought, and wondered what it might mean *to be the mother whose sons have been killed.* She wondered too what it might mean to be a wife, a wife whose husband had been killed. Johannes had not fought; he had volunteered but he had been thirty-four at the outbreak and, besides, like herself, was an alien. But yes he had presented himself, making known that he had languages, that he was ready to prosecute the War with words.

Letter from the War Office
August 22nd 1917
    Dear Sir,
In answer to your application, I have placed your name on the War Office Waiting List for services as an interpreter.
    Yours faithfully,
R.K. Mott.

Her tomb, she thought, was indeed an empty tomb – having no dead sons to mourn, no buried husband over whom to weep. Empty, perfectly empty. And, as the boys in uniform disappeared toward Whitehall, she remembered the autumn silence, the silence on the radio, last November and the November before. Throughout the two minutes she had sat and covered her ears. Johannes had stood, his arms at his side. It was, she had said, at the end, as if he were still waiting to serve as an interpreter. He had told her not to make light of the silence.

The Swiss Observer
November 17th 1923
We Swiss are as deeply concerned in Armistice Day as any other nation. (Editor).

The Swiss, Johannes had added, were a people always readied for war. He had pointed to a letter from the linguist; here, even as the linguist spoke of words, he whispered of achieving 'victory all . . . along the line . . . and . . . advancing with all . . . big guns.' Johannes had run his finger along the words, saying that the war *had* reached the Alps, albeit the Dolomite Alps, and that all the bloodless scars of war (the bones, barbed wire, and machines) could still be seen. This perpendicular Flanders, this vertical Somme, he said, could still be seen, seen in the snow. 'Snow,' Johannes had said, 'is itself an engine of war.' (*She had read late at night of the retreat from Moscow*). Napoleon, he had said, knew what it meant to lose an army in the snow; and Moscow had remained untouched, unspoiled.

    Yes, true, but now it was Spring, and she must head for Regent Street where the windows would be glorious, full of the coming season. And, as she walked, she thought once more of the Alps and the dead. Yes, there had been the young men, the soldiers, but there were others. She had read of them in *The Swiss Observer*, a London paper that Johannes used to buy, the 'organ of the colony' as he called it. Each week, it seemed, someone would fall to a death whilst walking the Alps. Pleasure-seekers they were, like Miss Lina Schwarz, a telephonist from Geneva who had ascended the Pointe Pelouse in Savoy when, suddenly seized with dizziness, she fell over a precipice and was shattered to death.

A man in a passing omnibus nodded from the lower deck. The bride, she said to herself, is married to another man. She paused to open the bag she carried; an over-night bag, Johannes had called it. Yes, all she might need.

But why, she thought, mourn just one victim of the Alps? The Alps, Johannes had said, were crowded with calvaries; over the years so many had fallen to their deaths that, at almost every turn, every climb, there seemed to be a cross, a Golgotha, yet another Saviour. '*Health,*' said Sir William, '*is proportion; so that when a man comes into your room and says he is Christ . . . you invoke proportion.*'

The man on the lower-deck might nod but people would continue to die falling. (*It is the hottest day of the year; & so it was last year, almost on this day, & I was at Long Barn & there was the Eton tutor, a nice young man . . . & he now lies at the bottom of a crevasse in Switzerland . . . crushed beside his [fiancée] Mary . . . . There are the two bodies for ever . . . frozen, near together*). And what, she wondered, might it be like to fall beside another? The telephonist had fallen, whirled, descended alone, but what would it be like to plummet hand-in-hand? And how would you be remembered, the two of you? Would it mean that not one cross but two would mark the place where you would finally shatter? And if the two of you were married might a future passer-by interpret the two crosses as witness to both a Christ and a Christess? Or even, dare she say it, a Mr and Mrs Christ? (*The friends and relations of [Sir William's] . . . patients felt for him the keenest gratitude for insisting that these . . . Christs and Christesses . . . should drink milk in bed*). She liked the idea of married Saviours; a single cross had always puzzled her. (*A seedy-looking nondescript man . . . stood on the steps of St Paul's Cathedral . . . why not enter in? he thought, [and] put this leather bag stuffed with pamphlets before . . . a cross, the symbol of something*).

Marie paused before St James's Church. Why not enter in? she thought. Why not? Because its cross would be empty, and she could not bear the Resurrection – that poor woman being told not to hold on tight, being told not to touch her risen Saviour. No, she would not enter in. It is true that she was re-born, that she was washed in the Blood, that *she had seen the light two years and three months ago*, but today she might see the dark.

VECTIA: But Heron, don't you see the horror . . . . He could win his case
quickly if he had a little evidence . . . . You don't know what it is
to be driven into real badness.

Marie looked behind, wondering if he were following her, the linguist.
He had followed her before, she was sure of it.

VECTIA: I have read in the newspapers that, to collect evidence, a husband
gets detectives to spy on his wife.

She turned again. Still the linguist followed, but she would not quicken
her step. 'TEETH. TEETH,' said the sign above the window. *He started
after her. . . . Was she, he wondered, . . . respectable?* And *was* she? *Was*
she respectable? There were, of course, all those nights spent apart. But
then *he . . . insisted, after her illness, that she must sleep undisturbed* and,
besides, Dr Stopes, the famous Dr Marie Stopes (again Marie), had always
advised that husband and wife should have separate bedrooms.

Her own room, in the mornings, had the light. It would wake her early,
assuming she had slept. Johannes's room was just across the landing. *The
supreme mystery . . . was simply this: here was one room; there another.*
Not a mystery, Johannes would say, merely an arrangement, an arrangement of souls; he would quote Dr Stopes who had said that 'No soul could
grow to its full stature without spells of solitude.' Marie missed him nevertheless, the warmth of his body; but she could always telephone – another
jest, or joke, of his; Honeymoon Land, Johannes would say, was possessed
of an excellent telephone exchange. Once, just once, he added, as if to
prove his point, that *people were talking behind the bedroom walls.* Yes,
she had said, where else could people talk? She had read in the local paper,
the *Recorder* that, in Palmers Green, girls who went into service discussed
their mistress's failings with freedom.

Marie suspected that their own girl spoke freely; and, more than once,
Marie had aired her suspicion. 'Breathes there a woman with tongue so
tied she never discusses the servant problem?' the *Recorder* had asked.
No, she had murmured; her tongue was never so tied, least not her French
tongue, for if she and Johannes ever wished to keep words to themselves,
to puzzle their girl, they would talk in French. Yes, French. She thought
of the linguist. 'Suppose,' he once had said, '- suppose someone
pronounces the French word *nu* (naked).' Suppose indeed. And suppose,
just suppose, one was overheard by a girl who understood French and
who might then *see* someone naked, and with another? What then?

HERON: Come, let him find us here together.
VECTIA: What must I do?
HERON: Slip into one of those lacy things. Quick for our pretence!
(Inaudible murmur from the bedroom).

But a word overheard, even the word 'naked,' what would that betray? What could that prove? (*Outside the door was Miss Kilman . . . listening to whatever was said*). Besides, she thought, what could a spoken word *ever* prove? As the linguist had once whispered, 'It would be impossible to photograph the utterance of a word.'

But enough of words. *On and on she went . . . up Regent Street* now thinking of teeth and the x-rays she used to take, in the surgery in Paris. And she had seen much, so much in the wide open mouths. (*The spirit of religion was abroad . . . her lips gaping wide*). Just the other day she had read, in the *Recorder*, the question, 'Do you periodically examine your children's teeth?' No. No, she did not. Her qualifications were not recognised here in England. So, no, she examined nobody's teeth and had no desire to do so, for what could be seen within the wide-open mouth was unbearable, unthinkable. (*I have pneumonia in my throat – the germs copulating . . . vigorously*).

She walked on, as another shower whipped her cheek. And through the rain she saw a woman who wore a mackintosh, a green mackintosh. It was *Miss Kilman standing still in the street for a moment to mutter, 'It is the flesh.'* Marie nodded her assent; *this . . . Christian – this woman* was right, so very right; but not the green mackintosh, in that respect Miss Kilman erred. She, Marie, like Miss Kilman, was, of course, born again, she too was now married to Christ; but the bride was still beautiful and so would never wear such a mackintosh, not even where none could see. Miss Kilman, she had heard, was given to *standing . . . upon the landing in her mackintosh*. A large dark motorcar crept by, its new tyres piano black.

Yes, Miss Kilman stood on the landing, and yes she, Marie, had also dwelled, some nights, upon the landing. And there, right there, *she would think what in the world she could do to give him pleasure (short always of the one thing).* Some nights she would even go into his room, *and he could see her with tears running down her cheeks going to her writing table and dashing off that one line.* Strange, how it always ended that way. Sometimes she would write that same one line again and again for much of the night.

HERON: But now I want you to tell me about Will's behaviour – here – in this room. (*He leans across the bed, offering a pencil and indicating that she is to write her answers*).

In the morning, after such a night, she would wonder at her writing. Page after page, and always that one line. The night of truth, she used to say. The linguist, however, had always said of writing, 'We must be aware of its defects and its dangers.' The linguist had not liked writing, not liked to set things down. To her he had, in fact, never written; though he would whisper – through the traffic. Writing, he believed, was a kind of poison, and one that was slowly infecting speech. 'In Paris,' he had sighed, '- in Paris one already hears *sept femmes* with the "t" pronounced.'

But, why 'sept *femmes*' she had asked. Why not 'sept hommes'? Or 'sept rues'? Why seven *women*? Were there only women in Paris? The linguist had said nothing, and she had apologised. She had been speaking like one of Mrs Pankhurst's women. Such women were legion in Palmers Green and had, indeed, set fire to the letterbox on the corner of Fearnley Road. Its gaping mouth had smoked like a gun, and when the box was opened there had been nothing but ash. It had been a kind of treason. England had trembled.

On she walked, all the while thinking of how, long ago, she had chosen, at her coming-of-age, when still in Paris, not to be English. Her mother was French, her father was English, and she had chosen France. A blow had been struck; a window broken; a brick dislodged. She had betrayed the Kingdom, connived against *this isle of men, this dear, dear land,* had chosen to be not English. (*To be not English even among the dead – no, no! Impossible!*).

Marie smiled to herself. She had long continued her betrayal. It had become a secret treason, a secret un-weaving, a nightly work of nothing and tears, a nightly not-thinking of England. And it made her smile at a policeman, the very thought, who had just stopped the traffic.

How little the policeman knew; how little could he have guessed, for instance, that she was a friend of the eminent linguist or that he, the linguist, had a wife who was also called Marie. How little, too, could the policeman have guessed that within but half an hour she, Marie, Johannes' Marie, as it were, would undress. *Women must put off their rich apparel. At midday they must disrobe.* Her finest lace underclothes would be cast across a chair, her body cast in Russian perfume, and she would be alone in a room with a man, not her husband.

HERON: This doesn't look very convincing.
VECTIA: What ought we to do? Make the pillows look untidy?

Marie smiled again, then laughed, and *laughing . . . she . . . crossed Oxford Street . . . and turned down one of the little streets . . . now, and now, the great moment was approaching.* Yes, she had found Queen Anne Street, and on she walked. She stood before a door and rang the bell. An ambulance passed by. The door was opened by a girl who led her along a corridor and into a somewhat faded room. She declined the invitation to remove her coat and stared at a door that led into another room. *She made to hide her dress, like a virgin protecting her chastity . . . . Now the door opened, and . . . for a single second she could not remember what he was called!* The man in the doorway was known to both her and Johannes; known, though not well, she would not say well. He smiled. All would be fine, he said. They would not be alone; there would be a witness. It was the only way and would be for the best. He then withdrew.

There were, she now noticed, two others in the room – a man and a woman. They looked up as if she were a guest and this their drawing-room. The man stood up and introduced himself as Hugh Whitbread, the woman beside him being Mrs Whitbread. *They had just come up*, he said, *to see doctors. Other people came to see pictures, go to the opera . . . ; the Whitbreads came 'to see doctors.'* Marie nodded, sat down, and drew from her bag a book. Mr Whitbread coughed, desiring to speak. *His wife*, he explained, *had some internal ailment.* How openly the stranger spoke. Johannes never spoke of ailments, or of problems, but then *Dr Holmes said there was nothing the matter with him.*

The High Court of Justice
May 27th 1924
I do order that Thomas Stevens, F.R.C.S. of 20 Queen Ann Street, W1 be appointed to examine Johannes Schad to report whether he is capable of the act of generation; and also to examine Marie Schad and to report whether she hath or hath not any impediment on her part to prevent the consummation of Marriage.

W. Inderwick
Registrar.

Something had changed. It was the Whitbreads; they had gone; and in their place stood an older woman, a nurse, a kind of angel, in grey. Would Mrs Schad care to follow her? The grey angel was beckoning her back toward the entrance hall and, once there, led her to a staircase. *Like a nun withdrawing, or a child exploring a tower, she went upstairs.* At the third turn, or break, in the stairs Marie paused. It was a little larger than the landing at home. Marie looked out. Our lives, she thought, are Swiss. At last, she could see forever.

But what could *he* see? Johannes. He had always said that, according to the Zionists, from Basel one could see the milk and honey of Israel. From Basel, he would say, the Promised Land could at least be seen, if not entered. Such, she thought, was the nature of Paradise; she had heard much of Heaven and knew it was not for all. Dr Stopes, for instance, had recently written about a newly married couple who had thought they were 'entering Paradise together' but were, apparently, mistaken.

A horn sounded in the street, and she followed the nurse up another flight of stairs, then through an open door. Here, at last, she would be seen and saved. The doctor looked up from his desk, rose to his feet, and moved toward a basin of water. He washed his hands in silence. The nurse motioned Marie toward a curtain. *Women . . . at midday . . . must disrobe.* The policeman would stop the traffic and she would now undress. The bride, she whispered, is beautiful. The linguist had smiled when first she had said this, as if he too were drawn to talk of beauty; but she had been wrong. 'To speak of a linguistic law,' he had remarked, 'is like trying to lay hands on a ghost.' The doctor washed his hands a second time.

> 20 Queen Ann Street
> April 16, 1924

Report on the condition of Mrs Marie Schad wife of Mr Johannes Schad both being known to me.

I examined Mrs Schad on April 7th 1924 and found that she had infantile sexual organs. Even the insertion of a small finger into the vagina caused very great pain, and I am convinced that sexual connection has never taken place. Mrs Schad states that she has not menstrated since November 1904.

> Thos. C. Stevens
> Gynaecological Surgeon.

Once outside, she stood in the door-frame, and here she might have stayed forever. But there were the flowers to buy, and so she would walk. She *must* buy the flowers, she thought, as two men passed by, the very best. As the two men walked, one spoke. '*I have come over,*' he said, '*to see lawyers about the divorce.*' She knew there was a flower-stall near-by; she had passed it on her way. And there it was, vivid with terrible colour. Yes, she would have them wrapped. Thank you. Behind her, two smart women waited, one laughing and the other talking of '*men . . . who sent their wives to Court.*'

Marie would *not* be sent. She would go of her own volition. And she would take flowers. 'Are flowers,' she asked, 'allowed in court?' The women, behind her, smiled. 'The High Court,' added Marie, staring at the letter she had drawn from her bag. The High Court, in the Strand.

Part Three
(NOVEMBER 25TH 1924)

Marie had bought the flowers, and held them tight. Her coat matched the grey of the vast stone-built entrance hall. She loved the echoes, the foot-falls, and the splendid whispers. A cathedral, she thought, and sat down. The bench was cold.

Beside her was a tall, angular woman. 'It is to be an annulment,' whispered the woman. She paused, then began again: 'Dr Stopes herself has had an annulment.' Marie lay her flowers at her feet. 'It happens, you know,' whispered the woman. 'Dr Stopes has written, I believe, about a nullity case that took place after twenty years of supposed marriage.'

Marie did not care for the word 'supposed.' It was true they had rarely made public their affection; true they had not always spoken over dinner, unless Johannes had invited guests. But a couple need not exhibit affection; need not speak, nor even touch. Two can, sometimes, simply lie together, hearing the same sounds, feeling the same air press upon their cold, bare limbs. And two can, surely, sleep apart, dream apart, sleep and dream through nineteen years. *A little independence there must be between people living together.*

Yes, she thought, yes, a little independence; *a room of one's own*, a bedroom of one's own, and a bed in which to inhale un-breathed air. She sighed, but would not cry, for she was enraptured by the mosaic floor. Her shoes, she thought, were still not as she would like. She then looked up, and across the hall stood Johannes wearing the same dark suit he had worn in that first-ever summer of theirs, in Paris, *dans la belle époque*, on the very day they had stood side-by-side, before God and Man. A miracle it had been. She raised her hand, but only for an instant.

As she lowered her hand, a clear, light voice was heard above the whispers, and echoes of whispers. It was his name and hers. And should they enter together? She would have liked to hold his hand, but she had the flowers and thus her arms were full. She made her way alone. The courtroom was dark and, once within, a court usher, a pale man, showed her to a seat. The judge, it would be Sir Thomas Horridge, should soon appear. She caught Johannes' eye. *The business of copulation was filth to him before the end.* But this was not the end. The world could turn. Sir Thomas may yet see to that. And here he came. She straightened her hat. Had the usher admired her hat? Or *was it that she had taken off her wedding ring?*

'Marriage,' began Sir Thomas, 'is founded on words of Divine authority.' To dissolve a marriage, she inferred, would be to dissolve God. She looked around. *Perhaps, after all, there is no God?* But God, she knew, existed. Her marriage was, therefore, as secure as God, her Saviour God.

Sir Thomas now called upon the evidence of Dr Stevens, to be read by Johannes's solicitor, a thin man. The first testimony concerned herself, but she would not lower her eyes. Some words she heard, some she did not. 'Very great pain,' she heard; 'not since November 1904,' she heard; 'both being known to me,' she heard. Was it not strange, she thought, to be seen by one to whom she was already known.

'Not since November 1904' – she heard the words again. 'Not since November 1904.' She closed her eyes tight shut, and Paris, and Johannes, and their courtship froze beneath her eyelids, bloodless. No trace of blood, none at all. She had known what this could mean, but it could not have been the case. And she had bled no more, thereafter. No more the Curse.

She wished to say something but the thin man had begun to read again, informing the court that the petitioner had successfully demonstrated himself capable of the act of generation. But *how*, Dr Stevens had not said; or under what conditions, or before whom. And did this, she wondered, prove beyond all doubt that Johannes had always been capable of the act?

> VECTIA: Ah, I wonder how many childless women are like me? Unsuspicious wives of men unable to be fathers.

But she must now speak, address the court, risk contempt. All would turn, all behold the beautiful bride, the still un-ravished bride, and though she might suffer a rush of November blood, she would yet speak. She rose to her feet, still holding her flowers, and lifted her head. But Sir Thomas had gone, and the courtroom was already beginning, in silence, to empty. She looked across at Johannes, who mouthed a word that was, she thought, 'Goodbye,' his lips kissing the air. (*He has left me; I am alone for ever*). She had, she now understood, been nobody's wife; there had been no marriage to end. And she wondered by what English magic the court had erased something which had never been. Nothing, she thought. It was just as Mr Eliot had written. Nothing again.

'But what,' she said, quietly tearing at the silence, '- but what of the statement? Dr Stevens' statement, it contains errors, the finest of errors.' Her solicitor was already leaving. 'Dr Stevens,' she continued, 'meant to say "menstruated," but what the typist had set down is "menstrated." The "*u*" is not there.' It had gone, she thought, like a letter only ever drawn in the sky. The assertion that she 'had not *menstrated* since November 1904' was, surely, inadmissible, illegitimate, a kind of bastard?

Her solicitor had now gone. Marie would, though, continue to speak. 'His name,' she said, '- his name is also wrong, the *doctor's* name. It says "Thomas C. Stevens" but it should say "Thomas G. Stevens." Where there should be a "G" there is a "C."'

Silence. There was silence. She looked around the court. Only the usher had remained. But he had listened; she felt sure he had listened.

And now, yes now, he spoke, reminding her that the eminent linguist (he too, the usher, seemed to know the linguist) had always warned that words would change, and letters disappear. The word 'menstruated' might lose the letter 'u' but such, said the usher, is merely the forgetfulness of language.

'Kindly recall,' he said, 'the linguist's observations regarding the German word, *Bethaus*, meaning "temple."'

She nodded.

'And kindly also recall,' continued the usher, 'how he had said that the word had once been spelt *betahus*.'

Marie sat down, and the usher drew to his gentle conclusion: this particular change, the linguist had said, was 'the result of an accident . . . the fall of the "*a*" in *betahus*.'

But no! she protested; the linguist had, for once, been mistaken; had clearly been wrong to talk of the *fall* of the "a" – the "a" had not *fallen* but moved, migrated. Whilst once the 'a' came *before* the letter 'h' now it came *after*. It had passed through the letter 'h' as if it were scarcely there; as the linguist might surely have guessed, for had he not also once said that the 'aspirate *h* . . . is an orthographic ghost'? The 'a' was not, therefore fallen, was not gone. No, it was elsewhere, in another room, as it were.

The usher was perturbed; the woman, she was right. Within the word 'Betahus' there was no crevasse, no place to fall; it was as if the linguist had been thinking of an accident somewhere in the Alps. The usher, deeply troubled, sat down; this woman would now develop her case.

'And so,' she said, 'if the letter "a" had not disappeared, then how could *she*, flesh and blood, ever disappear?' The usher said nothing. 'Might she not,' she continued, 'pass, like the "a," through some door, some wall, and there, *like a nun who has left the world,* find asylum?' She had risen to her feet, but was possessed by a terrible dizziness. The usher offered her his arm, and inquired if she would like him to telephone for a cab. Yes, she said; to Victoria, for she would go South that night, toward Paris, where she would meet the linguist, who would arrive there on the 8.45 from Geneva.

But did she not know, inquired the usher, his face torn in two, did she not know that the linguist was dead? That he had died in 1913? She did not move, her face as still as a doll.

Yes, she said. Yes, she had known, had always known; but the linguist, she said, when last they met, had whispered, 'Let us *begin* with death.' Begin, she said, begin – not end.

There was, once more, a dizziness. The usher again offered his arm, and inquired if she was quite well enough to travel alone. He paused, then spoke again. Could he not (here he hesitated and even blushed) – could he not *accompany* her? Marie, for a moment, said nothing. Such kindness; she had never encountered such kindness. No, she then said, gently.

The man had not quite understood, had not quite understood this leaving like a nun, this leaving the world, this beginning with death. *This killing oneself.* She would, though, give to the man her flowers. He thanked her.

Outside, the cries of the street welcomed Marie. *This killing oneself,* she thought, *does one set about it with a table knife?* She walked on. Or, she wondered, could one simply walk in front of a motor car? *In the midst of traffic there was the habitation of God.* And this killing oneself, she thought, should one set about it today, next week, or, exactly a year and a day after one's undressing, one's disrobing?

The Diary of Virginia Woolf
April 8th 1925

London . . . is shot with the accident I saw this morning . . . a woman crying Oh oh oh faintly, pinned against the railings with a motorcar on top of her.

Postscript

We do not know what actually happened to Marie following the annulment. In August of that year Johannes married, or re-married. His bride, with whom he had three children, one being my father, was also called Marie. Johannes chose, though, always to call her 'Marnie,' adding an 'n.'

XI

A Chronology of Bewilderment and
Bedevilment. Or, How Literary
Criticism Has Variously:
Misbehaved, Become Distracted,
Been Beside the Point, Fallen About
Laughing, Wept, Grown
Autobiographical, Thrilled at its
Own Superfluity, and
Aspired to the Fateful Condition
of Literature Itself.
Some Key Dates.
(2013)

1865 Matthew Arnold writes, 'Literature is the promised land toward which criticism can only beckon. That promised land it will not be ours to enter, and we shall die in the wilderness; but to have decided to enter it, to have saluted it from afar, is already perhaps the best distinction . . . .' The critic may not, for Arnold, be creative; however, the critic's failure, his falling short, his dying salutation of an impossibly-distant promised land, is itself so exquisite a thing, so sad a thing, as to be itself a kind of poetry, indeed the most dangerous kind of all.

1890 Oscar Wilde imagines a man called Gilbert who sits at a piano in a house in Piccadilly and remarks that 'criticism is itself an art . . . , it . . . need not . . . bear any . . . obvious resemblance to the thing it criticises.' Gilbert thus take a hammer (or piano) to the mirror of criticism.

1890 Remembering Arnold's claim that the true function of criticism is 'to see the object as in itself it really is,' Gilbert insists the function of criticism is 'to see the object as in itself it really is *not*.' The point is to miss the point. Have you got that?

1890 Gilbert adds that 'Criticism . . . is the only civilised form of auto-biography.' He also observes that 'It is always Judas who writes the biography.'* If Judas were, then, to write an *auto*biography would he not turn his hand to criticism? Perhaps he has done so.

1928 Walter Benjamin observes that 'citation wrenches the word from its context but thereby calls the word back to its origin.' To quote is, necessarily, to quote out of context and, in doing so, words are set free, are once more themselves.

1929 Ludwig Wittgenstein encounters in Cambridge the father of modern academic literary criticism, F. R. Leavis, and cries, 'Give up literary criticism!' Dr Leavis does not take the advice, nor does literary criticism – not yet, leastwise.

1939 Jorge Luis Borges publishes a short-story featuring a character who copies out word-for-word Miguel de Cervantes' novel *Don Quixote* (1605), thus ably demonstrating what a truly realist mode of literary criticism would be.

1940 (18th September) Virginia Woolf began to set down 'Notes for Reading at Random.' Six months later she walks into the River Ouse with a pocket full of stones, but no notes.

1949 John Cage, the avant-garde composer and music critic, reads part of *Finnegan's Wake* upside down. It is a beautiful gesture, but no one notices.

1949 Cage gives 'A Lecture on Something.' When the subject of the lecture, Morton Feldman, was asked if he agreed with it, he replied, 'That's not me; that's John.'

1951 Cage finally realises that his name is an anagram of 'Jo Change.' Please remember that Karl Marx once said 'The philosophers have only interpreted the world, in various ways; the point is to change it.' Might the same be said of literary critics? Might we change the world by the force of our reading? After all, Robert Browning once wrote, 'Read the text right, emancipate the world.' Note: to read rightly is not, necessarily, to read correctly.

1954 Cage gives a lecture titled '45' For a Speaker.' The lecture is accompanied by piano, and the text of the lecture incorporates a number of actions that the lecturer is required to perform. These include: snore, lean on elbow, slap table, hiss, blow nose, brush hair, light match, bang fist. There is no requirement to pray. Not yet.

1956 T. S. Eliot, giving America a lecture called 'The Frontiers of Criticism,' insists that 'you cannot fuse creation with criticism.' He is, though, keen to italicise the word 'literary' whenever he speaks of 'literary criticism.' What, by the way, would a genuinely *literary* criticism be?

1971 Roland Barthes writes that 'the discourse *on* the text should

---

*Kiss and tell. Kiss and tell Jesus.

itself be nothing other than text.' Nine year later he dies after being hit by a laundry van in Paris. Who is in the van?

1973 Norman O. Brown, the avant-garde literary critic (thus a critic in the van, you might say) meditates upon Karl Marx's eccentric 1852 essay, 'The 18th Brumaire of Louis Napoleon'; Brown concludes that 'What Karl Marx really meant is *Finnegan's Wake.*' A remarkable discovery.

1976 A book called *The Romantic Sublime* is published posthumously by Thomas Weiskel, a young Yale scholar. In the winter of 1974, just after completing the manuscript, Weiskel went skating on a frozen lake near his New Haven home, pulling his three-year old daughter on a sledge behind him – both fell through the ice and died. His wife writes in the Preface: 'Tom, in his death, following by seconds his daughter's, . . . knew in an instant both the sublime and the terror of the nature he wrote about.'

1980 Geoffrey Hartman writes, 'Literary commentary may cross the line and become as demanding as literature.' Hartman knew Weiskel well.

1980 Hartman adds, 'Criticism is driven by the sin of envy and the drive for primacy; like Satan or Iago, the critic has a penchant for reversal which is near daemonic.' There is such a thing as *bad* reading. Perhaps there is only *bad* reading.

1980 Hartman also adds that 'The essay form is a secret relation of the Romantic fragment.' It is, I think, a secret relation of fragments and ruins in general; I have in mind such ruins as the aphorism, the epigram, and the joke.

1980 Hartman *also also* adds, 'The only critic who we must take seriously is one who may not yet exist: who extends his art, having decided that his role is creative.' I wouldn't take him seriously if I were you.

1983 Gregory Ulmer announces what he calls post-criticism; 'the break with . . . realism,' he says, 'which revolutionised the modernist arts, is now underway (belatedly) in criticism.' We must no longer hold up a glass to the text. Break your glasses now.

1983 Ulmer adds that post-criticism performs its own meanings; it 'functions,' he says, 'within an epistemology of performance – [it is] knowing as . . . producing. Post-criticism writes "on" its object in the way that Wittgenstein's knower exclaims: Now I know *how to go on!*' Note: to know is to know how to go on. On, on.

1984 Julian Barnes publishes a novel called *Flaubert's Parrot* about a doctor obsessed with Gustave Flaubert; as the novel develops we slowly realise that the doctor-critic may well have killed his adulterous wife. Literary critics, or at least literary theorists, have been known to kill their wives – I think of Louis Althusser, and do *not* know how to go on.

Still Not Here – By Way of an Afterword

(2013)

> John Schad, also sometimes known as 'John Shad,' [is] a scholar who –
> despite appearing as a character in Nabokov's *Pale Fire* under the name
> 'John Shade' – is real, and not made up by me at all. In the slightest.
> Really.
>
> (A.R.R.R. Roberts, The Va Dinci Cod)

To return to the theme of my Foreword, I am afraid to report that Schad
has still not been found, and that some grow concerned. Others, more
sanguine, suggest that he may simply have heeded the words of Louis
MacNeice, a poet of another low and dishonest decade, who once, in
despair, sang 'But I will escape, with my dog, on the far side of the Fair.'
Schad has no dog, but the fairground might just appeal to our prodigal
given his reputed interest in Walter Benjamin's astonishing discovery that
for 'the masses, education is a series of catastrophes that befall them at
fairs.' Schad, ever the exodist, has certainly dreamt of a university-
without-walls, leading some now to say he has been spotted manning a
fairground attraction called 'The University of Catastrophe' and bedecked
with inspiriting mottos such as 'Only everybody can know the truth'
(Goethe).

This may seem improbable but it does in some ways tally with what
is, I think, the most substantial evidence we have as to Schad's whereabouts. Just the other night I was pacing through his shrouded library
when I came across the Indiana edition of *The Letters of G.W.F. Hegel*.
As I prised open up the large grey volume I chanced upon one particular
sentence that Schad had underlined; it was in a letter dated August 16,
1803, and runs as follows:

> Schad is having a physical apparatus made for himself and will lecture
> on experimental physics in the winter; others think he is in the process
> of going mad.

The Schad to whom Hegel here refers is Johann Baptist Schad (1758–
1837), Professor of Philosophy and contemporary of Hegel's at the
University of Jena. It should be noted that at no point, here or elsewhere,

does Hegel make any attempt whatsoever to identify 'the physical appa-ratus.' This sentence does, therefore, intrigue in and of itself; but what makes the sentence still more important for us is that it suggests, I believe, that our prodigal Schad has, characteristically, confused himself with his 1803 Jena namesake. If so, and *our* Schad is himself now having an appa-ratus being made then, pray, what is it? What? There are a number of hypotheses.

Some, for instance, say that the apparatus is a comedy piano designed to fall apart in triumphant disaster whilst Schad, *à la* John Cage, teases out a comic tune or two to accompany a lecture entitled 'Higher Misreading.' It is thought that, drawing on the long tradition of the seaside 'Professor' (as in, for example, Professor of Punch and Judy), he may be giving the lecture as an end-of-the-pier entertainment at various, half-remembered seaside resorts. He invariably concludes, it is said, with a rousing, honky-tonk setting of Friedrich Nietzsche's dictum, 'I should believe only in a god who understood how to dance.'

Others agree that the apparatus in question *is* musical but argue that it is a violin; primarily because historical research reveals that Schad's 1803 namesake, Johann, did himself play the violin, the most tearful of instruments, of course, and thus a more likely instrument for our prodigal, given his fascination with the 'still, sad music of humanity.' According to this theory, Schad has limped off, fiddling plaintively as he goes, in search of the 'far-off interest of tears'; he has, as it were, invested in tears and is concerned to see what profit they may yield, what they might yet tell him of the nature of Man and the purpose, if any, of a life devoted to literary criticism. On his back, it is reputed, someone has pinned the words: 'The true essence of eyes is not to see but to cry.'

Another, closely related theory is that the apparatus Schad has had made is a cross, and that he has taken to 'carrying it about the world in general.' Some, in fact, say that he does so in pale imitation of Odysseus, he who chose to end his days, after a lifetime of seafaring, not in easeful Ithaca but upon the road, taking up the oar of a ship, which he placed on his shoulders, and travelling inland on a journey that would only end, he vowed, when he had travelled so very far from the coast that he finds a man who does not know what it is that he, Odysseus, carries. Our prodigal, they say, has likewise disappeared with his cross in search of the first person who does not know what *it* is; at which point, of course, the cross might finally cease to be a symbol and thus be reborn as a thing, a thing that kills. 'A cross?' inquires Oedipa Maas, 'Or the initial T?' – I quote Thomas Pynchon's novel *The Crying of Lot 49*, a favourite of our runaway.

There is, though, a view among certain anonymous textual scholars that there is a corruption in the Hegel letter as published in the Indiana edition quoted above, and that the apparatus in question is not 'physical' (*physikalisch*) but rather 'psychical' (*psychisch*). Some critics have, then, suggested that we should have in mind a *textual* apparatus; for, what could be more psychical, more (let us say) telepathic, than the written word? This view is sometimes supported by reference to another favourite of Schad's, namely Vladimir Nabokov's 1962 novel *Pale Fire* which features, of course, a character known as John Shade. This coincidence is in itself, I think, germane to our inquiry, but our interest is redoubled when we observe that the character Shade, a fictional poet, composes a long narrative poem that is described precisely as if it were some kind of machine; note how we read of 'the magic action of Shade's poem . . . the very mechanism and sweep of verse, the powerful iambic motor.' As it happens, the magic action of John Shade's iambic machine is to cause a figure called Gradus, aka 'Jacques Degree,' a vagabond from middle-Europe, to travel across the Atlantic in order to shoot John Shade dead. Shade's poem is, you see, a kind of suicide machine, a psychical apparatus that draws toward its author his very own killer.

But I press on, press on to observe that, if textual, the apparatus in question is as likely to be a work of scholarship as of imagination. Indeed, the long editorial commentary that frames Shade's poem does, in fact, refer to itself as an '*apparatus criticus*' – quite a coincidence, I think. Doubters might insist on my quoting the context for this self-reference, and to appease the tribe of Thomas I shall do so here: 'I have,' [says Shade's editor] 'no desire to twist and batter an unambiguous *apparatus criticus* into the monstrous semblance of a novel.' The spectacular irony of these words is that the 250-page 'apparatus criticus' *does* quite literally take on the monstrous semblance of a novel, for the annotation gradually becomes a full-scale narrative concluding, of course, in Jacques Degree's shooting of Shade.

However, I digress; and must return to the mystery of 'the apparatus.' In this connection we should recall that Hegel follows his reference to 'the apparatus' with the observation that Schad, Johann Schad, our Schad of 1803, plans 'to lecture on experimental physics in the winter.' This suggests, I believe, that if the apparatus is indeed an 'apparatus criticus' it might well be, in some sense, experimental, or at least allow for the possibility of experiment. This, of course, is exactly what we have in *Pale Fire* where the 250 pages of seeming annotation serve in fact as an experiment in novel-writing, a novel the like of which had not been seen before. Indeed, just one year before, in 1961, (no coincidence, I think) C.S. Lewis publishes a book called *An Experiment in Criticism*, wherein after no less than 100 pages of learned preamble, Professor Lewis finally declares that 'the *apparatus* which my *experiment* required has now been assembled and we can get to work.' My hypothesis, therefore, is that the mysterious apparatus at the heart of our inquiry into the whereabouts of Schad is some kind of experimental work of criticism.

I am, by the way, intrigued by the fact that Professor Lewis was (and indeed, for some, still is) known as 'Jack' and that he dies, in 1963, on the very same day as John F. Kennedy is famously shot dead by a vagabond. Another Jack, and another John with a bullet in his head. Coincidence?

I am sorry – again I digress, and will now return to our central inquiry by considering the nature of the experiment our prodigal Schad may have in mind. Might it, in some way, be related to 'experimental *physics*' as was, it seems, the case for his 1803 namesake, model, and inspiration? And, if so, what kind of experimental physics could it be? To help answer this latter question, we should pause to consider how philosophy related to physics in Jena at the beginning of the nineteenth century. Here our best clue is the work of Hegel himself who, in order to formally acquire his 'Habilitation,' the qualification that licensed one to give university lectures, had submitted in 1801 a treatise called *De Orbitus Planetarum* (*On The Orbit of Planets*). The treatise is a critique of Newtonian physics in which the young Hegel audaciously argues that Newton's 'celestial mechanics,' an account of the universe as predictable and orderly, does not conform to his (Hegel's) peculiarly dialectical view of all things – the treatise opens with the classic Hegelian thesis that 'contradiction is the rule for truth.' It may come as no surprise that the Newtonian worldview survived Hegel's initial critique; however, Newtonian physics would not survive experimental physics *per se*, nor indeed the rule of contradiction, or paradox. I have in my sights here the sub-atomic investigations of Werner Heisenberg, Niels Borg *et al.*, investigations which issued in quantum physics, a mode of physics famously riddled with contradiction (light being, for example, both wave and particle, or things being in more than one place at the same time); as we all know, this contrarian new physics finally dismantled Newton's orderly, clockwork, and – dare one say it – very English universe. Professor Johann Schad's lectures on experimental physics, those which he planned to give in the winter of 1803, if ever actually given, may well then have been worth attending, worth risking the snow and ice of a frozen Jena; for these, I contend, would have been lectures not only given by a man reportedly going mad but also lectures that might, might just, have foreshadowed the miraculous world of quantum theory.

If so, then it could just be that our prodigal Schad, our very own dear, lunatic Schad, is even now re-enacting these uncanny lectures and indeed deploying the apparatus that he has had made for himself to make real, or practical, the theory that the lectures foreshadow. I am sure I need not remind you what terrible apparatus exists to make real the theory of quantum physics, also known of course as nuclear physics. In short: Schad may, I fear, be a *dangerous* clown. You will perhaps retort that a hapless professor of literature such as Schad could not possibly be concerned with quantum physics, but I regret to say that our prodigal has blundered into this particular dark before. See, for instance, an essay he once wrote on that vagabond Jacques Derrida which develops the claim that Derridean deconstruction is analogous to nuclear fission, a claim based on Derrida's own remarkable insistence that (and I quote) 'each textual atom bursts.' It should be noted that Derrida is also a dangerous figure, even possibly a murderous one; you may recall that he once wrote 'Right here I kill you,' adding 'there is someone in me who kills.'

Given all this, we may yet become thankful for Schad's continuing absence. It may just be that the Republic of Letters, or State of Criticism will be better off without the Great Misreader. Please note that, late in life, our Professor *Johann* Schad, *Hegel*'s Schad, as it were, was expelled from Tsarist Russia, led out by secret police under cover of night. True, all true. I am not, of course, for a moment suggesting that we expel our own Professor Schad; indeed, sadly, it may not be necessary since he might just have, I regret to say, passed from this world altogether.

I am, you see, beginning to suspect, perhaps like you, that just as *John Shade* fell prey to *Jacques Degree* so *John Schad* has fallen prey to *Jacques Derrida*. If names tell us anything – and remember: one's name is one's fate, *nomen est omen*, as the ancients say – then this morbid thought has to be considered, entertained. Please bear in mind Oscar Wilde's declaration that 'Anything may happen to a person called John.'

Another fearful possibility is, however, that our prodigal has taken his own life, or at least simply wasted away. After all, as a critic he is a man doomed to such a fate; I here glance toward Matthew Arnold's insistence that 'literature is the promised land toward which criticism can only beckon. That promised land it will not be ours to enter, and we shall *die* in the wilderness.'

Geoffrey Hartman once wrote that 'criticism is not the place where language goes to die'; however, it may, I fear, be the place where *our prodigal* dies – and where better, perhaps, for one so in love with language, one so eager to be a 'hostage of the Word'; indeed, such are the peculiar fancies of our runaway scholar that he may even believe he dies alongside the Word himself, alongside Christ, that is to say, at Golgotha, on a cross.

But what, in truth, *is* a cross? What *are* two pieces of wood that happen to intersect? What do they become? What the apparatus? What the thing? What?

These, I confess, are questions I put, somewhat frantically, to our prodigal even as he passed away, breathed his last; for, as I must now finally reveal, he *is*, sadly, dead. Moreover, he had no answer to my questions. In reply, all the dying man could offer was a kind of prayer, saying 'Dear Jesus, do something.'

'But these,' I protested, 'are second-hand words, *quoted* words, words stolen from that novel about John Shade.'

He said nothing.

'Besides, I added, seeking to console him, 'Jesus has better things to do than save a critic.'

Again the clown said nothing.

'Criticism,' I continued, still attempting to ease his passing, 'is driven by sin, the sin of envy, a Satanic drive for primacy, a daemonic penchant for reversal.' He did not, however, seem to understand, and so I added: 'My friend, you are dying of the sin of reversal, the law of contradiction.' His eyes grew blank and so I bent to kiss him goodbye saying, 'In reversal there is no salvation.' And, in reply, the poor man whispered, 'Dear Jesus, dear Jesus, dear Jesus.'

Fool, bloody and poor fool.

Notes

All biblical references are to the King James Version unless otherwise stated. 'NIV' is the New International Version.

Epigraphs
ix   In the beginning . . . The Gospel of St John, 1:1.
x   Anything may happen . . . *De Profundis* [1905] in Oscar Wilde, *Plays, Prose Writings Poems*, ed. Anthony Fothergill (London: Everyman, 1996), p. 478.

Not Here – by Way of Foreword
1   when a certain . . . Hugo St Victor, 'On Study and Teaching' [12th Century] in James Bruce Ross and Mary Martin McLaughlin (eds), *The Portable Medieval Reader* (Harmondsworth: Penguin, 1949), p. 583.
1   Man has become . . . Quoted in Joseph A. Smith and Susan Handelman (eds), *Psychoanalysis and Religion* (Baltimore: Johns Hopkins University Press, 1990), p. 71.
1   Robert Burton's . . . *The Anatomy of Melancholy* [1621], (New York: New York Review Books, 2001), p. 16.
2   When we are . . . Jacques Derrida, *Without Alibi*, ed. and tr. Peggy Kamuf (Stanford: Stanford University Press, 2002), p. 196.

I Waiting in Unhope
3   What is laid . . . Franz Kafka, *The Great Wall of China: Stories and Reflections*, tr. Willa and Edwin Muir (New York: Schocken, 1946), page 167.
3   unsight . . . *The Complete Poems of Thomas Hardy*, ed. James Gibson (London: Macmillan. 1976), 38.5, 106.37, 136.24, 141.44 – references are, and will be, to poem and line numbers respectively.
3   nothing is . . . *Poems*, 137.11.
3   the self is always . . . T. D. Armstrong, 'Supplementarity: Poetry as the Afterlife of Thomas Hardy,' *Victorian Poetry* 26 (1988): 392.
3   Childlike . . . *Poems*, 135.9–12.
4   I have no . . . Ibid., 44.2, 75.13, 141.48.
4   the mind is . . . David Hume, *A Treatise of Human Nature* [1739], ed. L. A. Selby-Bigge (Oxford: Clarendon Press, 1978), p. 253.
4   for Hardy . . . J. Hillis Miller, *The Linguistic Moment: From Wordsworth to Stevens* (Princeton: Princeton University Press, 1985), p. 290.
4   sense of severance . . . *Poems*, 55.5.
4   already dead . . . Armstrong, p. 382.

4   benumbed . . . *Poems*, 78.31, 9.10.

4   none replies . . . Ibid., 30.45, 40.29.

4   it is mind . . . Miller, p. 310.

4   Nescience . . . *Poems*, 30.48.

4   Unknowing God . . . Ibid., 88.

4   Lord Most . . . Ibid., 87.2–11.

4   too oft unconscious . . . Ibid., 89.21.

4   the true formula . . . Jacques Lacan, *The Four Fundamental Concepts of Psychoanalysis* [1973], tr. Alan Sheridan (London: Hogarth Press, 1977), p. 59.

5   each feels incomplete . . . Deborah L. Collins, *Thomas Hardy and His God: A Liturgy of Unbelief* (London: Macmillan, 1990), p. 103.

5   Yet, maybe . . . *Poems*, 78.26–35.

5   I fear we . . . Friedrich Nietzsche, *Twilight of the Idols* [1889], tr. R.J. Hollingdale (Harmondsworth: Penguin Books, 1990), p. 48.

5   the world knew . . . John 1:10.

5   made himself . . . Philippians 2:7 (NIV).

5   God chose things . . . 1 Corinthians 1:28.

6   I danced . . . *Poems*, 135.12,9.

6   Many people . . . Juliet Mitchell and Jacqueline Rose, *Feminine Sexuality: Jacques Lacan and the école freudienne* (London: Macmillan, 1982), p. 140.

6   when wilt thou . . . *Poems*, 85.1,3.

6   work[ing] . . . Thomas Hardy, *Tess of the D'Urbervilles* [1891] (Harmondsworth: Penguin, 1978), p. 414.

6   the activity of . . . Karl Marx, *Selected Writings*, ed. David McLellan (Oxford: Oxford University Press, 1977), p. 80.

6   within the family . . . Cited in Hélène Cixous and Catherine Clément, *The Newly Born Woman* [1977], tr. Betsy Wing (Manchester: Manchester University Press, 1986), p. 143.

6   strange orchestras . . . *Poems*, 85.7.

6   quite forgot . . . Ibid., 110.13–14, 27, 24.

6   those unimportant . . . Cited in Trevor Johnson, *A Critical Introduction to the Poems of Thomas Hardy* (London: Macmillan, 1991), p. 129.

6   a dominion . . . *Poems*, 90.1–9

7   political unconscious . . . See Fredric Jameson, *The Political Unconscious* (London: Methuen, 1981).

7   Should that morn . . . *Poems*, 85.9–14.

7   wait[ing] in unhope . . . Ibid., 136.24.

7   knew / And [yet] . . . Ibid., 119.31–2.

7   one wild shock . . . Collins, p. 70.

7   Communist consciousness . . . See David McLellan, *The Thought of Karl Marx* (London: Macmillan, 1980), pp. 225–6.

8   Between us now . . . *Poems*, 100.1.

8   Some words . . . Ibid., 9.7.

8   the ache of . . . *Tess of the D'Urbervilles*, p. 180.

II   The End of the End of History

10   The historian . . . Michael W. Jennings, Howard Eiland and Gary Smith (eds),

Walter Benjamin: Selected Writings, 4 vols (Cambridge, Mass.: Harvard University Press, 1996–2003), 4.405

10 Postmodern theories . . . Michel Foucault, for example, writes that 'the forces operating in history are not controlled by destiny or regulative mechanisms, but respond to haphazard conflicts . . . they always appear through the singular randomness of events' – Michel Foucault, *The Foucault Reader*, ed. Paul Rabinow (Harmondsworth: Penguin, 1986), p. 88.

10 the only important . . . Graham Swift, *Waterland* (London: Picador, 1984), p. 6.

10 disrupt disruption . . . Ibid., p. 51.

10 distances himself . . . Douglas Kellner, *Jean Baudrillard: From Marxism to Postmodernism and Beyond* (Cambridge: Polity 1989), p. 173.

10 in the middle . . . *Waterland*, p. 2.

10 there are no . . . Ibid., p. 117.

10 the true historical . . . Foucault, p. 89.

11 history . . . creates . . . *Waterland*, pp. 118–19.

11 the dissolution of . . . Gianni Vattimo, 'The End of History' in Ingeborg Hoesterey (ed.), *Zeitgeist in Babel* (Bloomington: Indiana University Press, 1991), p. 133.

11 saviour of the . . . *Waterland*, p. 198.

11 a landscape which . . . Ibid., p. 11.

11 Reality is . . . Ibid., p. 34.

11 waiting for . . . Ibid., p. 255.

11 what is the future . . . Ibid., p. 308.

11 Women are the . . . Christine Crosby, *The Ends of History: Victorians and 'The Woman Question'* (London: Routledge, 1991), p. 1.

11 shortens its vision . . . Foucault, pp. 89–90.

11 literally unthinkable . . . Having abandoned rational thought, along with the rest of the Enlightenment project, the postmodernist finds herself in a world that quite literally does not bear thinking.

12 that desert 'America' . . . For Baudrillard, the postmodern hyperreality of empty signs and value-free images means that there is no truth, only the true-seeming, and that therefore all political beliefs become equally invalid. In his book *America* (1986) Baudrillard describes a depthless, image-fixated society and interprets its election of an actor as President (Ronald Reagan) as the grand realization of the political indifference that inevitably succeeds the postmodern dissolution of all truth claims.

12 But Mary [is] . . . *Waterland*, p. 228.

12 Sartre's vision . . . For Sartre, history is a nightmare of 'blood guilt' since it is, above all, a record of domination and exploitation.

12 the nightmare . . . Fredric Jameson, *The Ideologies of Theory: Essays, 1971 to 1986*, 2 vols (Minneapolis: University of Minnesota Press, 1988), 2.162.

12 Mary Mother . . . *Waterland*, p. 266.

12 within the family . . . Friedrich Engels, *The Origin of the Family, Private Property and the State* [1884], tr. Alec West (London: Lawrence and Wisehart, 1972), p. 137.

12 the curses . . . See Genesis 3:16–19.

13 If . . . the now . . . Jacques Derrida, *Margins of Philosophy* [1972], tr. Alan Bass (Brighton: Harvester, 1982), p. 39.

13 He's here . . . *Waterland*, p. 308.
13 Nietzschean amnesia . . . I have in mind Nietzsche's intermittent anti-historicism, or stress on the therapeutic unhistorical in man.
13 dredgery drudgery . . . *Waterland*, p. 299.
13 'History' is . . . Gayatri Spivak, 'The New Historicism, Political Commitment and the Post-Modern Critic' in Aram Veeser (ed.), *The New Historicism* (London: Routledge, 1989).
13 a revolutionary [and] . . . *Waterland*, p. 228.
13 immaculate conception . . . Ibid., p. 226.
13 the end of . . . Vattimo, p. 140.
13 postmodern literature . . . Cited in Charles Newman, *The Post-Modern Aura. The Act of Fiction in an Age of Inflation* (Evanston: Northwestern University Press, 1985), p. 22.
14 every second . . . Walter Benjamin, *Illuminations*, tr. Harry Zohn (London: NLB, 1973), p. 266; I have taken the liberty of substituting 'is' for Benjamin's / Zohn's 'was' for the simple reason that I understand Benjamin to be voicing the belief as a very present one. Although Christine Crosby and others would disagree (Crosby, pp. 149–50), Jameson does not, as is made clear in his essay 'Marxism and Historicism' where he similarly misquotes 'was' as 'is' (*Ideologies*, 2.164-165).
14 revolutionary [or] Messianic . . . Benjamin, *Illuminations*, p. 120.
14 epistemological scepticism . . . For the literary theorist such scepticism derives, in the main, from structuralism's claim that language does not so much represent reality as construct it. For the historical materialist, the scepticism is a function of 'the cultural logic of late capitalism' – Jameson's definition of postmodernism and its preoccupation with image, simulation, and hyperreality. Baudrillard, however, along with others, such as Richard Rorty and Gianni Vattimo, would relate the scepticism to a Nietzschean or Heideggarian rejection of Enlightenment confidence in reason and objectivity.
14 in natural and . . . George Steiner, *Real Presences: Is There Anything in What We Say?* (London: Faber, 1989), p. 57.
14 its 'master code' . . . Jameson, p. 149; the transcendental signified of which he speaks is, of course, historical materialism.
14 It is no . . . Dick Hebdige, 'After the Masses,' *Marxism Today*, January 1989, p. 51.
14 where do we . . . *Waterland*, pp. 120–1.
14 the dredger . . . Ibid., p. 310.
15 We row back . . . Ibid., p. 310.
15 the irony of . . . David Revill, 'Star in Love Triangle,' *Times Higher Education Supplement*, 21 December 1990, p. 14.
15 empty triumph . . . For Baudrillard, the subject as the foundation of knowledge is defunct and overthrown by the object. Douglas Kellner, puts it this way: 'Baudrillard's theme in *Les Strategies Fatales*, is the triumph of objects over subjects within the obscene proliferation of an object world so completely out of control that it surpasses all attempts to understand, conceptualise and control it' (p. 155).
15 the saviour . . . *Waterland*, p. 308.
15 twenty-first century metaphysic . . . Revill, p. 14; something of this meta-

physic is indicated by Baudrillard's talk of 'the ecstatic form of the pure object' (*Fatal Strategies*, [1983] tr. Phil Beitchman and W. G. J. Niesluchowski (New York: Semiotext(e), 1990), p. 9)).

15   to buy it . . . See *Waterland*, p. 210.

15   not the disappearance . . . Fredric Jameson, 'Introduction' to Jean François, *The Post-Modern Condition* [1979] (Manchester: Manchester University Press, 1984), p. xii.

15   trace of the . . . Philippa Berry, 'Deserts of the Heart,' *The Times Higher Education Supplement*, 28 December 1990, p. 7.

16   God came down . . . *Waterland*, p. 269.

16   mobs [of] . . . Ibid., p. 271.

16   *Vox populi* . . . Ibid., p. 121.

16   God doesn't talk . . . Ibid., p. 232.

16   there are no . . . Ibid., p. 108.

16   negative theology . . . In the essay 'Différance,' Derrida remarks that 'the detours, locutions and syntax in which I will often have to take recourse will resemble those of negative theology even to the point of being indistinguishable from negative theology' (*Margins*, p. 6).

16   negative political theology . . . Terry Eagleton, *The Ideology of the Aesthetic* (Oxford: Blackwell, 1990), p. 326.

16   negative theology [and] . . . Terry Eagleton, *Walter Benjamin, or Towards a Revolutionary Criticism* (London: Verso, 1981), p. 148.

16   just as the . . . Eagleton, *Ideology*, p. 216.

16   the knowledge of . . . Ibid., p. 183.

17   chromium-plated confessor . . . *Waterland*, p. 221.

17   Dick's sexual desire . . . See ibid., p. 33.

17   stopped cycling . . . Ibid., p. 224.

17   is where history . . . Ibid., p. 229.

17   the suppression of . . . Karl Marx, *Grundrisse* [1939], tr. Martin Nicolaus (Harmondsworth: Penguin, 1972), p. 511.

17   at its most . . . Theodor W. Adorno, *Negative Dialectics* [1966], tr. E. B. Ashton (London: Routledge, 1973), p. 207.

17   the new society . . . Karl Marx, 'The Civil War in France' [1871], in Marx, *Selected Writings*, p. 540.

17   chronology go . . . *Waterland*, p. 229.

17   aborted embryo . . . See ibid., p. 50.

17   nonfather . . . Ibid., p. 282.

17   the land girls . . . Ibid., p. 39.

18   the more modern . . . Marx, *Selected Writings*, p. 227.

18   to . . . get . . . *Waterland*, p. 33.

18   writers [have begun] . . . Ibid., p. 70.

18   bourgeois society [that] . . . Marx, *Selected Writings*, p. 227.

18   womb of history . . . Eagleton, *Ideology*, p. 326.

18   the attempt to . . . Adorno, p. 3.

18   no originating seed . . . Raman Selden, *A Reader's Guide to Contemporary Literary Theory* (London: Harvester 1989), p. 39.

18   under the capitalist . . . Marx, *Selected Writings*, p. 502.

18   rewrite certain religious . . . Fredric Jameson, *The Political Unconscious* (London: Methuen, 1981), p. 285.

19   the puppet called . . . Walter Benjamin, *Illuminations*, p. 255.
19   the revolution has . . . Adorno, p. 205.
19   Value differentiates itself . . . Karl Marx, *Capital* [1867], tr. Ben Fowkes (New York: Vintage, 1973), p. 256.
19   instead of possessing . . . Karl Marx, *Selected Writings*, p. 117.
19   God came down . . . *Waterland*, p. 206.
19   I got it . . . Ibid., p. 229.
19   revolutionary act . . . Ibid., p. 228.
19   babe in the . . . Ibid., p. 269.
19   abounding in theological . . . Karl Marx, *Selected Writings*, p. 435.
20   the commodity is . . . Eagleton, *Ideology*, p. 374.
20   white greasepainted . . . *Waterland*, p. 109.
20   ghostly price . . . Ibid., p. 292.
20   the phantasmagoric form . . . See Ned Lukacher, 'Benjamin's Chthonian Revolution,' *Boundary 2*, 11 (1982–3): 45.
20   wants to change . . . *Waterland*, p. 108.
20   son-who's-not . . . Ibid., p. 282; according to orthodox belief, of course, Christ is 'our son-who's-not-a-son' to Joseph.
20   ghostly charges . . . Ibid., p. 292.
20   Harry . . . The novel draws, I am suggesting, on the familiar colloquial phrase 'any Tom, Dick or Harry.'
20   Christ the mediator . . . Karl Marx, *Selected Writings*, p. 326.
21   disrupt[s] disruption . . . *Waterland*, p. 51.
21   disruptions of the . . . Joseph O'Leary, 'Theology on the Brink of Modernism,' *Boundary 2*, 13 (1985): 150.
21   the Spirit . . . John 3:8.
21   Inasmuch as . . . Matthew 25:40.
21   ye [shall] have . . . Mark 14:7.

III   The Divine Comedy of the Sign

Please note that all references to Tennyson's poetry are taken from *The Poems of Tennyson*, ed. Christopher Ricks, 3 vols (Berkeley: University of California Press, 1987); references to *In Memoriam* [1850] are given as canto and line.

22   I sometimes . . . *In Memoriam*, 5.1–4.
22   lesser griefs . . . Ibid., 20.1.
22   truth in closest . . . Ibid., 36.6.
22   there is a . . . Isobel Armstrong, *Language as a Living Form in Nineteenth Century Poetry* (Brighton: Harvester, 1982), p. 173.
22   As, above all . . . Elizabeth Hirsch, '"No Record of Reply": *In Memoriam* and Victorian Language Theory,' *ELH* 55 (1988): 234.
22   the loss of . . . Alan Sinfield, *Alfred Tennyson* (Oxford: Blackwell, 1986), p. 102.
22   dear words . . . *In Memoriam*, 85.83.
22   familiar names . . . Ibid., 18. 7.
22   closest words . . . Ibid., 36. 6.
22   the sad words . . . Ibid., 58.1.
22   measured language . . . Ibid., 5.6–7.
22   an infant crying . . . Ibid., 54.19–20.

22 In the beginning . . . Gerhard Joseph, *Tennyson and the Text: The Weave and the Shuttle* (Cambridge: Cambridge University Press, 1992), p. 25.

22 the symbol . . . Jacques Lacan, *Écrits* [1966], tr. Alan Sheridan (London, 1977), p. 104.

23 This structuralist . . . Jacques Derrida, *Writing and Difference* [1967], tr. Alan Bass (Brighton: Harvester, 1978), p. 292.

23 the sad incompetence . . . William Wordsworth, *The Prelude or Growth of a Poet's Mind* [1805], ed. Ernest de Selincourt (Oxford: Oxford University Press, 1926), 6.593.

23 when composition . . . *The Complete Works of Percy Bysshe Shelley*, ed. Roger Ingpen and Walter E. Peck (New York, 1965), 7.135.

23 bleeding words . . . *The Poetical Works of Edmund Spenser*, ed. J. C. Smith (Oxford: Oxford University Press, 1909), 1.7.38.

23 the word of . . . *The Poems of Gerard Manley Hopkins*, ed. Norman H. MacKenzie (Oxford: Oxford University Press, 1990), p. 124.

23 recent research . . . Roland Barthes, *Image-Music-Text*, tr. Stephen Heath (London: Fontana, 1977), p. 148.

23 Let tears of . . . 'Early Spring,' lines 53–54.

23 the void . . . Sinfield, p. 88.

23 is often in . . . Ibid., p. 74.

23 a hint of . . . Ibid., 98. As Joseph remarks, 'even if we accept Peirce's "inadequacy of the sign" or Wittgenstein's "What we cannot speak about we must pass over in silence," does not such acceptance finally betray in the very language of its expression a certain nostalgia, the repressed desire to cross beyond the epistemological bar . . . ?' (Joseph, p. 23).

23 no word less . . . For George Steiner, 'there is no word less deconstructible' than 'the name of hope' – *Real Presences: Is there anything in what we say?* (London: Faber, 1989), p. 232.

24 divinest anguish . . . 'R. Alcona to J. Brenzaida,' *The Complete Poems of Emily Jane Brontë*, ed. C. W. Hatfield (New York: Columbia University Press, 1941), p. 223, line 31.

24 the nobleness of . . . 'Stanzas from the Grande Chartreuse,' *The Poems of Matthew Arnold*, ed. Miriam Allott (London: Longman, 1979), p. 306, line 107.

24 the far-off . . . *In Memoriam*,1. 8.

24 what Carlyle . . . Isobel Armstrong, 'Re-Reading Victorian Poetry,' in Joanne Shattock (ed.), *Dickens and Other Victorians* (London: Macmillan, 1988), p. 126. I acknowledge that this account, as Hirsch points out, is also informed by the Victorians' – and, in particular, John Donaldson's – phonocentric denigration of writing itself as 'always degenerate and outward' (p. 241). I recognize too that, as Linda Dowling has argued, the new philology's scientific approach to language likewise seemed to the Victorians 'to make language disturbingly independent' ('Victorian Oxford and the Science of Language,' *PMLA* 97 (1982): 1.167). However, although phonocentrism and new philology both influence Tennyson my claim is that the poem's sense of an alienated language is also informed by the 'iron' hour of the machine.

24 remorseless *iron* hour . . . *In Memoriam*, 84.14–16 (my italics).

24 with a flitting . . . Tennyson, *Maud* [1855], 2.2.81–85.

24   was meant to . . . Cited in Hallam Tennyson, *Alfred Lord Tennyson: A Memoir* (London, 1897), 1.304–305.

24   truth in closest . . . *In Memoriam*, 36. 6–8 (my italics).

25   *In Memoriam* longs . . . Armstrong, *Language*, p. 184.

25   in both the . . . Hirsch, p. 253.

25   Man's word is . . . 'The Coming of Arthur,' line 132.

25   matter-moulded forms . . . *In Memoriam*, 95.46.

25   conviction that the . . . Katerina Clark and Michael Holquist, *Mikhail Bakhtin* (London: Harvard University Press, 1984), p. 225.

25   Christ, uniquely, is . . . Terry Eagleton, *The Body as Language: Outline of a New Left Theology* (London: Sheed and Ward, 1970), p. 12.

25   The most ancient . . . M. M. Bakhtin, *The Dialogic Imagination: Four Essays*, ed. Michael Holquist (Austin: University of Texas Press, 1981), p. 50.

25   ring out my . . . *In Memoriam*,106.19–20.

25   Sorrow . . . sports . . . Ibid., 48. 1–9.

25   Lesser griefs . . . Ibid., 20.1.

25   Love . . . played . . . Ibid., 125.11.

25   grief with symbols . . . Ibid., 85.95.

25   the poem . . . Armstrong, *Language*, p. 173.

25   My words . . . *In Memoriam*, 52.3–4.

25   The lightest wave . . . Ibid., 49.5.

26   Mute symbols of . . . Ibid., Epilogue, 58.

26   there oft seemed . . . Ibid., 125.3–4.

26   Tennyson's strategy for . . . Sinfield, p. 86.

26   empiricism of Locke . . . To be more specific, it has to do with Locke's empiricist insistence that words may be traced back to sense data, and Chambers' naturalistic view that human language only developed through an accident of evolution. For a discussion of Locke's influence on *In Memoriam*'s account of language see Donald S. Hair, '"Matter-moulded forms of speech,"' *Victorian Poetry* 27 (1989): 1–16.

26   the vulgar dialects . . . See Dowling, pp. 166–71; although Dowling's main concern is with developments in the 1860s, the new philology was well represented in the 1830s and 40s by Benjamin Thorpe and John Kemble. For an excellent discussion of Kemble's influence on *In Memoriam*, see William A. Wilson, 'Victorian Philology and the Anxiety of Language in Tennyson's *In Memoriam*,' *TSLL* 30 (1988): 28–48.

26   the Word [that] . . . *In Memoriam*, 36.9–14.

27   without him . . . John 1:3.

27   that in poetry . . . Sinfield, p. 89.

27   practice . . . expert . . . *In Memoriam*, 75.5–6.

27   force that would . . . Ibid., 73.16.

27   signification . . . is . . . Raymond Williams, *Marxism and Literature* (London: Oxford University Press, 1977), p. 38.

27   so pure a . . . *Robert Browning: The Poems*, ed. John Pettigrew and Thomas J. Collins (Harmondsworth: Penguin, 1981), line 189, lines 590–591, 575–576.

27   language [is] the . . . Lord Macaulay, *Essays, Historical and Literary* (London, n.d.), p. 3; William Johnson Fox, review of *Poems, Chiefly Lyrical*

(1830) in the *Westminster Review*, reprinted in Isobel Armstrong (ed.), *Victorian Scrutinies* (London: Athlone, 1972), p. 71.

27 Is this an . . . *In Memoriam*, 21.13–16.

28 He is not . . . Ibid., 7.9–12 (my italics).

28 comedy tends to . . . Northrop Frye, *Anatomy of Criticism: Four Essays* (Harmondsworth: Penguin, 1990), p. 27.

28 the monetary sign . . . As Smith writes, 'Labour . . . is the real measure of the exchangeable value of all commodities' – *An Inquiry Into the Nature and Causes of the Wealth of Nations* [1776], (New York: Random House, 1937), p. 34.

28 the grand old . . . *In Memoriam*, 111.22.

28 shape[s] the whisper . . . Ibid., 64.12.

28 all within was . . . Ibid., 87.18–20.

28 But iron dug . . . Ibid., 118.20–5.

28 like coarsest clothes . . . Ibid., 5.10.

28 sealed within the . . . Ibid., 56.20.

28 every kiss of . . . Ibid., 117.11.

28 out of darkness . . . Ibid., 124.23.

28 all . . . is toil . . . Ibid., 128.24.

28 offered . . . the space . . . Sinfield, p. 19.

29 Not on the . . . Robert Browning, 'Rabbi Ben Ezra,' lines 133–134.

29 the under-classes . . . Thomas Carlyle, *The Works*, ed. H. D. Traill, 31 vols (London, 1896–1901), 29.122.

29 the radical distinction . . . Williams, p. 22.

29 Saussure's notion of . . . See Eagleton, *Benjamin*, p. 152.

29 noble letters . . . *In Memoriam*, 95.24.

29 noble type . . . Ibid., Epilogue, 138.

29 the wealth / Of . . . Ibid., Epilogue, 102–103.

29 griefs that may . . . Ibid., 20.1.

29 that roar which . . . George Eliot, *Middlemarch* [1874], ed. W. J. Harvey (Harmondsworth: Penguin, 1965), p. 226.

29 nameless trouble . . . *In Memoriam*, 4.13.

29 I am nameless . . . *Maud*, 1.4.118.

29 a new name . . . Carlyle, *The Works*, 29.119.

29 the lesser griefs . . . *In Memoriam*, 20.1–4.

30 I cannot think . . . Ibid., 123.12.

30 'T is . . . Robert Browning, *The Ring and the Book* [1868–9], ed. Richard D. Altick (Harmondsworth: Penguin, 1971), line 32.

30 objects brought to . . . 'Death in the Desert,' lines 230–232.

30 a world where . . . Martha Vicinus, *The Industrial Muse: A Study of Nineteenth-Century British Working Class Literature* (London: Croom Helm, 1974), p. 276.

30 as the triumph . . . As paraphrased by Douglas Kellner, *Jean Baudrillard: From Marxism to Postmodernism and Beyond* (Cambridge: Polity, 1989), p. 155.

30 That [which] may be . . . *In Memoriam*, 20. 9–10.

30 My words are . . . Ibid., 52.2–3.

30 word by word . . . Ibid., 95.33–34.

30 love's dumb cry . . . Ibid., 95.27–32.

31   love . . . is . . . A. Dwight Culler, *The Poetry of Tennyson* (New Haven: Yale University Press, 1977), pp. 12–13.

31   the only consummation . . . Herbert F. Tucker, *Tennyson and the Doom of Romanticism* (Cambridge, Mass.: Harvard University Press, 1988), p. 36.

31   man's desire . . . Lacan, *Écrits*, p. 175; Lacan, *Four Fundamental Concepts*, p. 154. As Eagleton remarks, the 'potentially endless movement from one signifier to another is what Lacan means by desire' (*Literary Theory*, p. 167).

31   [up]on that which . . . *In Memoriam*, 95.36–39 (my italics).

31   the wish too . . . Ibid., 95.13.

31   'woman' [is] that . . . As quoted and translated by Toril Moi, *Sexual/Textual Politics* (London: Methuen, 1985), p. 163.

31   Dumb is that . . . *In Memoriam*, Epilogue, 106.

31   And rise, O . . . Ibid., Epilogue, 109.

31   and strangely on . . . Ibid., 95.27, 25–6.

31   lets the other . . . Hélène Cixous, 'The Laugh of the Medusa' (1976) in Elaine Marks and Isabelle de Courtivron (eds.), *New French Feminisms* (Brighton: Harvester, 1980), p. 250. I acknowledge two riders to this argument: firstly, that Cixous often claims that by 'she' is meant not 'femininity' but 'bisexuality'; and secondly, that *écriture féminine* is at times decidedly homogeneous rather than heterogeneous (see Moi, p. 119).

31   work[s] on the . . . As quoted and translated by Moi, p. 108; by this Cixous means, as Moi puts it, 'texts that . . . revel in the pleasures of textuality.'

32   capable of [being] . . . Cixous, 'Medusa,' p. 251.

32   the Word wrought . . . *In Memoriam*, 36.9–11.

32   the spouse and . . . *The Book of Common Prayer* (London, n.d.), p. 367.

32   woman must write . . . Hélène Cixous, '*Sorties*: Out and Out: Attacks/Ways Out/Forays,' in Catherine Belsey and Jane Moore, eds., *The Feminist Reader* (London: Macmillan, 1989), p. 113.

32   that articulated body . . . Eagleton, *Body as Language*, p. 67.

32   single church . . . *In Memoriam*, 104.3–4.

32   priestess . . . Ibid., 3.2.

32   chalice . . . Ibid., 10.15.

32   altar . . . Ibid., 55.15.

32   catacombs . . . Ibid., 58.4.

32   endless feast . . . Ibid., 47.9.

32   the dark church . . . Ibid., 67.15.

32   the joyous affirmation . . . Derrida, *Writing*, p. 292.

32   the most living . . . *In Memoriam*, Epilogue, 52–56.

33   The fool that . . . Ibid., 69. 8–12.

33   One body . . . *Common Prayer*, p. 380.

33   One church . . . Edward Plumptre (1921–91), 'Thy hand, O God, has guided,' *The New English Hymnal* (Norwich: England, 1986); for examples of very similar phrasing in Victorian hymns see nos. 346, 468, 484; Carlyle, *Works*, 2.369. This continuing interest of Carlyle's is located and discussed by David Riede in 'Transgression, Authority, and the Church of Literature in Carlyle' where Riede also quotes Carlyle's assertion that 'the history of Literature . . . is our proper Church History' – Jerome McGann (ed.), *Victorian Connections* (Charlottesville: University of Virginia Press, 1989), p. 109.

33 makes the Church . . . In so doing the poem only returns to its opening stanza, which is very reminiscent, in syntax and diction, of a collect.

33 negatively theological . . . I say 'negatively theological' in that, as several commentators have recently remarked, there is a distinct similarity between the infinite deferral of signification in the Derridean scheme and the *via negativa*'s perpetual refusal finally to describe God.

IV Hostage of the Word

34 to speak logoi . . . Michael Edwards, *Of Making Many Books* (London: Macmillan, 1990), p. 179.

34 belief that language . . . T. R. Wright, *Theology and Literature* (Oxford: Blackwell, 1988), p. 32.

34 God is what . . . Robert P. Scharleman, 'The Being of God When God is not Being God,' in Thomas J. J. Altizer *et al.*, eds. *Deconstruction and Theology* (New York: Crossroads, 1982), p. 102.

34 The death of . . . Charles Winquist, 'Body, Text and Imagination' in Altizer, p. 73.

34 Man has become . . . Lecture delivered on 17 June 1961, quoted in Smith and Handelman, *Psychoanalysis and Religion* (Baltimore: Johns Hopkins University Press 1990), p. 71.

35 In the beginning . . . Jacques Derrida, *Writing*, p. 67.

35 it was certainly . . . Jacques Lacan, *Écrits: A Selection* [1966], tr. Alan Sheridan (London: Tavistock, 1977), p. 61.

35 In the beginning . . . Julia Kristeva, *Au commencement était l'amour: psychanalyse et foi* (Paris: Hachette, 1985).

35 violently selected . . . Jacques Derrida, *Glas* [1974], tr. John P. Leavey and Richard Rand (Lincoln: University of Nebraska Press, 1986), pp. 196b-197b. For examples of the recurring interest in John's Gospel, see *Glas*, pp. 74a -77a, 107b, 148b.

35 for us the . . . Lacan, cited in Smith and Handelman, p. 70.

35 Literature . . . by refusing . . . Barthes, *Image-Music-Text*, p. 147.

35 the Other . . . Jane Mitchell and Jacqueline Rose (eds), *Feminine Sexuality: Jacques Lacan and the école freudienne* (London: Macmillan, 1982), p. 140.

35 the intelligible face . . . Jacques Derrida, *Of Grammatology* [1976], tr. Gayatri Chakravorty Spivak (Baltimore: Johns Hopkins University Press, 1976), p. 13.

35 one may hold . . . Kevin Hart, *The Trespass of the Sign: Deconstruction, Theology and Philosophy* (Cambridge: Cambridge University Press, 1989), p. 28

36 John's Gospel . . . Edwards, pp. 183–4.

36 Just as Heidegger . . . Heidegger's distinction is made clear by G. J. Seidel, who writes that 'for Heidegger . . . there is the true Logos ['the . . . Heraclitean . . . Logos so intimately connected with Physis'] . . . and there is the Logos which has been falsified to mean reason, concept, judgement, etc.' (G. J. Seidel, *Martin Heidegger and the Pre-Socratics* (Lincoln: University of Nebraska Press, 1964), pp. 87–8). For René Girard's distinction, see *Things Hidden Since the Foundation of the World* [1978], tr. S. Bann and M. Metteer (London: Athlone, 1988), pp. 263–9. One must not

forget that 'the New Testament writers never use the term Logos to denote of "reason" or "thought" . . . but always denote by it "speech," "utterance," or "word"' (H. D. M. Spence and J. Sell, *The New Pulpit Commentary: The Gospel of St John* (London, 1907), p. 5). I acknowledge that one must also distinguish within the Greek *Logos* since in the writings of Heraclitus, for instance, it is by no means a necessarily totalising or foundational term. This is made clear, of course, by Heidegger who translates the Heraclitean *Logos* as 'the Laying that gathers' and that therefore 'assembles . . . by bringing things and letting them lie before us . . . [in such a way that] each being can be joined and sent into its own' – Martin Heidegger, *Early Greek Thinking: The Dawn of Western Philosophy*, tr. D. F. Krell and F. A. Capuzzi (San Francisco: Harper, 1975), p. 72. 'Thus,' as John Caputo comments, 'the [Heraclitean] *Logos* does not refer to some kind of systematic principle which imposes a unity of order upon things in the manner of Hegel's *Vernunft*, of Spinozistic necessity, or of Newtonian determinism' – John D. Caputo, *Heidegger and Aquinas: An Essay on Overcoming Metaphysics* (New York: Fordham University Press, 1982), p. 195.

36   [although] John writes . . . Derrida, *Glas*, p. 75a.

36   a God not . . . John-Luc Marion, *God Without Being: Hors-Texte* [1982], tr. Thomas A. Carlson (Chicago: University of Chicago Press, 1991), p. 61; see also Robbins p. 127.

36   faith does not . . . Marion, p. 61.

36   original, heterogeneous . . . Jacques Derrida, 'Deconstruction and the Other' (1981) in Richard Kearney (ed.), *Dialogues with Contemporary Continental Thinkers: The Phenomenological Heritage* (Manchester: Manchester University Press, 1988), p. 117.

36   things which are . . . 1 Corinthians 1:28.

36   I am quite . . . Simone Weil, *Waiting for God* [1950], tr. Emma Craufurd (New York: Harper and Row, 1973), p. 34.

36   if God [were] . . . Derrida, *Writing*, p. 108.

36   Ye shall seek . . . John 7:34.

37   outer darkness . . . Derrida, *Of Grammatology*, pp. 45, 101.

37   What I have . . . John 19:22.

37   he is not . . . Mark 16:6.

37   the presence of . . . Stephen D. Moore, *Literary Criticism and the Gospels: The Theoretical Challenge* (New Haven: Yale University Press, 1989), p. 162.

37   risk[s] death in . . . Jacques Derrida, *Speech and Phenomena and Other Essays on Husserl's Theory of Signs* [1967], tr. David B. Allison (Evanston, Ill.: Northwestern University Press, 1973), p. 77.

37   have we ever . . . *Spurs: Nietzsche's Styles / Éperons: Les Styles de Nietzsche* [1978], tr. Barbara Harlow (Chicago: University of Chicago Press, 1979), p. 90.

37   God has not . . . Mitchell, p. 154.

37   Reb Derrissa . . . He thus signs his two essays on Edmond Jabès – see Derrida, *Writing*.

37   has been exploring . . . Graham Ward, 'Why is Derrida Important for Theology,' *Theology* 95 (1992): 268.

37   graveyard [or] perhaps . . . Geoffrey Hartman, *Saving the Text: Literature /*

Derrida /Philosophy (London: Johns Hopkins University Press, 1981), pp. 9, 19.

37   crown of thorns . . . Katerina Clark and Michael Holquist, *Mikhail Bakhtin* (London: Harvard University Press, 1984), p. 250.

37   I am dispersed . . . *Roland Barthes by Roland Barthes* [1975], tr. Richard Howard (London: Macmillan, 1977), p. 143.

38   Descartes inaugurates . . . Lacan, *The Four Fundamental,* p. 226.

38   where I do . . . Clark, p. 144.

38   we are approaching . . . Edwards, pp. 101–24.

38   yet not I . . . Galatians 2:20.

38   Christ made himself . . . Philippians 2: 5,7 [NIV].

38   the kenotic Christ . . . 'One man, at least, has understood her [the mystic] . . . that most female of Men, the Son. . . . In his crucifixion he opens up a path of redemption to her. . . . She is transformed into Him in her love. . . . In her and/or outside her, as, in her jouissance, she loses all sense of corporeal boundary' – Luce Irigaray, *Speculum of the Other Woman* [1974], tr. Gillian C. Gill (Ithaca: Cornell University Press, 1985), pp. 199–201. As Toril Moi comments, 'Christ undoes specular logic, and the mystic's self-abasement re-enacts his passion' (p. 137).

38   Christian theology . . . Hart, p. 93.

38   it is where . . . Cited in John B. Cobb, Jr., 'A Theology of Story: Crossan and Beardslee' in Richard Spencer (ed.), *Orientation by Disorientation* (Pittsburgh: University of Pittsburgh, 1980), p. 153.

38   new version of . . . Wright, p. 30.

38   negative atheology . . . Derrida, *Speech,* p. 135; *Writing,* p. 297.

38   the world knew . . . John 1:10–11.

38   the Johannine logos . . . Girard, p. 271.

39   living with the . . . David Jasper, *The Study of Literature and Religion* (London: Macmillan, 1989), p. 106.

39   do not hold . . . John 20:17 [NIV].

39   I pray God . . . Meister Eckhart, *The Essential Sermons, Commentaries, Treatises, and Defense,* tr. E. College and B. McGinn (New York: Paulist, 1981), p. 202.

39   deconstruction . . . Eric Ives, 'Modern Historical Scholarship and the Christian Gospel,' *The Glass* 6 (1972): 42.

39   this is the . . . John 3:19.

39   Verily, I say . . . John 10:7.

39   these things I . . . John 15:17.

39   a dionysian Christianity . . . Cited in Altizer, p. 75.

39   we do not . . . John Dominic Crossan, *The Dark Interval: Toward a Theology of Story* (Niles, Ill.: Argus Communications, 1975), p. 39.

39   deconstruction is among . . . Eagleton, *Walter Benjamin,* p. 133.

40   What is laid . . . Kafka, *The Great Wall,* p. 167.

40   everyone on the . . . John 18:37 [NIV].

40   I am come . . . Luke 12:52.

40   there was a . . . John 7: 43, 9:16.

40   I will not . . . John 14: 30.

40   My time is . . . John 7: 6.

40   [always] has some . . . Bakhtin, cited in Clark, p. 225.

40   this conviction that . . . Clark, p. 86.
40   Christ, uniquely, is . . . Eagleton, *Body as Language*, p. 12.
41   overlook the phase . . . Derrida, *Positions*, tr. Alan Bass (Chicago: University of Chicago Press, 1972), pp. 41–2.
41   saddened, negative . . . Derrida, *Writing*, p. 292.
41   in the final analysis . . . Altizer, p. 3.
41   the death of God . . . Derrida, *Writing*, p. 184.
41   it would not . . . Derrida, *Of Grammatology*, p. 68.
41   ground of . . . Robert Detweiler (ed.), 'Derrida and Biblical Studies,' *Semeia* 23 (1982): 16.
41   My God . . . Matthew 27.46.
42   saddened and . . . Derrida, *Writing*, p. 292.
42   Good Friday . . . Derrida, *Glas*, p. 96a.
42   Derrida's theory . . . As Nealon writes, 'for Derrida, the privilege is momentary – the first of two gestures. The upshot of undecidability is the ethical gesture toward alterity, the necessary structuring position of difference within sameness' – Jeffrey T. Nealon, 'The Discipline of Deconstruction,' *PMLA* 107 (1992): 1277, n.19.
42   Paul de Man . . . 'A deconstruction,' writes Paul de Man, 'always has for its target to reveal the existence of hidden articulations and fragmentations within assumedly monadic totalities' – *Allegories of Reading. Figural Language in Rousseau, Nietzsche and Proust* (New Haven: Yale University Press, 1978), p. 249.
42   unquestioned possibility . . . Jacques Derrida, *Of Spirit: Heidegger and the Question* [1987], tr. Geoffrey Bennington and Rachel Bowlby (Chicago: Chicago University Press, 1989), p. 10.
42   nontruth . . . Jacques Derrida, *Dissemination* [1972], tr. Barbara Johnson (London: Athlone, 1981), p. 168.
42   a violent, parodic . . . Derrida, *Glas*, 147b.
42   Golgotha . . . As we have seen, Hartman talks of a 'Golgotha of dissociated names and notions,' while Raschke argues that 'writing . . . is the ongoing enfleshment and displacement – shall we say the "crucifixion"? – of the eternal "Word" by its diffusion within and through time' – Carl A. Raschke, 'The Deconstruction of God' in Altizer, p. 15.
42   is not the . . . Derrida, *Writing*, p. 297.
42   It is finished . . . John 19:30
42   namely, sin . . . See 2 Corinthians 1: 5, 21.
42   cup pass . . . Matthew 26:39.
43   one naked . . . Derrida, *Writing*, p. 107.
43   the bad solitude . . . Ibid., p. 91.
43   God's name . . . 'The subordination,' writes Derrida, 'of the trace to the full presence summed up in the logos . . . such are the gestures required by an onto-theology determining the . . . meaning of being as presence . . . as life without difference: another name for death, historical metonymy wherever God's name holds death in check' (*Of Grammatology*, p. 71).
43   Calvary of . . . Derrida, *Glas*, p. 261a. Hegel's phrase comes at the end of the 'Absolute Knowing' chapter of *Phenomenology of Spirit*.
43   If any man . . . Matthew 16:24.

43 the shrine . . . Frank Kermode, *The Genesis of Secrecy: On the Interpretation of Narrative* (Cambridge, Mass.: Harvard UP, 1979), p. 123.

44 the joyous . . . Derrida, *Of Grammatology*, p. 292.

44 a certain . . . Derrida, *Margins*, p. 27.

V Why Wait for an Angel?

47 I define . . . Lyotard, *The Postmodern Condition*, p. xxiv.

47 I am . . . John 14.6.

47 the question . . . For a fuller summary of the novel see Tony Tanner, *Thomas Pynchon* (London: Methuen, 1982), pp. 56–7.

47 communication is . . . Thomas Pynchon, *The Crying of Lot 49* (London: Picador, 1979), p. 72.

48 wait[s in vain] . . . Ibid., p. 73.

48 the television . . . See ibid. pp. 74, 6,10.

48 swung among . . . Ibid., p. 24.

48 the time she'd . . . Ibid. p. 14.

48 the phone buzzed . . . Ibid., p. 62.

48 *miracle* of . . . Ibid. p. 124 – my italics.

48 the trace . . . Philippa Berry, 'Deserts of the Heart,' *Times Higher Educational Supplement*, 28 December 1990, p. 7.

48 several critics . . . See, for instance, Valentine Cunningham, *In the Reading Gaol* (Oxford: Blackwell, 1994), pp. 363–410; Kevin Hart, *The Trespass the Sign* (Cambridge: Cambridge University Press, 1989); and Phillipa Berry and Andrew Wernick (eds.), *Shadow of Spirit: Postmodernism and Religion* (London: Routledge, 1992).

48 to refuse . . . Roland Barthes, 'Death of the Author' in *Image-Music-Text*, p. 147.

48 another mode . . . *Lot 49*, p. 126.

48 frightful Pentecost . . . Ibid., p. 45.

48 49 days . . . See Edward Mendelson, 'The Sacred, the Profane, and *The Crying of Lot 49*' in Kenneth Baldwin and David K. Kirby (eds.), *Individual and Community* (Durham, North Carolina: Duke University Press, 1975), p. 208.

49 zany paraclete . . . *Lot 49*, pp. 45, 81, 82.

49 the later Greeks . . . It is important to note that, for the early Greeks, in particular Heraclitus, the *logos* does not necessarily have this meaning: as John D. Caputo comments, 'the [Heraclitean] *logos* does not refer to some kind of systematic principle which imposes a unity of order upon things' – *Heidegger and Aquinas* (New York: Fordham University Press, 1982), p. 195. Perhaps, then, *Lot 49*'s 'epileptic Word' recovers something of the earlier Heraclitean meaning of *logos*.

49 odd, religious . . . *Lot 49*, p. 15.

49 all manner . . . Ibid., p. 12.

49 ladies' john . . . Ibid., p. 61.

49 high magic . . . Ibid., p. 89.

49 cue[s] the . . . Ibid., pp. 15,19,84.

49 seek[s] . . . the Word . . . David Seed, *The Fictional Labyrinths of Thomas Pynchon* (London: Macmillan, 1988), p. 132.

50 Word, or speech . . . In John's Gospel the *Logos* speaks *logoi*; thus the same word is used to describe both Christ and utterance, or speech.

50 distorted by power . . . Foucault argues that '"Truth" is linked in a circular relation with systems of power which produce and sustain it' – Michel Foucault, *Power/Knowledge*, ed. Colin Gordon (Brighton: Harvester Wheatsheaf, 1980), p. 84.

50 a hieroglyphic sense . . . *Lot 49*, p. 15 (my italics).

50 project a world . . . Ibid., p. 56.

50 made to hold . . . Ibid., p. 46.

50 the stillness . . . Ibid., p. 31.

50 the angel descends . . . See John 5:1–9.

50 a descending angel . . . *Lot 49*, p. 127.

51 promise of hierophany . . . Ibid., p. 20.

51 feel[s] him close . . . Ibid., p. 21.

51 busful of Negroes . . . Ibid., p. 84.

51 it was a . . . Ibid., p. 85.

51 mutuality, or community . . . For a good summary of the debate surrounding this possibility see Terry Eagleton, *The Ideology of the Aesthetic* (Oxford: Blackwell, 1990), pp. 403–5.

51 the . . . face of . . . *Lot 49*, p. 62.

51 a circle of . . . Ibid., pp. 81–2.

52 Anarchosyndicalist . . . Ibid., p. 83.

52 Trystero . . . symbolised . . . Ibid., pp. 107–8.

52 a real alternative . . . Ibid., pp. 117–18.

52 Oedipa settled back . . . Ibid., p. 127.

52 its own image . . . For many cultural theorists, the cultural imperialism of America is a crucial aspect of postmodernism – see Peter Brooker (ed.), *Modernism/Postmodernism* (London: Longman, 1992), p. 24.

52 there either was . . . *Lot 49*, p. 126.

52 the oldest building . . . Ibid., p. 127.

52 El Desheredado . . . Ibid., p. 110.

53 tried to find . . . Ibid., p. 27.

53 facially deformed . . . Ibid., p. 85.

53 I can't help . . . Ibid., p. 57.

53 a jet flying . . . Ibid., p. 88.

53 a cross . . . Ibid., p. 62.

53 Inasmuch as . . . Matthew 25: 40.

53 spreads his arms . . . Ibid., p. 127.

54 spent finding . . . Ibid., p. 80.

54 she was meant . . . Ibid., p. 81.

54 the night's profusion . . . Ibid., p. 85.

54 Oedipa . . . had . . . Ibid., p. 83.

54 Oedipus *Maas* . . . It is, of course, the Anglican Book of Common Prayer that refers to the eucharist as a 'perpetual memorial.' In the portion of *Lot 49* that was first published in *Esquire Magazine* our 'heroine' was called Oedipa Mass.

54 holy man . . . *Lot 49*, p. 15.

54 like a host . . . Ibid., p. 46.

54 as if the . . . Ibid., p. 68.

54 body of Christ . . . See 1 Corinthians 1: 12–27.

54 Your fly . . . Ibid., p. 126.

54 Calavera . . . Mendelson, p. 192.

54 the . . . chlorine . . . *Lot 49*, p. 84.

54 tabernacle . . . According to *Oxford English Dictionary*, a tabernacle is not only a 'canopied niche' but a 'receptacle for . . . eucharistic elements.'

54 like the church . . . Ibid., p. 83.

54 encrypted . . . Ibid p. 123.

54 really tuned in . . . Ibid., p. 15, my italics.

55 the Tristero also . . . Mendelson, p. 190.

56 it is more . . . Walter Benjamin, 'Surrealism' [1929] in *One Way Street*, p. 230.

VI Reading the Long Way Round

57 It may . . . William Makepeace Thackeray, *Vanity Fair* [1847–8], ed. J. I. M. Stewart (Harmondsworth: Penguin. 1968), p. 497.

57 finds itself . . . *Vanity Fair*, p. 213.

57 We do not . . . Ibid., p. 346.

57 Grand Tour . . . Thackeray himself describes his visit to Weimar in 1830–31 as 'a curtailed version' of the Grand Tour' – see William Makepeace Thackeray, *Memoirs of a Victorian Gentleman*, ed. Margaret Forster (London: Seeker and Warburg, 1978), p. 35.

57 Roundabout Chapter . . . *Vanity Fair*, p. 516; see *The Roundabout Papers* (*The Works of William Makepeace Thackeray*, 26 vols (London: Smith Elder, 1898–99), xii), which are a collection of sham histories written in the form of memoirs.

57 narrative is linear . . . Thomas Carlyle, *The Works*, ed. H.D. Traill, 30 vols (London: Chapman and Hall, 1896–1901), xxvii. 89.

57 the time . . . Derrida, *Of Grammatology*, p. xc.

57 We are [left] . . . *Vanity Fair*, pp. 453, 557.

57 go[es] backwards . . . Ibid., p. 293.

57 amiable object . . . Ibid., p. 229.

57 What were the . . . Ibid., pp. 559–60.

58 live 'without God' . . . *The Letters and Private Papers of William Makepeace Thackeray*, ed. Gordon N. Ray, 4 vols (Cambridge: Cambridge University Press, 1945–46), 2. 309.

58 Veneering [. . .] instructed . . . Charles Dickens, *Our Mutual Friend* [1864-5], ed. Stephen Gill (Harmondsworth: Penguin, 1970), p. 295.

58 the 'massacre of . . . David Thomson, *England in the Nineteenth Century* (Harmondsworth: Penguin, 1950), p. 39.

58 associations with Waterloo . . . See Clive Emsley, *British Society and the French Wars* (London: Macmillan, 1979), p. 176 and Joyce Marlow, *The Peterloo Massacre* (London: Rapp and Whiting, 1970), pp. 13, 93–4.

58 John Lees . . . Marlow, p 13.

58 so little nineteenth . . . Emsley p. 171.

58 august jobbers . . . *Vanity Fair*, p. 328.

59 go no farther . . . Ibid., pp. 346–7.

59 our women . . . Ibid., p. 216.

59   this is what . . . Ibid., p. 792.

59   the English line . . . Ibid., p. 386.

59   the sense of . . . Robin Gilmour, *Thackeray: Vanity Fair* (London: Edward Arnold, 1982), p. 28.

59   [The] final onset . . . Ibid., p. 386.

59   Becky is a . . . Gilmour for instance, remarks that 'like Napoleon, Becky is an upstart challenging the old order,' Gilmour, p. 14.

59   In flinging . . . *Vanity Fair*, p. 45.

59   standardized English . . . 'Johnson's *Dictionary* [. . .] was what its age demanded – a standard and standardizing dictionary' – James Sledd and Gwin Kolb, *Dr Johnson's Dictionary* (Chicago: University of Chicago Press, 1955), p. 44.

59   The whole structure . . . Cited in Anthony Froude, Thomas *Carlyle: A History of His Life in London*, 2 vols (New York: Harper, 1855), 1. 21.

59   Continental tour . . . *Vanity Fair*, p. 740.

60   des sangviches . . . Ibid., p. 716.

60   Newmero . . . Ibid., p. 756.

60   The little . . . Ibid., p. 766.

60   the Tower . . . Ibid., p. 714.

60   though he was . . . Ibid., p. 716.

60   Innumerable Philosophies . . . Carlyle, *Works*, xxviii, 32–33.

60   Count de . . . *Vanity Fair*, p. 726.

60   Princess . . . Ibid., p. 732.

60   letters in the . . . J. Hillis Miller, *Ariadne's Thread: Story Lines* (New Haven, CT: Yale University Press, 1992), p. 8.

60   taken together . . . Joseph F. Graham (ed.), *Difference in Translation* (Ithaca, NY: Cornell University Press, 1985), p. 206.

60   letter *can* always . . . Derrida, *The Post Card*, p. 123.

60   a lady who . . . *Vanity Fair*, p. 774.

61   our little wanderer . . . Ibid., p. 747.

61   this little Ishmaelite . . . Ibid., p. 779.

61   Celestial City . . . In Bunyan's *Pilgrim's Progress* (1678–84) 'Vanity Fair' is, of course, just a stop on the way to Christian's ultimate destination – namely, the 'Celestial City' that is heaven.

61   he was nowhere . . . *Vanity Fair*, p. 551.

61   was accustomed to . . . Ibid., p. 497.

61   Rebecca thought about . . . Ibid., p. 487.

61   she had been . . . Ibid., p. 49.

61   blushed . . . Ibid., p. 67.

61   thinking of old . . . Ibid., pp. 486–7.

61   awes and terrors . . . Ibid., p. 46.

61   Mr Hammerdown . . . Ibid., p. 205.

61   Sir Huddlestone . . . Ibid., p. 531.

61   Sir Something . . . Ibid., p. 64.

61   you and I . . . Ibid., p. 385.

62   each respected . . . Ibid., p. 186.

62   reader[s] of a . . . Ibid., p. 186.

62   If the Doctor . . . Ibid., p. 46.

62   we should all . . . Ibid., p. 229.

62   Thackeray's pervasive . . . Jack P. Rawlins, *Thackeray's Novels: A Fiction that is True* (Berkeley: University of California Press, 1974), pp. 202–15.

62   the doctor will . . . *Vanity Fair*, p. 700.

62   Your end . . . Ibid., p. 701.

62   Two months after . . . Ibid., p. 753.

62   a protection . . . Michel Foucault, *Language, Counter-Memory, Practice: Selected Essays and Interviews*, ed. Donald F. Bouchard and Sherry Simon (Ithaca, NY: Cornell University Press), p. 117.

63   our own funeral . . . *Vanity Fair*, p. 704.

63   the addressee . . . Derrida, *Margins*, p. 315.

63   living substance . . . Freud, *Works*, xviii, 38–9.

63   The great glass . . . *Vanity Fair*, p. 502.

63   cannot be written . . . Derrida, *Of Grammatology*, p. 87.

63   hollowed into . . . Lacan remarks that language is 'what hollows being into desire,' quoted in Eagleton, *Literary Theory*, pp. 167–8.

63   the long *indirect* . . . Freud, *Works*, xviii, 10.

63   annual tour . . . *Vanity Fair*, p. 714.

64   Ah! *Vanitas Vanitatum!* . . . Ibid., p.797.

64   suffer the . . . Mark 10:14.

64   Come back . . . *Vanity Fair*, p. 185.

64   G.O. . . . Ibid., p. 711.

64   Even so . . . Charlotte Brontë, *Jane Eyre*, ed. Q. D. Leavis (Harmondsworth: Penguin, 1966), p. 477; she quotes, of course, from Revelation 22.20.

VII   Half-Way House

67   Philosophy . . . represents . . . Jacques Derrida, *The Truth in Painting* [1978], tr. G. Bennington and I. McLeod (Chicago: University of Chicago Press, 1987), p. 39.

67   Hardy's most . . . Martin Seymour-Smith, *Hardy* (London: Bloomsbury, 1994), p. 266.

67   melodrama and philosophy . . . Review of *A Laodicean* in *The Observer*, 2 April 1882.

67   a notable . . . Thomas Hardy, *A Laodicean* [1881], ed. John Schad (Harmondsworth: Penguin, 1997), p. 86.

67   philosopher's stone . . . Ibid., p. 39.

67   stylistic eclecticism . . . J. B. Bullen, *The Expressive Eye: Fiction and Perception in the Work of Thomas Hardy* (Oxford: Clarendon Press, 1986), p. 122.

67   restoration . . . She initially plans to add 'a Creek colonnade' (*A Laodicean*, p. 71) to this Norman castle.

67   the bottomless depth . . . Ibid., p. 77.

67   grounded structure . . . The Enlightenment philosopher Immanuel Kant asserts, for example, that 'it is the common fate of human reason to complete its speculative structures as speedily as may be, and only afterwards to enquire whether the foundations are reliable' – *Critique of Pure Reason* [1787], tr. N. K. Smith (London: Macmillan, 1929), p. 47.

67   flights of . . . *A Laodicean*, p. 242.

67   philosophical . . . Ibid., p. 263.

67 gymnastics . . . Ibid., p.150.

67 human beings . . . Ibid., p. 104.

68 reworking of philosophy . . . See ibid., p. 206 notes 5–6.

68 kill[ed] the Spirit . . . Friedrich Nietzsche, *Thus Spoke Zarathustra* [1883–5], tr. R.J. Hollingdale (Harmondsworth: Penguin, 1961), p. 68.

68 compelled [him] . . . Florence Emily Hardy, *The Life of Thomas Hardy 1840–1928* [1928–30] (London: Macmillan, 1962), p. 145.

68 an enchanted . . . *A Laodicean*, p. 105.

68 unpedastaled . . . Ibid., p. 125.

68 a man [at] . . . Ibid., p. 215.

68 refus[al of the] . . . Annie Escuret, 'Thomas Hardy and J. M. W. Turner' in L. St. John Butler (ed.), *Alternative Hardy* (London: Macmillan, 1989), p. 214.

68 lack [or suspicion] . . . Michael Millgate, *Thomas Hardy: A Biography* (Oxford: Oxford University Press, 1985), p. 132.

68 it was brought . . . *A Laodicean*, p. 3.

68 of a thickness . . . Ibid., p. 83.

68 metaphysic . . . Hardy to Roden Noel, 3 April 1892, *The Collected Letters of Thomas Hardy*, ed. Richard Little Purdy and Michael Millgate, 7 vols (Oxford: Clarendon Press, 1978–1988), 1. 261.

68 without any . . . Ibid., p. 227.

68 sun and air . . . Ibid., p. 39.

68 lighthouse . . . Ibid., p. 312.

68 trading houses . . . Ibid., p. 327.

68 house of cards . . . Ibid., p. 62.

68 the house of . . . Ibid., p. 322.

68 This is [both] . . . Ibid., p. 26.

68 unhomely . . . Sigmund Freud, 'The Uncanny' [1919], *Works*, xxvii.219–52.

68 '*Unheimlich*' is the . . . Ibid., p. 224.

69 they are more . . . *A Laodicean*, p. 42.

69 sinister . . . It is only in the serial edition that she is so described (see ibid., p. 395, n. 9).

69 Ah, I begin to . . . Ibid., p. 69.

69 from the beginning . . . Marsilio Ficino, 'Commentary on the Symposium,' cited in E. Panolsky, *Idea: A Concept in Art Theory* (New York: Harper and Row, 1968), p. 137.

69 haunted house . . . Freud, *Works,* xvii. 241.

69 half-charmed . . . *A Laodicean*, ibid., p. 250.

69 figures . . . lines . . . Ibid., p. 250.

70 an art which . . . Ibid., p. 61.

70 Saxon abbey . . . See p. 388, n. 1.

70 built ere the . . . Ibid., p. 24.

70 She pulled off . . . Ibid., p. 77.

70 In his meditation . . . Ibid., p. 222.

70 absolutely empty . . . Ibid., p. 353.

71 the house of . . . Martin Heidegger, 'Letter on Humanism' [1947], tr. F. A. Capuzzi in *Martin Heidegger: Basic Writings* (London: Routledge, 1993), p. 217.

71 Being a dwelling . . . Ibid., p. 36.

71   he seized her . . . Ibid., p. 77.

71   general [and simple] . . . Mark Wigley, *The Architecture of Deconstruction: Derrida's Haunt* (Cambridge, Mass.: MIT Press, 1993), p. 102.

71   battlemented parapet . . . Ibid., p. 3.

71   a shadow of . . . Ibid., p. 46.

71   a streak of . . . Ibid., p. 65.

71   in the darkness . . . Ibid., p. 82.

71   octagonal chamber . . . Ibid., p. 271.

71   painting room . . . Ibid., p. 63.

72   complicated apparatus . . . Ibid., p. 186.

72   abstract forms . . . See Plato, *The Republic*, tr. H.D. P. Lee (Harmondsworth: Penguin, 1955), pp. 278, 86.

72   phantasmic double . . . Gunning cites a digression in Balzac's novel *Le Cousin Pons* (1846) which states that Daguerre's invention has proved 'that a man or a building is. . . continuously represented by a picture in the atmosphere . . . which can be captured' – 'Phantom Images and Modern Manifestations' in P. Petro (ed.), *Fugitive Images* (Bloomington: Indiana University Press, 1995), p. 420.

72   both take their . . . Edward Cadava, 'Words of Light' in *Fugitive Images*, p. 222.

72   the absolute form . . . Plato, *Republic*, p. 282.

72   God's sun should . . . *A Laodicean*, p. 335.

72   I want to . . . See Gillian Beer, '"The Death of the Sun": Victorian Solar Physics and Solar Myth' in J. B. Bullen (ed.), *The Sun is God: Painting, Literature and Mythology in the Nineteenth Century* (Oxford: Clarendon Press, 1989), p. 159; unpublished letter to E. R. Milnes, 19 November 1862, cited in Dinah Birch, '"The Sun is God": Ruskin's Solar Mythology' in ibid., p. 112.

72   the sun-god . . . Ibid., pp. 111–13.

73   spirit photographs . . . See *Fugitive Images*, pp. 42–71.

73   the German Emperor . . . *A Laodicean*, p. 336.

73   a maker of . . . Ibid., p. 63.

73   his hair hung . . . Ibid., p. 45.

73   I can't think . . . Ibid., p. 63.

73   the profound . . . Roland Barthes, *Camera Lucida: Reflections on Photography* [1980], tr. R. Howard (New York: Hill and Wang, 1981), p. 13.

73   black and white . . . *A Laodicean*, p. 234.

73   transcript of . . . Ibid., p. 137.

73   libellous . . . Ibid., p. 336.

73   not to arrive . . . According to Derrida, 'a letter can always not arrive at its destination' – Jacques Derrida, *The Post Card: From Socrates to Freud and Beyond* [1980], tr. A. Bass (Chicago: University of Chicago Press, 1980), p. 123.

73   dull if not . . . For example, in A. C. Baugh's, *A Literary History of England* (London: Routledge, Kegan and Paul, 1967) we read that '*A Laodicean* . . . is quite worthless' (p. 1466), whilst even Jane Gatewood in her Introduction to the World's Classics edition (Oxford: Oxford University Press, 1991) writes that it is 'an experiment that failed' (p. xviii).

73   libellous . . . *A Laodicean*, p. 336.
73   unarchitectural . . . Ibid., p. 365.
74   heliographic science . . . Ibid., p. 283.
74   the trick of . . . Ibid., p. 213.
74   In the beginning . . . Jacques Derrida, 'Ulysses Gramophone' [1987], tr. T. Kendall and S. Benstock in D. Attridge (ed.), *Acts of Literature* (London: Routledge, 1992), p. 270.
74   It was the . . . *A Laodicean*, p. 332.
74   to fulfil the . . . Ibid., p. 12.
74   unintelligible . . . Ibid., p. 35.
74   mum's the word . . . Ibid., p. 332.
74   Emma had some . . . See Seymour-Smith, *Hardy*, p. 265.
74   writing [that] . . . Derrida, *Dissemination*, p. 144.
74   the house of . . . See Henry James, Preface to *The Portrait of a Lady* [1881] (Harmondsworth: Penguin, 1966), p. ix.
75   Paula visits the . . . *A Laodicean*, p. 267.
75   the capitals in . . . Ibid., p. 164.
75   gravestone epitaphs . . . Ibid., p. 139.
75   names . . . cut . . . Ibid., p. 65.
75   working with stone . . . See Miller, *Ariadne's Thread*.
75   literature went to . . . *A Laodicean*, p. 144.
75   the . . . message sped . . . Ibid., p. 186.
75   Somerset's telegrams to . . . Ibid., p. 255.
75   too are intercepted . . . Ibid., pp. 243, 255.
75   a newspaper is . . . Ibid., p. 222.
75   one invitation is . . . Ibid., p. 89.
75   another is sent . . . Ibid., p. 194.
75   a letter is . . . Ibid., pp. 111–12.
75   a newspaper announces . . . Ibid., p. 222.
75   a non-homogenous . . . See Jacques Derrida, *Limited Inc* [1977], tr. S. Weber (Evanston: Northwestern University Press, 1988), p. 3.
75   the footsteps . . . *A Laodicean*, p. 181.
75   an arrow-slit . . . Ibid., p. 18.
76   the house [merely] . . . See Wigley, p. 109.
76   a magazine of . . . *A Laodicean*, p. 336.
76   two [sentinels stand] . . . Ibid., p. 158.
76   there is history . . . Paul de Man, *Aesthetic Ideology*, ed. A. Warminski (Minneapolis: University of Minnesota Press, 1996), p. 133.
76   Will to Power . . . This phrase first emerges in Nietzsche's work around 1882.
76   English civil wars . . . *A Laodicean*, p. 38.
76   wars of the . . . Ibid., p. 95.
76   some of the . . . Ibid., p. 246.
76   of a thickness . . . Ibid., p. 18.
76   there is no . . . Benjamin, *Illuminations*, p. 258.
76   in the line . . . *A Laodicean*, p. 135.
76   Anglo-South-American . . . Ibid., p. 329.
76   Greek . . . statues . . . See Ibid., p. 390, note 2.
77   morocco case . . . Ibid., p. 190.

77 Dare's cigarettes . . . Ibid., p. 117.
77 cotton thread . . . Ibid., p. 27.
77 the print of . . . Ibid., p. 137.
77 white baptismal robe . . . Ibid. p. 12.
77 dress of ivory . . . Ibid., p. 99.
77 white hat . . . Ibid. p. 37.
77 white signal . . . Ibid., p. 66.
77 white parasols . . . Ibid., pp.55, 357.
77 white . . . fragment . . . Ibid., p. 92.
77 white feather . . . Ibid., p. 358.
77 watery white . . . Ibid., p. 373.
77 saw a white . . . Ibid., p. 15.
77 spot of white . . . Ibid., p. 78.
77 the spot of . . . Ibid., p. 373.
77 directed point-blank . . . Ibid., p. 327.
77 ask[s] . . . point-blank . . . Ibid., p. 361.
77 tell him point-blank . . . Ibid., p. 350.
77 her black-and-white . . . Ibid., p. 99.
77 overhears the news . . . Ibid., p. 177.
78 in the middle . . . Ibid., p. 82.
78 here rose the . . . Ibid., p. 377.
78 a finished writer . . . Ibid., p. 379.
78 *A Laodicean* contained . . . W. L. Phelps, *Autobiography With Letters* (London: Oxford University Press, 1939), p. 391.
78 the author of . . . *A Laodicean*, p. 337.
78 house and lineage . . . Ibid., p. 322.
78 Nebuchadnezzar's . . . Ibid., p. 353.
78 the map . . . Ibid., p. 145.
78 where men burn . . . Heinrich Heine, *Almansor* [1823], *The Complete Poems* (Boston: Suhrkamp, Inc.,1992), p. 302, line 245.
78 burnt the manuscript . . . See R. L. Purdy, *Thomas Hardy: A Bibliographical Study* (Oxford: Clarendon Press, 1954), p. 38.
78 ere the art . . . *A Laodicean*, p. 24.
79 the framed gentleman . . . Ibid., p. 374.
79 motion pictures . . . See Beaumont Newhall, *The History of Photography* (London: Secker and Warburg, 1982), p. 121.
79 Game? Call it . . . *A Laodicean*, p. 177.

VIII Leavis Spells Pianos

82 'life' is a . . . Quoted in Michael Bell, *F. R. Leavis* (London: Routledge, 1988), p. 110.
82 every creative . . . F. R. Leavis, *Valuation in Criticism and Other Essays* (Cambridge: Cambridge University Press, 1986), p. 287.
82 Leavis Spells . . . See Ronald Hayman, *Leavis* (London: Heinemann, 1976), p. 1.
82 the front cover . . . See Jacques Derrida, *Points . . . Interviews, 1974-1994*, ed. Elisabeth Weber (Stanford, CA: Stanford University Press, 1992).
82 playing the . . . See Geoffrey Bennington and Jacques Derrida, *Jacques*

Derrida [1991], tr. Geoffrey Bennington (Chicago: University of Chicago Press, 1993), p. 191.

82 history of the . . . Barthes, *Image-Music-Text*, p. 163.

83 poststructuralism and jazz . . . Valentine Cunningham, *Reading After Theory* (Oxford: Blackwell, 2002), pp. 69–71.

83 accompaniment . . . Derrida performed alongside Ornette Coleman at the 1995 La Villette Jazz Festival – see Catherine Malabou and Jacques Derrida, *Jacques Derrida: La Contre-Allée* (Paris: La Quinzaine Litteraire, 1999), p. 101.

83 at the piano . . . Oscar Wilde, *Plays, Prose Writings and Poems* (London: Everyman, 1996) p. 99.

83 play Chopin . . . Ibid., p. 105.

83 to see the . . . Ibid., p.124.

83 without prelude . . . See F. R. Leavis, *The Critic as Anti-Philosopher*, ed. G. Singh (London: Chatto & Windus, 1982), p. 137.

83 sense of an ending . . . See Frank Kermode, *The Sense of an Ending: Studies in the Theory of Fiction* (Oxford: Oxford University Press, 1967).

83 Professor of Life . . . *The Essays of Virginia Woolf*, ed. Andrew McNeillie, 4 vols (London: Hogarth Press, 1994), 4.342–8.

84 by the early . . . Eagleton, *Literary Theory*, p. 27.

84 Mr Norris . . . See Christopher Norris, *William Empson and the Philosophy of Literary Criticism* (London: Athlone Press, 1978), p. 205.

84 changed not trains . . . I allude, of course, to Christopher Isherwood's novel, *Mr Norris Changes Trains* (1935).

84 doing this kind . . . See Michael Payne and John Schad, *life.after.theory* (London: Continuum, 2003), p. 56.

84 'Le Parjure' . . . This essay is a reading of Henri Thomas' *Le Parjure* (1954), a novel which Paul de Man once advised Derrida to read as a way of under-standing something of de Man himself – see Jacques Derrida, *Without Alibi*, tr. Peggy Kamuf (Stanford: Stanford University Press, 2002), pp. 161–2.

84 criticism is as . . . T. S. Eliot, *Sacred Wood: Essays on Poetry and Criticism* (London: Methuen, 1960), p. 48.

84 the end of . . . Sigmund Freud, *Beyond the Pleasure Principle* [1920], ed. James Richards, Penguin Freud Library, 15 vols (London: Penguin, 1984), 11.311.

84 it is, already . . . Derrida, *The Post Card*, p. 285.

84 the absolute idea . . . Derrida, *Glas*, p. 82a.

84 when the German . . . See Payne and Schad, p. 64.

85 structure of the . . . Derrida, *Glas*, pp. 77a, 15b.

85 autobiothanatoheterographical . . . Bennington and Derrida, p. 213.

85 Criticism . . . is . . . Wilde, p. 121.

85 writes in order . . . Michel Foucault, *The Archaeology of Knowledge* [1969], tr. A.M. Sheridan Smith (London: Routledge, 1972), p. 17.

85 I have always . . . 'L'intellectuel et les pouvoirs,' *La Revue Nouvelle* 80 (1984): 339.

85 everybody's autobiography . . . Bennington and Derrida, p. 311

85 'autobiography' is perhaps . . . Jacques Derrida, *Acts of Literature*, ed. Derek Attridge (London: Routledge, 1992), p. 34.

85 blast open . . . Benjamin, *Illuminations*, p. 254.

85 any attempt . . . Paul de Man, *Blindness and Insight*, 2nd edn (London: Routledge, 1983), p. 55.

86 the joyous affirmation . . . Derrida, *Writing*, p. 292.

86 behind the . . . Terry Eagleton, *The Function of Criticism* (London: Verso, 1984), p. 101.

86 it is still . . . Jacques Derrida, *Specters of Marx* [1993], tr. Peggy Kamuf (London: Routledge, 1994), p. 14.

86 Leavis' veneration for . . . See William Empson, *Argufying*, ed. John Haffenden (London: Chatto & Windus, 1987), p. 41.

86 the semantic connection . . . John Ayto, *Bloomsbury Dictionary of Word Origins* (London: Bloomsbury, 1991), p. 323.

86 when Lacan's wife . . . See Catherine Clément, *The Lives and Legends of Jacques Lacan*, [1981] tr. Arthur Goldhammer (New York: Columbia University Press, 1983), p. 19.

86 prisoner of war . . . See Althusser, *The Future Lasts a Long Time*.

86 sight[s] we had . . . Quoted in David Macey, *The Lives of Michel Foucault* (London: Vintage, 1993), p. 347.

86 a whole book . . . See Jacques Derrida, *The Work of Mourning*, eds. Pascale-Anne Brault and Michael Naas (Chicago, IL: Chicago University Press, 2001).

87 I seem to . . . Ibid., p. 215.

87 pathetic and human . . . Derrida, *Without Alibi*, p. 182

87 wanting sentence . . . Derrida himself here quotes Pierre Fontanier, *Les figures du discours* (Paris: Flammarion, 1968), p. 315.

87 death is a . . . Paul de Man, *The Rhetoric of Romanticism* (New York: Columbia University Press, 1984), p. 81.

87 Paul de Man . . . Payne and Schad, p. 28.

87 In life . . . Jacques Derrida 'Le Parjure' – lecture given as part of 'life.after.theory' conference, Loughborough University, November 2001.

87 person on business . . . Samuel Taylor Coleridge, *Poetical Works*, ed. Ernest Hartley Coleridge (Oxford: Oxford University Press, 1912), p. 296.

88 And it came . . . Luke 24:30–1.

88 the door that . . . Frank Kermode, *Not Entitled: A Memoir* (London: Flamingo, 1995), p. 219.

88 Leave the door . . . Derrida, *The Post Card*, pp. 127–8.

88 God has . . . Jacques Lacan, 'A Love Letter' (1975), in Juliet Mitchell and Jacqueline Rose (eds), *Feminine Sexuality: Jacques Lacan and the école freudienne* (London: Macmillan,1982), p. 154.

88 theory's theological turn . . . For an excellent survey of this development, see Graham Ward, *Theology and Contemporary Critical Theory* (Houndmills: Palgrave, 1999).

88 expressed a disquiet . . . See Payne and Schad, p. 128.

88 from the Left . . . See ibid., p. 138.

88 the history of . . . Frank Kermode, *Essays on Fiction, 1971–82* (London: Routledge, 1983), p. 31.

88 secularisation multiplies . . . Frank Kermode, *The Classic* (London: Faber, 1975), p. 138.

89 the blindman's bluff . . . Frank Kermode, *The Genesis of Secrecy* (Cambridge, MA: Harvard University Press, 1979), p. 14.

89 surprised by joy ... See *Wordsworth: Poetical Works*, p. 204.

89 surprised by sin ... See Stanley E. Fish, *Surprised by Sin* (London: Macmillan,1967).

89 one always asks ... Bennington and Derrida, p. 46.

89 I didn't earn ... Hélène Cixous, *Coming to Writing and Other Essays* [1989], tr. Sarah Cornell *et al.* (Cambridge, MA: Harvard University Press, 1991), p. 45.

89 right here ... Derrida, *The Post Card*, p. 33.

89 We are the ... See above, p. 49.

89 the Text cannot ... Barthes, *Image-Music-Text*, p. 157.

90 by preferring my ... Jacques Derrida, *The Gift of Death* [1992], tr. David Wills (Chicago, IL: Chicago University Press, 1995), p. 69.

90 everything is related ... Sigmund Freud, *Introductory Lectures on Psychoanalysis*, Penguin Freud Library, 1.53.

90 There are ethics ... Payne and Schad, p. 31.

90 Can We Say ... Kermode, *Essays on Fiction*, pp. 156–67

90 the space of ... Derrida, *Acts of Literature*, pp. 36–7.

90 the work of ... Jean-Paul Sartre, *What is Literature?* [1949], tr. Bernard Frechtman (London: Methuen, 1967), p. 45.

90 he ... is condemned ... Jean-Paul Sartre, *Existentialism and Humanism* [1946], tr. Philip Mairet (London: Methuen, 1973), p. 34.

90 Just imagine ... Payne and Schad, p. 4.

91 the possibility ... Derrida, *Without Alibi*, p.191.

91 much theory is ... Payne and Schad, pp. 57–8.

91 What is called ... Derrida, *Without Alibi*, p. 161.

91 I think where ... Lacan, *Écrits*, p. 166.

91 What is Called ... See *Basic Writings: Martin Heidegger*, ed. David Farrell Krell (London: Routledge, 1993), p. 366.

91 bring back ... Derrida, *Without Alibi*, p.191.

91 the unconscious of ... Pierre Macherey, *A Theory of Literary Production* [1966], tr. Geoffrey Wall (London: Routledge, 1978), p. 94.

91 the madman's speech ... Michel Foucault, 'The Order of Discourse' [1970] in Robert Young (ed.), *Untying the Text* (London: Routledge, 1981), p. 53.

91 this sex which ... Luce Irigaray, *This Sex Which Is Not One* [1977], tr. Catherine Porter (Ithaca, NY: Cornell University Press, 1985).

91 Nothing exists ... Jacques Lacan, *Écrits*, 2 vols (Paris: Editions du Seuil, 1977), 1.392.

91 What characterises each ... Ferdinand de Saussure, *Course in General Linguistics* [1916], tr. Roy Harris (London: Duckworth, 1983), p. 115.

91 Every sign is ... Eagleton, *Literary Theory*, p. 110.

91 What deconstruction is ... Jacques Derrida, 'Letter to a Japanese Friend' [1987] in Peggy Kamuf (ed.), *Derrida Reader* (London: Harvester Wheatsheaf, 1991), p. 275.

91 the cross ... Lacan, *Écrits*, pp. 154-5.

92 is not a ... I. A. Richards, *Principles of Literary Criticism* (London: Routledge, 1960), p. 84.

92 the break with ... Gregory Ulmer, 'The Object of Post-Criticism,' in Hal Foster (ed.), *The Anti-Aesthetic: Essays on Postmodern Culture* (Port Townsend, WA: Bay Press, 1983), p. 83.

92 the possibility of . . . Quoted by Ulmer, p. 83.

92 I forgot my . . . Jacques Derrida, *Spurs / Éperons* [1978], tr. Barbara Harlow (Chicago, IL: Chicago University Press, 1979), pp. 122–43.

92 the impossibility of . . . Quoted in Frank Kermode, *The Uses of Error* (London: Collins, 1990), p. 117.

92 it's . . . grave . . . Derrida, *The Post Card*, p. 154

92 it is [still] . . . Ibid. , p. 176.

92 thought for . . . Ibid., p. 32.

93 the strength of . . . Søren Kierkegaard, *Fear and Trembling* [1843], tr. Alistair Hannay (Harmondsworth: Penguin, 1985), p. 67.

93 the critic as . . . See Terry Eagleton, *Against the Grain, Essays 1975–1985* (London: Verso, 1986), pp. 149–66.

93 importance of doing . . . Wilde, p. 97.

93 noise in which . . . Lacan, *Écrits*, p. 388.

93 the high and . . . Heidegger, *Basic Writings*, p. 389.

93 is . . . capable of . . . Hélène Cixous, 'The Laugh of the Medusa' [1976], tr. Keith Cohen and Paul Cohen in Elaine Marks and Isabelle de Courtivron (eds), *New French Feminism* (London: Harvester Wheatsheaf, 1981), p. 60.

93 Here Comes . . . Derrida, *Post Card*, p. 142.

93 when we are . . . Derrida, *Without Alibi*, p. 196

94 the companionship . . . Derrida, *Specters*, p. xviii.

94 Like ghosts amid . . . Peter Scheckner (ed.), *An Anthology of Chartist Poetry* (London: Associated University Presses, 1989), p. 199.

IX Someone Called Derrida

97 The book . . . The 'book,' as I misname it, is 'Envois' which is, more properly speaking, part of Derrida's *The Post Card / La Carte Postale: de Socrate à Freud et au-delà* (Paris: Flammarion, 1980). In the notes that follow all quotes are to this text, unless otherwise stated; in each case I shall give the page reference to the English translation first.

97 inaudible murmurs . . . Ibid., p. 230 / p. 246.

97 I truly believe . . . Ibid., p. 143 / p. 156.

97 Suppose that at . . . Ibid., p. 78 / p. 86.

98 That's me . . . Ibid., p. 96 / p. 106.

98 Why am I . . . Ibid., p. 77 / p. 86.

98 They did not . . . Ibid., p. 191 / p. 206.

98 an odd couple . . . Ibid., p. 148 / p. 161.

98 haunting has no . . . Letter to the author, 28 May 1999.

98 I hadn't noticed . . . Derrida, *The Post Card*, p. 167 / p. 181.

98 these interlaced . . . Ibid., p. 135 / p. 148.

98 the only school . . . Ibid., p. 87 / p. 97.

99 Disaster – we . . . Ibid., p. 77 / p. 85.

99 Is it what . . . Ibid., p. 167 / p. 180.

99 Tell my mother . . . All references to the words my father spoke in his final years are as transcribed by my mother. This transcript appears as an appendix in the book of which this is the opening chapter.

99 I tried to . . . Ibid., p. 210 / p. 225.

100 my 'poor father' . . . Ibid., p. 247 / p. 265.

100 On the morning . . . Ibid., p. 21 / pp. 25–26.

100 all the cruelty . . . Ibid., p. 143 / p. 156, p. 43 / p. 49.

100 To the devil . . . Ibid., p. 25 / pp. 29–30.

100 Who is he . . . Ibid, p. 115 / p. 126.

100 The police . . . Ibid., p. 82 / p. 91.

100 in literature everything . . . Ibid., p. 144 / p. 157.

100 all these cops . . . Ibid., p. 33 / p. 38.

100 Dupont and Dupond . . . Ibid., p. 112 / p. 123.

100 twins who are . . . It is said, very elegantly, by Peggy Kamuf, as a footnote to Jacques Derrida's 'Biodegradables: seven diary fragments,' tr. Peggy Kamuf, *Critical Inquiry* 15.4 (1989): 848, n. 19.

100 I have just . . . Derrida, *The Post Card*, p. 246 / p. 263.

101 For the children . . . Ibid., p. 68 / p. 75.

101 Holocaust of the . . . Ibid., p. 143 / p. 155.

101 Norbert . . . Ibid., p. 190 / p. 205.

101 Paul . . . Ibid., p. 254 / p. 272.

101 *Prognostica Socratis* . . . Ms. Ashmole 304, Bodleian Library, University of Oxford. To learn more about the author of the fortune-telling book see Suzanne Lewis, *The Art of Matthew Paris* (Berkeley: University of California Press, 1987) and Francis Wormald, 'More Matthew Paris Drawings,' *The Walpole Society* 31 (1946): 109–12.

101 *Si puer vivet* . . . Ibid., p.218 / p. 233.

102 give ear closely . . . Ibid., p. 225 / p. 241.

102 whoever you are . . . Ibid., p. 223 / p. 239.

102 destroyed by fire . . . Ibid., pp. 3–4 / pp. 7–8.

102 lost causes . . . It was Mathew Arnold who said this – see Matthew Arnold, *Selected Prose*, ed. P. J. Keating (Harmondsworth: Penguin, 1970), p. 130.

103 labyrinth between . . . Derrida, *The Post Card*, p. 15 / p. 20.

103 sanctuary of . . . Ibid., p. 216 / p. 227.

103 Are you following . . . Ibid., p. 217 / p. 233. It is true that the 'you' who is predicted to one day enter the Duke Humfrey Room is, by virtue of the verb form, feminine in the French original; however, Derrida goes out of his way to warn us against believing in such grammatical signs and wonders: 'Letters,' he writes, 'are always post cards: neither legible nor illegible, open and radically unintelligible (unless one has faith in "linguistic," that is gramm-matical, criteria: for example to reach the conclusion from the fact that I say "It's nice that you are back [*revenue*]" that I am certainly writing to a woman' . . .)' (p. 79 / p. 88).

103 One day . . . Derrida, *The Post Card*, p. 217 / p. 225.

103 the radio . . . Ibid., p. 109 / p. 120.

103 Did I tell you . . . Ibid., pp. 211–16 / p. 227, p. 208 / p. 224.

103 Letters, knowledge . . . Ibid., p. 96 / p. 106.

103 I visited the Duke Humphrey Room on Tuesday, 22 March 2005.

104 I felt myself . . . Derrida, *The Post Card*, p. 209 / p. 224.

104 archivists [who] . . . Ibid., p. 84 / p. 93.

105 I arrived . . . Ibid., p. 216 / pp. 227–28.

105 he was well . . . Ibid., p. 223 / p. 239.

105 You are my . . . Ibid., p. 174 / p. 188.

105 I intend to . . . Ibid., p. 173 / pp. 187–8.

105 It would be . . . Ibid., p. 210 / p. 226.

105 June 6th . . . Ibid., pp. 14–15 / p. 19.

106 The late Master . . . *The Letters of Mercurius* (London: John Murray, 1970), p. 6.

106 Gentlemen, it is . . . *The Collected Writings of Thomas de Quincey*, ed. Davis Masson, 14 vols (London A. & C. Black, 1889–1890), 13.24.

106 Gervase Fen . . . Fen, also an amateur sleuth, is a fictional character in a series of novels by Edmund Crispin. Lord Peter Wimsey is another amateur sleuth and fictional character, in his case in a series of novels written by Dorothy L. Sayers, including *Gaudy Night* (1935) which is set in Oxford. Detective Chief Inspector Morse is a fictional character in a series of Oxford-based novels written by Colin Dexter, many of which were adapted for television between 1987 and 2000.

106 Lewis . . . I revisited Oxford at the very beginning of August 2005, which happened to coincide with the filming of *Inspector Lewis*, a spin-off from the Morse television series, featuring the actor Kevin Whately as Lewis. The one-off episode was screened in 2006.

107 that bounder . . . Faith Wolseley, *Which Way Came Death?* (London: John Murray, 1936), p. 33.

107 I see – . . . Ibid., p. 329.

107 No school . . . Ibid., pp. 343, 152.

107 I will look . . . Derrida, *The Post Card*, p. 14 / p. 18.

108 someone gives the . . . Ibid., p. 248 / p. 266.

108 We had the . . . *School Magazine*, LXXXIX (December 1947).

108 Right here . . . Derrida, *The Post Card*, p. 33 / p. 38.

108 there is someone . . . Ibid., p. 80 / p. 89.

108 revolver-pocket . . . Ibid., p. 233 / p. 250.

110 rather like a . . . This remark has always been a vivid part of my memory of 'Envois'; however, every time I re-read it I fail to find the actual quote. I must now suspect myself of having dreamt it.

110 you know the . . . Derrida, *The Post Card*, p. 252 / p. 269.

110 that devil of . . . Ibid., p. 28 / p. 33.

110 Hell is in . . . Christopher Fry, *Three Plays* (London: Oxford University Press, 1960), p. 182.

111 The boy's dead . . . Ibid., p. 187.

111 It was a . . . Letter to my mother, April 1951.

111 madrigal . . . Derrida, *The Post Card*, p. 223 / p. 239.

111 Promise me . . . Ibid., p. 122 / p. 134.

111 Though I haven't . . . Letter, February 1951

112 there is none . . . William Shakespeare, *Henry V* [1599], ed. Gary Taylor (Oxford and New York: Clarendon Press, 1982), IV.iv.76.

112 I have to get . . . Derrida, *The Post Card*, p. 211 / p. 227.

112 That boy will . . . Ms Ashmole 304, fol.43v. I am very grateful to the Bodleian Library for kind permission to quote from the fortune-telling book; and I am especially indebted to Dr. Bruce Barker-Benfield, of the Bodleian, for kindly transcribing this particular extract. Professor Daniel Ogden of the University of Exeter very kindly helped me to translate it.

X Our Lives, Mrs Dalloway

I should like to thank both Professor David Bradshaw (Oxford) and a number of librarians at the British Library (Colindale), Enfield Library, and the National Archives for their assistance as I undertook the research for this text. I should also like to thank BBC Radio 3 for enabling me to read from on it on 'The Verb' on 15 June 2012.

114 On the Fourth . . . National Archives: HO 77/ 2080. C450964.

115 Mrs Dalloway said . . . Virginia Woolf, *Mrs Dalloway* [1925], ed. Stella McNichol (Harmondsworth: Penguin, 1992), p. 3.

115 Odd affinities . . . Ibid., p. 167

115 I want . . . *The Diary of Virginia Woolf*, 5 vols, ed. Anne Olivier Bell (London: Hogarth, Press, 1979–85), 2. 37.

115 She . . . never . . . *Mrs Dalloway*, p. 169.

115 I love walking . . . Ibid., p. 6.

115 the eminent linguist . . . William James referred thus to Saussure in 1892 – see John E. Joseph, 'He was an Englishman,' an essay on Saussure's visit to England in 1911 (*TLS*, 16 November 2007, p. 16).

115 a panorama of . . . Saussure, *Course*, p. 82 / *Cours de Linguistique Générale* [1916], ed. Charles Bally and Albert Sechehaye (Paris: Payot, 1964), p. 117.

115 ascend Mont Blanc . . . See Arnold Lunn, *The Swiss and their Mountains* (London: George Allen, 1963), pp. 68–9.

115 a city of . . . Percy Bysshe Shelley, 'Mont Blanc' [1817], *Poetical Works*, ed. Thomas Hutchinson (Oxford: Oxford University Press, 1970), p. 534.

115 the guest-book . . . See G. R. de Beer, *Escape to Switzerland* (Harmondsworth: Penguin, 1945), pp. 66–7.

115 Over the Strand . . . *Mrs Dalloway*, p. 152.

115 to hold on . . . See 'The Waste Land' [1922] in *The Complete Poems of T.S. Eliot* (London: Faber, 1969), lines, 15–18.

115 Our lives . . . Emily Dickinson, 'Our lives are Swiss' [c.1896], *The Complete Poems*, ed. Thomas H. Johnson (London: Faber, 1970), p. 41.

116 The British Empire . . . See Cathy Ross, *Twenties London* (London: Philip Wilson Publishers, 2003), p. 8.

116 April was indeed . . . See *The Waste Land*, line 1.

116 It is nature . . . *The Essays of Virginia Woolf*, 6 vols, ed. Andrew McNeillie (London: Chatto and Windus, 1986–2012), 3.410–12.

116 The curtain rises . . . Marie Stopes, *A Banned Play* [1916], (London: John Bale, 1926), pp. 56–8.

116 Johannes Schad has . . . National Archives: HO 144/ 6158. 230293.

116 Villians there must . . . *Mrs Dalloway*, p. 190.

116 We assign identity . . . Saussure, p. 107 / p. 151.

116 Every man fell . . . *Mrs Dalloway*, p. 148.

116 This cable . . . See Ghada Karmi, *Married to Another Man* (London: Pluto Press 2008) and H. Haumann (ed.), *The First Zionist Congress* (Basel: S. Karger AG, 1997).

117 lifted her up . . . *Mrs Dalloway*, p. 14.

117 the rubber . . . Johannes worked for Chautard, rubber merchants.

117 All down the . . . Ibid., pp. 21–2.

117 In its consistency . . . Joseph, p. 15.

117 K . . . R . . . *Mrs Dalloway*, pp. 22–3.

117 Honeymoon Land . . . See *The Recorder, for Palmers Green, Winchmore Hill and Southgate*, 7 December 1914.

117 an Italian airman . . . *Recorder*, 19 December 1912.

117 the ears of . . . *Collected Essays of Virginia Woolf*, ed. Leonard Woolf, 4 vols (London: Hogarth, 1966–67), 3. 332.

117 boys in uniform . . . *Mrs Dalloway*, p. 23.

118 to be the . . . Ibid., pp. 55–6.

118 Dear Sir . . . National Archives: HO 144/ 6158 230293.

118 We Swiss are . . . *Swiss Observer*, 17 November 1923.

118 victory all . . . See Jean Starobinski, *Words Upon Words: The Anagrams of Ferdinand de Saussure*, tr. Olivia Emmet (New Haven: Yale University Press, 1979), p. 9.

118 She had read . . . *Mrs Dalloway*, p. 34.

119 Miss Lina Schwarz . . . *Swiss Observer*, 16 July 1921.

119 crowded with calvaries . . . See Wilfred Noyce, *The Alps* (London: Thames and Hudson, 1963), pp. 183–4.

119 Health is . . . *Mrs Dalloway*, p. 108.

119 It is the . . . *The Diary of Virginia Woolf*, 3.314.

119 The friends and . . . *Mrs Dalloway*, p. 109.

119 A seedy-looking . . . Ibid., p. 31.

119 she had seen . . . Ibid., p. 136.

120 But Heron, don't . . . Stopes, *Banned Play*, p. 104.

120 I have read . . . Ibid., p. 101.

120 He started after . . . *Mrs Dalloway*, pp. 57–8.

120 He . . . insisted . . . Ibid., p. 34.

120 husband and wife . . . Marie Stopes, *Married Love* [1918], ed. Ross McKibbin (Oxford: Oxford University Press, 2008), p. 72.

120 the supreme mystery . . . *Mrs Dalloway*, p. 140.

120 No soul could . . . Stopes, *Married*, p. 72.

120 people were . . . *Mrs Dalloway*, p. 72.

120 girls who went . . . *Recorder*, 10 November 1907.

120 suppose someone . . . Saussure, p. 8 / p. 23.

120 Come, let him . . . Stopes, *Banned Play*, p. 109.

121 Outside the door . . . *Mrs Dalloway*, pp.134-5.

121 It would be . . . Saussure, p.15 / p. 32.

121 on and on . . . *Mrs Dalloway*, p. 58.

121 The spirit . . . Ibid., p. 15.

121 Do you periodically . . . *Recorder*, 17 November 1907.

121 I have pneumonia . . . *Letters of Virginia Woolf*, 6 vols, ed. Nigel Nicolson and Joanne Trautmann (London: Harcourt Brace Jovanovich, 1975–79), 2.549.

121 Miss Kilman standing . . . *Mrs Dalloway*, p. 140.

121 this . . . Christian . . . Ibid., p. 137.

121 standing . . . upon . . . Ibid., p. 136.

121 Yes, Miss Kilman . . . Ibid., p. 135.

121 She would think . . . Ibid., p. 170.

121 But now I . . . *Banned Play*, pp. 113–14.

121 We must be . . . Saussure, p. 24 / p. 44.

122 In Paris . . . Ibid., p. 31/ p. 54.

122 the letterbox . . . See *Recorder*, 5 November 1912.

122 Her mother was . . . See National Archives: HO 144/ 6158. 230293.

122 this isle of . . . *Mrs Dalloway*, p. 198.

122 also called Marie . . . Her maiden name was Faesch, and she died in 1950.

122 Women must put . . . Ibid., p. 33.

122 This doesn't look . . . *Banned Play*, p. 111.

122 laughing . . . she . . . *Mrs Dalloway*, p. 59.

122 She made to . . . Ibid., p. 43.

123 They had just . . . Ibid., p. 6.

123 Dr Holmes said . . . Ibid., p. 73.

123 I do order . . . National Archives: J 77 / 2080. C450964.

123 Like a nun . . . *Mrs Dalloway*, p. 33.

123 from Basel one . . . In 1897 Theodor Herzl declared 'In Basel, I have founded the Jewish state,' see Haumann, p. 134.

123 a newly married couple . . . See Stopes, *Married Love*, p. 25.

124 To speak of . . . Saussure, p. 90 / p. 130 – here the word translated as 'ghost' is 'fantôme.'

124 Report on the . . . National Archives: H0 144 / 6158 . 230293.

124 I have come . . . *Mrs Dalloway*, p. 49.

124 men . . . who . . . Ibid., p. 162.

124 November 25th 1924 . . . Date of the *decree nisi* hearing in the High Court.

124 Dr Stopes herself . . . See Marie Stopes, *Marriage in My Time* (London: Rich and Cowan, 1935), pp. 22–3.

124 a nullity case . . . Ibid., p. 23.

125 A little independence . . . *Mrs Dalloway*, p. 8.

125 A room of . . . 'A Room of One's Own' is an extended essay by Woolf based on lectures she gave at Cambridge in 1928.

125 Sir Thomas Horridge . . . Sir Thomas Gardner Horridge (1857–1938).

125 The business of . . . *Mrs Dalloway*, p. 97.

125 Was it that . . . Ibid., p. 73.

125 Marriage is founded . . . These words were written by Lord Merrivale (*Marriage and Divorce* (London: George Allen, 1936), p. 15) who pronounced the decree absolute in the High Court on 15 June 1925.

125 Perhaps, after all . . . *Mrs Dalloway*, p. 111.

126 Ah, I wonder . . . *Banned Play*, p. 135

126 He has left me . . . *Mrs Dalloway*, p. 51.

126 Nothing again . . . See *Waste Land*, l.120.

126 Thomas G. Stevens . . . See Aleck Bourne, 'Thomas George Stevens, Obituary,' *Journal of Obstetrics and Gynaecology of the British Empire* 61 (1954): 123–5.

126 Bethaus . . . Saussure, p. 226 / p. 311. I should point out that where Roy Harris uses the word 'fall' in his translation the original French has the word 'suppression.' Insofar as my reading hinges on the word 'fall' then the 'eminent linguist, Mr. X' (to quote William James, of course) is here not so much Saussure as Professor Harris; which is to say that the identity of Mr X slips precisely as we might expect of Mr X. In this connection we must never, of course, forget that even the 'original' French text, *Cours de Linguistique Générale* (1916) was authored not by Saussure himself – he had died three

year before – but by his students based on their notes from his lectures. In this sense Saussure, or at least the 'author' of *The Course*, has always been Mr X.

127 aspirate *h* . . . . Ibid., p. 30. I should point out that where Roy Harris uses the word 'ghost' the original French has the phrase 'un être fictif.' Here again, in this moment, the 'eminent linguist' of my narrative is, then, as much Professor Harris as Professor de Saussure.

127 like a nun . . . *Mrs Dalloway*, p. 31.

127 Let us begin . . . ['Commencons par la mort'] . . . Ferdinand de Saussure, *Écrits de linguistique générale* (Paris: Editions Gallimard, 2002), p. 153 / *Writings in General Linguistics* (Oxford: Oxford University Press, 2006), p. 101.

127 This killing . . . *Mrs Dalloway*, p. 101.

127 In the midst . . . Ibid., p. 146.

128 London . . . is . . . *The Diary of Virginia Woolf*, 3.6.

XI A Chronology of Bewilderment and Bedevilment . . .

129 Literature is the . . . Matthew Arnold, *Essays in Criticism* [1865] in R. H. Super (ed.), *The Complete Prose Works of Matthew Arnold* (University of Michigan Press: Ann Arbor, 1962), III, 285.

129 criticism is itself . . . *Oscar Wilde*, p. 120.

129 to see the . . . Arnold, III. 261.

129 to see the . . . Wilde, p. 124.

130 criticism . . . is . . . Ibid., p. 121.

130 It is always . . . Ibid., p. 99.

130 citation wrenches the . . . Benjamin, *One Way Street*, p. 286.

130 Give up . . . See *F. R. Leavis: The Critic as Anti-Philosopher*, ed. G. Singh (London: Chatto and Windus, 1982), p. 137.

130 Jorge Louis Borges . . . See *Labyrinths: Selected Stories and Other Writings*, ed. Donald Ayates and James E. Irby (Harmondsworth: Penguin, 1970).

130 'Notes for Reading . . . See Hermoine Lee, *Virginia Woolf* (London: Vintage, 1997), pp. 749– 51.

130 John Cage . . . See Ulmer, p. 102.

130 Cage gives . . . John Cage, *Silence. Lectures and Writings* (Cambridge, Mass.: MIT Press, 1961), p. 128.

130 Cage finally realises . . . Ulmer, p.107.

130 The philosophers have . . . Marx, *Selected Writings*, p. 158.

130 Read the text . . . Robert Browning, *The Poems*, 2 vols, ed. John Pettigrew (Harmondsworth: Penguin, 1981), 1.632.

130 Cage gives a . . . Cage, *Silences*, pp. 146–93.

130 you cannot fuse . . . Quoted in Geoffrey Hartman, *Criticism in the Wilderness: The Study of Literature Today* (New Haven: Yale University Press, 1980), p. 190.

130 the discourse on . . . Barthes, *Image-Music-Text*, p. 164.

131 What Karl Marx . . . Norman O. Brown, *Closing Time* (New York: Random House, 1973), p.53.

131 Tom in his . . . Thomas Weiskel, *The Romantic Sublime* (Baltimore: Johns Hopkins University Press, 1976), p. x.

131 Literary commentary may . . . Hartman, *Criticism*, p. 201.
131 Criticism is driven . . . Ibid., p.199.
131 The essay form . . . Ibid., pp. 193–4.
131 The only critic . . . Ibid., p. 215.
131 the break with . . . Ulmer, p. 83.
131 functions within an . . . Ibid p. 94.
131 Julian Barnes . . . See *Flaubert's Parrot* (London: Jonathan Cape, 1984).
131 Louis Althusser . . . See Louis Althusser, *The Future Lasts Forever* [1992], tr. Richard Veasey (New York: The New Press, 1995).

Still Not Here . . .
132 John Schad, also . . . A.R.R.R. Roberts [real name, Adam Roberts], *The Va Dinci Cod* (London: Gollancz, 2005), p. 2. It is indeed the case that 'John Schad' became 'John Shad' in 1965 when his father removed, by legal deed, the 'c' from the family name. Our runaway restored the 'c' in 1983 – see *Someone Called Derrida*, p. 79.
132 But I will . . . Louis MacNeice, 'The Individualist Speaks' [1933] in *Collected Poems* (London: Faber and Faber, 1979), p. 22.
132 the masses . . . *Benjamin: Selected Writings*, 2.1.136.
132 Only everybody . . . Though Schad generously attributes these words to Goethe I have found no evidence to justify the attribution. I am grateful to Dr Steffan Davies (University of Bristol), a Goethe specialist, for his assistance in this.
132 Schad is having . . . *Hegel: The Letters*, tr. Clark Butler and Christine Seiler (Bloomington: Indiana University Press, 1984), p. 67
133 I should believe . . . Friedrich Nietzsche, *Thus Spoke Zarathustra. A Book for Everyone and No One* [1885], tr. R.J. Hollindale (London: Penguin, 1961), p. 68.
133 play the violin . . . See Franklin A. Walker, '"Renegade" Monks and Cultural Conflict in Early Nineteenth-Century Russia: The Cases of I.A. Fessler and J.B. Schad,' *Religion, State and Society* 28 (2000): 352.
133 still, sad . . . R. L. Brett and A. R. Jones (eds), *Wordsworth and Coleridge. Lyrical Ballads* [1798] (London: New York, 1963), p. 116.
133 far-off interest . . . *In Memoriam*, 1.8.
133 the true essence . . . Jacques Derrida, *Memoirs of the Blind: The Self-Portrait and Other Ruins* [1991], tr. Pascale-Anne Brault and Michael Naas (Chicago: University of Chicago Press, 1993), p. 126.
133 Odysseus . . . See Homer, *The Odyssey*, tr. Walter Shewring (Oxford: Oxford University Press, 1980), p. 283.
133 A cross? . . . Pynchon, *Lot 49*, p. 62.
134 the magic . . . Vladimir Nabokov, *Pale Fire* (Harmondsworth: Penguin, 1962), p. 110.
134 Jacques Degree . . . Ibid., p. 241.
134 *apparatus criticus* . . . Ibid., p. 71.
134 the apparatus which . . . C.S. Lewis, *An Experiment in Criticism* (Cambridge: Cambridge University Press, 1961), p. 104.
135 same day . . . 22 November 1963.
135 *De Orbitus* . . . See Horst Althaus, *Hegel: An Intellectual Biography*, tr. Michael Trash (Cambridge: Polity, 2000), p. 61.

135 celestial . . . Ibid., p. 62.

136 each textual atom . . . Derrida, *Glas*, p. 86b.

136 right here . . . Derrida, *The Post Card*, p. 33.

136 there is someone . . . Ibid., p. 80.

136 expelled . . . See Walker, p. 353.

136 anything may . . . Letter to Robert Ross, Thursday [late March 1900], *The Letters of Oscar Wilde*, ed. Rupert Hart-Davis (London: Rupert Hart-Davis, 1962), p. 819.

136 literature is the . . . *Complete Arnold*, III. 285.

136 criticism is not . . . Geoffrey Hartman, 'Passion and Literary Engagement,' in *The Geoffrey Hartman Reader*, eds Geoffrey Hartman and Daniel T. O'Hara (Edinburgh: Edinburgh University Press, 2004), p. 454.

137 Dear Jesus . . . *Pale Fire*, p. 76.

137 criticism is driven . . . I confess that these words are Geoffrey Hartman's – see *Criticism in the Wilderness*, p. 199.

A Bibliography
Works by John Schad

Books

Authored

The Reader in the Dickensian Mirrors (London and New York: Macmillan, 1992).

Victorians in Theory: Derrida to Browning (Manchester and New York: Manchester University Press, 1999). Reprinted 2009.

Queer Fish: Christian Unreason from Darwin to Joyce (Brighton and Portland: Sussex Academic Press, 2004).

Arthur Hugh Clough, British Council Writers and Their Work Series (Tavistock: Northcote House, 2006).

Someone Called Derrida: An Oxford Mystery (Eastbourne and Portland: Sussex Academic Press, 2007).

The Late Walter Benjamin (London and New York: Continuum, 2012).

Edited

Dickens Refigured: Bodies, Desires and Other Histories (Manchester and New York: Manchester University Press, 1996).

Thomas Hardy, *A Laodicean* (Harmondsworth: Penguin, 1997).

Writing the Bodies of Christ: The Church from Carlyle to Derrida (Aldershot and Burlington, 2001).

Critical Inventions (Sussex Academic Press) a series of experimental monographs, 2007–2011. Titles include: Thomas Docherty, *The English Question*; Roger Ebbatson, *Heidegger's Bicycle*; James Holden, *In Search of Vintueil*; J. Hillis Miller, *The Medium is the Maker*; Kevin Mills, *The Prodigal Sign*; David Punter, *Rapture;* Jean-Michel Rabaté, *Being Given:1^0 Art, 2^0 Crime*.

Co-Edited

life.after.theory (London and New York: Continuum, 2003). Co-edited with Michael Payne.

Crrritic! Sighs, Cries, Lies, Insults, Outbursts, Hoaxes, Disasters, Letters of Resignation, and Various Other Noises Off in These the First and Last Days of Literary Criticism . . . Not to Mention the University (Brighton, Portland and Toronto: Sussex Academic Press, 2011). Co-edited with Oliver Tearle.

Plays

Someone Called Derrida (with Frederic Dalmasso), performed at Oxford Playhouse Drama

Studio, April 4th 2012; The Storey, Lancaster LitFest, Oct. 18th 2012; Maudsley Trust, London, November 10th, 2012.

Chapters and Introductions

'Why Wait for an Angel?: Pynchon's *The Crying of Lot 49*' in David Barratt *et al.* (eds.), *The Discerning Reader: Christian Perspectives on Literature and Theory* (Leicester and Grand Rapids, 1995), pp. 251–64.

'A certain foreign body.' Introduction to *Dickens Refigured* (1996), pp. 1–4.

'Dickens's Cryptic Church' in *Dickens Refigured* (1996), pp. 5–21.

'Philosophy/Architecture.' Introduction to *A Laodicean* (1997), pp. xvii–xxxiii.

'These are my bodies.' Introduction to *Bodies of Christ* (2001), pp. 1–7.

'Joycing Derrida, Churching Derrida' in *Bodies of Christ* (2001), pp. 41–58.

'Coming Back to "Life": Leavis Spells Pianos' in *life.after.theory* (2003), pp. 168–89.

'I Am Not Walter Benjamin' in Mark Knight (ed.), *Religion, Literature and Imagination* (London and New York: Continuum, 2009), pp. 87–105.

'Crrr— (by way of foreword)' in *Crrritic!* (2011), pp. 1–4.

'GodotOnSea' in *Crrritic!* (2011), pp. 250–273.

Foreword to Michael Crowley, *Closer to Home*, (2012), p. i.

Articles in Refereed Journals

'The I and You of Time: Rhetoric and History in Dickens,' *ELH* 56 (1989), 423–438.

'Waiting in "Unhope": Negation in Hardy's Early Poetry,' *Critical Survey* 5 (1993), 174-9.

'The End of the End of History in Graham Swift's *Waterland*,' *Modern Fiction Studies* 38 (1993) 911–25.

'The Divine Comedy of Language: *In Memoriam*,' *Victorian Poetry* 31 (1993), 171–86.

'"Hostage of the Word": Poststructuralism's Gospel Intertext' – *Religion and Literature* 25 (1993), 1–16.

'"no one dreams": Hopkins, Lacan and the Unconscious,' *Victorian Poetry* 32 (1994), 141–156.

'Reading the Long Way Round: Thackeray's *Vanity Fair*,' *Yearbook of English Studies* 26 (1996), 25–34.

'Someone Called Derrida: an Oxford Mystery,' *Textual Practice* 21 (2007), 135–48.

'Someone – a 20–minute radio play,' *International Literature Quarterly* 9 (2009).

'Queerest Book. A Dramatic Monologue,' *Literature and Theology* 26 (2012), 3–22.

Reviews

Michael Millgate, 'Testamentary Acts,' *The Higher* (2nd April 1993), 18.

Ken Newton (ed.), 'Theory into Practice,' *Notes and Queries* 238 (1993), 580–1.

Isobel Armstrong, 'Victorian Poetry,' *The Tennyson Research Bulletin* 6 (1994), 146–8.

Peter Thoms, 'The Windings of the Labyrinth,' *Review of English Studies* XLVI (1995), 293–4.

Geoffrey Galt Harpham, 'Getting it Right,' *The Modern Language Review* 90 (1995), 722–3.

Norman White, 'Hopkins,' *The Tennyson Research Bulletin* 6 (1995), 263–5.

John Maynard, 'Victorian Discourses,' *Literature and Theology* 10 (1996), 196–7.

Howard Fulweiler, 'Here a Captive Heart Busted,' *Review of English Studies* XLVII (1996),131–2.

Michael Payne, 'Reading Theory,' *The Review of English Studies* XLVII (1996), 131–2.

W. David Shaw, 'Elegy and Paradox,' *University of Toronto Quarterly* 66 (1996/97), 319–20.

Matthew Campbell, 'Rhythm and Will,' *Tennyson Research Bulletin* 11 (1999), 106–7.

David Alderson, 'Mansex Fine,' *Literature and Theology* 14 (2000), 96–7.

Kevin Mills, 'Approaching Apocalypse,' *The Glass* (2006), 59–60.

Index